Study Guide

to accompany

Essentials of Life-Span Development

John W. Santrock

University of Texas-Dallas

Prepared by
Jean Mandernach

University of Nebraska, Kearney

Boston   Burr Ridge, IL   Dubuque, IA   Madison, WI   New York   San Francisco   St. Louis
Bangkok   Bogotá   Caracas   Kuala Lumpur   Lisbon   London   Madrid   Mexico City
Milan   Montreal   New Delhi   Santiago   Seoul   Singapore   Sydney   Taipei   Toronto

The *McGraw·Hill* Companies

McGraw-Hill Higher Education

Study Guide to accompany
ESSENTIALS OF LIFE-SPAN DEVELOPMENT
John W. Santrock

Published by McGraw-Hill, an imprint of The McGraw-Hill Companies, Inc., 1221 Avenue of the Americas,
New York, NY 10020. Copyright © 2008 by The McGraw-Hill Companies, Inc. All rights reserved.

1 2 3 4 5 6 7 8 9 0 QPD/QPD 0 9 8 7

ISBN-13: 978-0-07-328791-1
ISBN-10: 0-07-328791-1

www.mhhe.com

Contents

What's in the Student Study Guide and How Can I Use it to my Advantage?

This Introduction suggests ways that you can use this Study Guide to help you learn the material in *Essentials of Life-Span Development, 1st Edition*, by John W. Santrock. You may already be familiar with some of these ideas—but at times one needs to be reminded of how helpful these tips can be.

The goals for the LifeSpan course include practice in critical thinking, the ability to apply class material to their own lives, and the ability to use integrative thinking (making connections). Critical thinking comes from reading, talking, and writing about the information you're learning. It includes being able to think about it from different perspectives, criticize the methodology used, and analyze the meaning of what you are reading. Critical thinking isn't a skill with which we are born; it takes time and effort to develop. As you read about the journey of cognitive development throughout the life span, you will see how very far you've already come in your thinking abilities! Because all the information in this text is about humans, it's about *you*. It is important for students to think about the implications of the material for their own lives, for raising their own children, and for understanding their families better. Also, each chapter builds on the information in the previous chapters. Therefore, it's necessary to stretch your integrative thinking skills in this course. See how theories learned early on can explain material learned a month later—for example, how do infants' abilities compare with teenagers' abilities?. Integrative thinking means you can make connections, see relationships, and not forget what you've learned when you move on to something new.

The first section of the Study Guide is **Learning Goals**, a set of statements about the ideas and the material you should be able to understand after reading the chapter. Read these learning objectives BEFORE you read the chapter, so you can have an idea of what you're trying to learn as you read; then read them again after you have read the chapter. By reviewing the learning objectives you can see if you did, indeed, "get it all."

The second section is a **Chapter Outline**. This is intended to help you to organize your thoughts and your reading and to be able to anticipate what you will encounter in the corresponding chapter of the text, and also to use the various sections of this Study Guide to be sure you have understood the material in each section of the chapter.

The third section serves as a **self-test** so you can make sure you understand the material. This includes five subsections: matching questions, multiple-choice questions, true/false questions, short-answer questions, and essay questions. The **matching** questions help you to assess your mastery of the key terms and concepts presented in the chapter. The **multiple-choice** section is a set of approximately 25 questions that cover the material in each chapter in a way that checks that you are not just memorizing terms, but are understanding the concepts. There are many "applied" questions that require you to think about how these ideas would work in real life.. Each question is keyed to one of the learning goals. This allows you to pinpoint particular concepts you may find difficult to understand. The **true/false** questions are similar to the multiple-choice questions but have only two answer choices, which requires you to really know the material and all the conditions under which each statement would be true or would be false. This helps you with your critical thinking abilities. The **short-answer** and **essay** questions are designed to help you crystallize the many concepts contained in the chapter so that you can explain and apply what you have learned. In about ten short-answer questions and two essay questions, the material from the entire chapter ties together so you can see how all the research, ideas, facts, and theories fit together. Answers to the short-answer questions often directly quote material from the text; but you should try to use your own words, because this will help to reinforce the material thoroughly. The answers to the essay questions are merely skeletal; you will have to write more expansive answers, drawing on the material in the chapter. Essay questions are designed to make students able to put together information from more than one chapter to answer the questions fully—so you may want to think about how you could do that. That type of studying will definitely help you develop your integrative thinking skills.

In the next two sections, **Research Projects** and **Personal Application Projects,** you will find suggested activities that require you to search out more information about the material in the chapter, by reviewing the literature, by doing your own empirical investigations (that is, by doing research), or by actively applying what you have learned to your own life. The best way to learn the course material of any class is to use it--to think about its application to your own life. These activities will force you to do just that. Ask your professor if you may choose one of these as a class project or for extra credit—or just do them for the fun of it to see how they work. Read through *all* the activities, from Chapter 1 through Chapter 17, at the beginning of the term because you may see one in later chapters that you might want to work on throughout the term. The activities that require surveying or observing other people include a warning to check with your professor before completing them. This is because that many colleges require an ethics committee to approve such studies/activities.

The last section includes **Internet Projects.** Note that the introductory section refers you to McGraw-Hill's Online Learning Center (website) for the Santrock Life-Span text and that you will find some great activities, learning aids, and exercises there (www.mhhe.com/santrockessls). The Internet section concludes with some websites appropriate to the chapter. (All website addresses in this Study Guide have been checked and are correct at the time of publication; however, websites are often discontinued, and addresses can change, so some sites may no longer work. If that occurs, please notify the publisher so that appropriate revisions can be made in future editions of this Study Guide.)

Let's talk about effective ways to study. You may already be familiar with some of these ideas, but often they bear repeating because something that did not work earlier may work now. Remember that we are all unique, so some strategies work better for some people than for others—try out a suggestion for a fair period of time (only you can decide what "fair" is), and if it works, great—if it doesn't, try something else.

WHAT "A" STUDENTS TYPICALLY HAVE IN COMMON (BESIDES BRAINS)

Unfortunately, many students do not do as well in college as they had hoped and expected. Let's examine some of the reasons for this disappointing outcome to see how to avoid it and to learn, instead, how to be a good student and to guide your behavior to improve your chances of achieving your goals.

Most students who are in college want to be good students, and most students have some particular goal in mind, which is probably why they chose the particular college or university they are attending. When you chose your college or university, and perhaps also an area of major interest or concentration, you had certain goals in mind, which likely included doing well in school, earning good grades, and graduating.

A common definition of education is that it is "how people learn stuff." The key to the definition of education is the word "how." Today, thanks to a wealth of research on the principles that guide the phenomenon of learning, and on the nature of learning and memory, we know much more about HOW learning occurs and HOW we can make it better. By using this knowledge, we can become better students. The following principles and techniques are often done intuitively by "A" students. The rest of us have to learn and then consciously apply these strategies. First, you need to make a plan . . .

Formulating the Plan

Anything worth having is worth planning for. Whether you hope to learn to teach, to fly, to write for profit, or to change diapers correctly, you have in mind a goal. Now that you are a college student, many people expect you to know what you want to do for a profession or career. Yet you may not have the foggiest notion, or you might have an idea that is still unclear. That is okay. What is clear, however, is that you want to succeed in your college courses. This is a relatively long-range goal and as such can serve to keep you on track.

However, our day-to-day behavior is often hard to connect to our long-range goals. We need short-term goals to keep us organized and to be sure that the flow of our activities is going in the right direction. To accomplish our long-range goals, we need to focus on three types of short-term goals. First, we need goals for the day; second, we need goals for the week; and third, we need goals for the semester or term. Let's look at each of these separately.

Goals for Today

Try keeping a daily checklist, diary, or schedule as a reminder of what must be done each day. Check off the things as you accomplish them. A pocket calendar or computerized organizer is particularly helpful for this task. After you complete your list, use numbers, asterisks (*), or letters to prioritize each item on the list, and be sure that you put most of your effort into completing those that have the highest priority.

Goals for the Week

"A" students usually also schedule their time weekly. Sometime during the course of registration, you made up a schedule showing your classes for the whole week. If you have a job, you must allow time for that, too. Also, many college or university students have family obligations that need to be considered as well. Finally, everyone needs some time for relaxing, eating, sleeping, and playing. With all these things in mind, it is no wonder many students find little time to study.

But "A" students do manage to do all these things. Do they have more time? No, we all have the same amount of time. But successful students USE their time wisely. To make the best use of your time, make a weekly schedule on a grid or table, and block off time for all necessary events: classes, work, relaxation, eating, sleeping, exercising, playing, family, errands, and studying. Students who schedule their time and keep to their schedules are usually amazed at how much time they find they have. Be sure to leave some blocks (10 to 20 minutes) that are unscheduled just to maintain some flexibility, because sometimes emergencies arise and you need some slack in your schedule to cope with them.

As you make up your weekly schedule, you may find your study time fits into a large block. If this is the case, remember to take short breaks every 20 to 30 minutes. This is called "distributed practice" and is far more efficient than studying for hours on end. After the first 20 or 30 minutes, most of us become much less efficient anyway. When you take that break, reward yourself somehow, then go back to your studying. NEVER try to read a whole chapter in one sitting. Study for only one class per day if possible, so that material stays organized in your mind. For example, Monday and Wednesday nights might be the best nights to study for a Tuesday/Thursday class. It's important to study EVERY DAY for at least a little while, so that you aren't forced to cram when big deadlines loom. Slow and steady is much more effective than fast and insane.

Also, learn to say "No" and not feel guilty about it. Students often find themselves giving up important study time to accommodate a friend or a family member, or they feel so guilty about NOT doing so that their guilt interferes with concentration as they try to study. Most of the time when people ask for our help, they could get help from someone else, solve the problem themselves, or work with you to accomplish the activity during one of your free periods. Of course, if it's really an emergency, such as a serious medical problem, then by all means forgo studying and help. But if it's not, you need to consider yourself and your education as high priorities. This keeps your eye on the prize at all times.

Goals for the Semester

At the beginning of each semester, we find ourselves immersed in many new courses and dealing with new professors, and it is often difficult to sort out all the new expectations and demands. However, to be successful, we must organize the information necessary for completing all the course requirements.

In the beginning of the semester, record due dates for all your course assignments, projects, and exams. That way you can schedule your weekend trips, parties, dates, and study time around important deadlines. Obtain a large wall calendar (available in any stationery store), date book, or computerized organizing tool and mark on it the dates of tests and exams and term-paper due dates, being sure to indicate the course for which each date applies. Now, estimate how long it will take you to make final preparations for those exams, and mark those dates as warning or alert dates. Look over the dates on which papers are due and see if they are bunched together. Remember that since mid-semester is the same for each class, the mid-term exams and papers will most likely be clustered. This can really create a problem unless you PLAN AHEAD. Cutting one class to finish work for another becomes an endless cycle. These students seem to have problems for the rest of the semester trying to catch up. You can help yourself to avoid the last-minute all-nighters if you simply determine a spread of due dates for yourself and mark those on the calendar, too. As you do this step, avoid any days that have personal significance for you, such as birthdays, anniversaries, upcoming weddings you'll be attending, and so on. This calendar gives you an overview of major dates in your semester. Remember the old saying, "If you fail to plan, you plan to fail."

If you have completed this step carefully, you now have a large semester calendar plastered on your wall, a weekly schedule of major life events, classes, and study times taped over your desk or entered into your computer, and a daily checklist of must-do items in your pocket or purse. Congratulations: you have made important strides toward using your time wisely. Let's now look at some other important strategies.

Attending Classes

Many students believe that, because they are in college, they can decide whether to go to class at all. This is true. Some students also believe that attendance in class is not important to their grade. This is NOT true. Some schools have attendance requirements, so that if students miss a given number of classes either it will lower their grade a full letter grade or the instructor may drop the student from the course. In other cases, instructors have in-class activities that count toward students' grades, so if students are not in class they do not get credit for participating. In any case, research shows that students who do not attend class sessions almost always do more poorly on the tests, quizzes, and exams. Perhaps they were absent when a crucial item was discussed or when the instructor discussed the material to be included on the test. Remember that more often than not, instructors include information in their lectures that is not in your textbook, and this "extra" information (from class lectures, videos shown in class, guest lectures, and so on) is fair game for tests. Moreover, if you are not there, the instructor cannot get to know you and therefore cannot give you the benefit of the doubt on your answers. It should come as no surprise that in study after research study, the data clearly show that students who attend class regularly receive the highest grades—and learn more, too. The first rule of being an effective student, then, is to attend classes. Besides, how else can you get your money's worth? There's an old saying that drives this point home: "Education is the only thing people are willing to pay for and not get." Now that you've determined you will go to class, what else will you do?

Benefiting from Lectures

Sometimes students think that if they come to class and "pay attention" they will remember what the instructor talked about; they think that if they take notes, they will miss much of what the instructor says. But sitting passively and staying attentive is difficult. For one thing, most people can think much faster than they can speak. While the instructor lectures at 80 words per minute, the student thinks at about 350 words per minute. It's fine if a student is using this extra "thinking capacity" to focus on what the instructor is saying, but this rarely lasts more than 5 minutes at a time. Most of the time, this extra "thinking capacity" is used in day dreaming.

Benefiting from lectures is best achieved by taking notes. Use plenty of paper, and leave blank lines at regular intervals, or leave wide side margins; you will use these spaces later. If your instructor takes questions during lectures, take advantage of this to clarify things that you do not understand. For the sake of the other students who didn't understand what the professor is talking about, each student should take on the responsibility of asking for clarification or to expand in a way that will help them understand. Remember that lectures have a way of progressing and building on earlier information. One must understand each point, or later points will be lost. But don't ask the person sitting next to you what the professor said; if you do this you'll disrupt the class, annoy the professor, and run a high risk of getting an inaccurate response.

When you take notes, write out the major points and try to make simple notations for the supporting minor points. If you miss something and you cannot ask a question about it, approach the instructor immediately afterward, when the question is likely to be fresh in your mind. Don't try to write down every word, and do try to use abbreviations. Also try using typographic symbols such as < and > (these are much shorter than writing out "less than" and "greater than"), and, last, develop your own form of shorthand or learn a traditional one. Also, write down anything that can help you remember the material later on. If the instructor tells a story related to a new concept, shows a video clip, does an in-class demonstration, answers a student question, or argues a point with a student, write it down. This will help you to remember the concept and will give you additional information to include in papers or essay questions on exams.

On the same day as the lecture, go back over your notes (or recording) and do two things. First, fill in the rest of the minor points. Second, write brief summaries and any questions that you now have in the blank spaces (lines or margins) you left earlier. Students using a tape-recorded lecture can recite the summaries and questions These few minutes spent reviewing and organizing your notes will pay off in greatly improved memory.

You can ask any questions you have in class or during the instructor's office hours and thus reap two benefits. First, you will get the answers; second, you will demonstrate that you are a serious student. Remember that although instructors are very busy people, most do not mind answering serious questions. First try to determine the answer for yourself. If your efforts are unsuccessful, then go to the instructor, making sure you are prepared to explain where and how you looked for the answer. (Avoid asking so many questions that your instructor begins to wonder how you were able to get to this point in your education.)

By the way, to get the most out of the lectures, do complete the assigned reading BEFORE the class begins so that you are familiar with the material. This will help you to keep up with what the instructor is talking about, will reduce the amount of information you do not understand, and will enable you to form questions to ask in class if the instructor does not talk about them. Asking "what page are you on?" or flipping pages over and over during the lecture is a very clear indication that you have not read the material.

Reading for Learning

We all know HOW to read. But different media require different reading strategies. Textbooks are unique and must be read with a strategy all their own.

There are many reading and studying strategies, and they all work to some extent. Perhaps you learned one or more in high school. Perhaps you even took a how-to-study course when you entered college. If so, you probably learned one or two of these systems. If you have one you like that works for you, keep it. If you are interested in learning a new one, read on.

The PQ4R Method

One of the most successful and most widely used methods of studying written material was the SQ3R method, which was introduced in 1941 by psychologist Francis P. Robinson at the Ohio State University. Researchers had noted that students who were more successful were more active readers. More recently, this method has been updated to the PQ4R method, which adds an additional step. This method teaches the skills that have made many thousands of students successful. If you use this method when you read and study, you will be more successful, too. The steps are outlined below.

The P stands for PREVIEW. After you have read the overview or chapter outline and the list of learning objectives, you should survey (preview) the chapter. This is also called *skimming*. Look at the headings and the subheadings, and get the gist of the major points in the chapter.

The Q stands for QUESTION. Reading is greatly enhanced if you are searching for the answers to questions. For this text, the Study Guide provides learning objectives that can serve as questions. For other texts, create questions yourself that are based on the chapter overview or on your own survey of the chapter. Be sure that you have at least one question for each major unit in the chapter; you will be less efficient at studying those units for which you do not have questions.

The first of the four Rs is for READ. As you read, look for the answers to the questions you posed, or to the study or learning objectives furnished for you. When you find material that answers these questions, put a mark (X) or a stick-on note in the margin next to that material. This will help now, as you are actively involved, and later, when you review. Wait to underline or highlight lines of text until after you have read the entire chapter at least once, so you will know what is and what is not important. Some experts suggest that you underline or highlight no more than 10% of what you are reading. If you are highlighting the majority of the text, perhaps you should not highlight at all. Choose a different method for emphasizing the main points in each section, such as taking notes, summarizing the entire page in your own paragraph, going over key words and the pictures and graphics again—whatever works for you.

The second R stands for REFLECT. As you are reading, stop every so often and reflect on the material to increase its meaningfulness. This includes analyzing the material, thinking about how to apply it to your own life, interpreting the information, and connecting it with information you already have in your long-term memory.

The third R is for RECITE. One of the oldest classroom techniques (Aristotle used it) is recitation. In the classroom version, the teacher asks the questions and the students answer them. Unless you can get your instructor to study with you regularly, you'll have to play both roles. Periodically, stop in your reading and say aloud (if possible) what the author is telling you. Try to put it in your own words, but be sure to use technical terms as you learn them. If you are not in a situation where you can recite out loud, do it in writing. *Just thinking it is not enough*. When should you pause to recite? A good rule of thumb is that each time you come to the end of a major subheading, you should recite. One professor encourages his students to recite at least one sentence at the end of each paragraph, and two or three or more sentences at the end of each subunit (when you come to a new heading).

People who do not use recitation usually forget half of what they read after one hour, and another half of the half they remembered by the end of the day. People who use recitation often remember from 75% to 90% of what they studied. This technique pays off. By the way, if anyone questions why you are talking to yourself, tell them that a psychologist recommended it.

The fourth R is for REVIEW. Review a chapter soon after you have studied it (using the PQ and the first 3 Rs). Then review it again the day or evening before the test. It is not usually helpful to cram the night before a test, and particularly not the day of the test. That type of studying does not produce good memory and is likely to make you more anxious during the test. It's best to review gradually over time and to try to *understand* what you are reading. Research shows that your memory is organized by MEANING networks, not isolated facts. Therefore, make meaning out of what you are studying. Flashcards and separate vocabulary lists can be a good first step in studying, but it is largely a time waster. You should spend your time studying to learn, not memorize. If you try to memorize, you will probably be overwhelmed by the sheer amount of information. Being overwhelmed often leads to stress and blanking out during the exam, which brings us to our next topic.

Taking Tests

One of the things students fear most is failure. Failure signifies that things are not going well and alerts us to the possibility that we may not achieve our goals. Unfortunately, many students see tests and exams as opportunities to fail, rather than as opportunities to shine. They prepare by becoming anxious and fearful, and by trying to cram as much as possible right before the exam. These students rarely do well on the exam. They often fail, thus accomplishing just what they feared.

Taking tests requires strategy and planning. First, it is helpful to know what type of test you will have. Your instructor probably told you during the first class meeting, or it may be in the class syllabus or course outline. If you do not know, ask.

If you are going to be taking essay exams, the best way to prepare is by writing essays. Before you do this, find out what types of questions the instructor asks and what is expected in a response. Again, it is helpful to ask the instructor for this information. Perhaps you can even see some examples of essay questions from previous years (some instructors at some colleges have copies of their exams on file in the department office or in the library). By finding out what is expected, you can formulate a model against which you can evaluate your answers.

Now, using the learning objectives, short-answer questions, or some essay questions you wrote, write out the answers. There are about ten short-answer questions and two essay questions for each chapter in this Study Guide. HINT: If you usually feel anxious during a test, practice writing your essays in the room in which the test will be given. See if you can determine a time when the room is vacant (your instructor or department administrator may be able to help you); then make yourself at home.

If your instructor gives multiple-choice tests, then you should practice taking multiple-choice tests. For each chapter, either use questions provided in the Study Guide, or make up your own. You may find it helpful to work out an arrangement to pool questions with other students, thereby reducing the amount of work you have to do and at the same time developing a network of friends.

However you do it, the important thing is to prepare for tests and exams. Yes, some luck and chance are involved in test scores, as even your instructor will admit, but the fact remains that preparation is about 95% of the secret to getting a good grade. Preparation is not only a good study and review technique but also a way to reduce anxiety.

Dealing with Test Anxiety

Anxiety can be a helpful response when it occurs at low levels because it may drive you to become well-prepared. In 1908, Yerkes and Dodson showed that the amount of anxiety that could benefit performance was a function of the difficulty and complexity of the task. As the difficulty of the task rose, anxiety became less helpful and more likely to interfere with performance.

If you have ever been so anxious in a test situation that you were unable to do well, even though you knew the information, you have test anxiety. If you get your exams back and are surprised that you marked wrong answers when you knew the correct answers, or if you can remember the correct answers only after you leave the examination room, you, too, may have test anxiety and need to work on it.

One thing students seem to forget when dealing with text anxiety is their health. If you are hungry, ill, sleepy, or just over tired, you can probably count on having problems with the test. All-night sessions the night before the test can really cause you to be too tired to think properly. Be good to yourself, and the test will be much easier.

Your campus counseling center or testing center probably provides workshops on dealing with test anxiety, effective test-taking skills, and relaxation techniques. For example, research shows that exercise and meditation are effective ways to manage stress and calm the mind before big events such as exams.

Strategy Number 1: Effective Study

Use study habits that promote learning and make the best use of time. Strategies such as scheduling your time and using the PQ4R method reduce anxiety by increasing confidence. As you come to realize that you know the material, your confidence rises and anxiety retreats.

Strategy Number 2: Relaxation

Each of us develops a unique pattern of relaxation. Some people relax by going to a specific place, either in person or mentally. Others relax by playing music, by being with friends, by using antigenic relaxation phrases, or by meditating. Whatever you do, try to practice relaxation techniques. If you are good at relaxing, try thinking about those situations that make you anxious, and relax while you think of them. To do this, allow yourself to think only briefly (15 to 30 seconds at a time) of the situation that makes you anxious, and then relax again. After a number of such pairings, you will find that thinking about that situation no longer makes you anxious. At this point, you may be surprised to find that the situation itself also no longer produces anxiety. You may find it helpful to move from thinking about anxiety-provoking situations that produce very little anxiety to those that are more anxiety-evoking. For example:

1. Your instructor announces that there will be a test in 4 weeks.
2. Your instructor reminds you of the test next week.
3. As you study, you see on the course outline the word "test," and remember next week's test.
4. One of your friends asks you if you want to study together for the test, which is the day after tomorrow.
5. You choose not to go out with your friends because of the test tomorrow.
6. As you get up in the morning, you remember that today is the day of the test.
7. You are walking down the hall toward the classroom, thinking about what questions will be on the test.
8. The instructor enters the classroom carrying a sheaf of papers in hand.
9. The instructor distributes the papers and you see the word "test" or "exam" at the top.
10. After reading the first five questions, you have not been able to think of the answers to any of them.

If you work at it gradually and consistently, pairing these types of thoughts (briefly) with relaxation and remembering to let go and relax after each one, you can dispel test anxiety and make test taking a more productive and successful experience.

Strategy Number 3: Thinking Clearly

Most students who have test anxiety think in unclear and unproductive ways. They say to themselves things like: "I can't get these answers correct . . . I don't know this stuff . . . I don't know anything at all . . . I'm going to fail this test . . . I'm probably going to flunk out of school . . . I'm just a dumb nerd." These thoughts share two unfortunate characteristics: they are negative and they are absolute. They should be replaced.

When we tell ourselves negative and absolute thoughts, we find it impossible to focus on the test material. The result is that we miss questions even when we know the answers. Our thinking prevents us from doing well.

A good strategy for replacing these negative and absolute thoughts is to practice thinking positive and honest thoughts, such as, "I may not know all the answers, but I know some of them . . . I don't know the answer to that right now, so I will go on to the next one and come back to it . . . I don't have to get them all right . . . I studied hard and carefully, and I can get some of them correct . . . I am a serious student and have some abilities . . . Hmm. This is a hard question, so I'll skip it, come back, and look for any clues in other questions that might help me answer this one . . . I am prepared for this test and know many of the answers . . . This test is important, but it is not going to determine the course of my entire life, and if I don't do well it doesn't mean I'm a horrible person or a dummy."

By thinking clearly, honestly, and positively, we quiet the flood of anxiety and focus on the task at hand. Students who use this technique invariably do better on tests. It takes practice to think clearly, but it is worth the effort. After a while, you will find that it becomes natural and does not take any noticeable effort. And as anxiety is reduced, more energy is available for studying and doing well on examinations. The eventual outcome is more enjoyment with learning, better learning, more success in college, and the achievement of your goals.

Strategy Number 4: Do the Easy Ones First

Another technique is to read each question, answer the ones you know, then go back to the harder ones. But watch out for two things: First, be sure you get the answers in the right place. Sometimes when we skip a question or two, we wind up marking the wrong space, so make sure that your answer to question 10 is in space 10. Second, you may find you're stumped by the first several questions. Don't let that throw you, just keep going because there is bound to be one you jump on and say, "Yes! I know that one!" Answer the easy ones first, then go back to the others after you've built up your confidence. Then, always go back over the whole test to be sure you answered every question.

Strategy Number 5: Take a Break

If you find yourself getting stressed out during the test, take a break. Put your pencil down and breathe deeply; you may even want to put your head down on the desk. Use a relaxation technique; or visualize yourself looking at the test and suddenly realizing that you DO know the answers to most of the questions. Then return to the test.

Remember that with all these test-taking strategies, if you don't do the first one, none of the others will help. Passing the course requires that you actively study the material!

Memory Techniques

No matter how much you read, it won't help you if you don't remember WHAT you read. The most critical factor in remembering is being able to apply what you have learned. Of course, some things, such as people's names or certain dates or statistical information, are not easily applied to your life, so you'll have to use other techniques for that information. But first, let's talk about the "easy way."

Apply It to Your Life

If you can use the material you are learning and in your everyday life, you will remember it without any problem. Instructors often show films, do activities in class, give homework assignments, assign projects, and as you to integrate what you are learning with your own life so that you can make real-world connections. Take advantage of the opportunities your instructors provide you. They are not just hoops to jump through to get a grade; they will help you to develop skills you can use in real life.

Another method of applying the material to your life is to connect it with what you already know, either from life experience or other courses you have taken. Sometimes what you are learning fits nicely with what you already know, sometimes it will contradict what you learned before, and sometimes it appears to be brand new. This is an opportunity for you to look at how the new information fits in with the old: Were there new research findings? Or, is it merely a difference of opinion? Make these associations! Don't keep the information for any class neatly compartmentalized; if you do, you'll have a hard time trying to find it when you need it.

Teach It to Someone Else

When we start teaching something to someone else, we find we HAVE TO learn it, and by trying to explain the material to another person, we examine it and think about it differently. So, take the material you are learning in this class (or any class) and teach it to someone else. When that person asks you questions, look them up and find the answers, or think them out together, or ask someone else. When you explain concepts to someone else, you will see them in a totally different light.

Less formally, ask your friends to "indulge" you by listening to what you learned in your life-span development class (or any other class).

Mnemonic Techniques

Some things are just really difficult to apply to your own life. Dates, names, places, statistics, and such may not have a great deal of meaning for you. In that event, use the tricks that memory specialists use: mnemonics. There are many different types. For example, one famous mnemonic is an acronym for remembering the Great Lakes: HOMES = Huron, Ontario, Michigan, Erie, and Superior; the colors of the spectrum is someone's name: ROY G. BIV = red, orange, yellow, green, blue, indigo, and violet. You can make up your own acronyms by taking the first initial of any term, person, and so on. It's easiest, though, if it's something that makes sense to you.

Another mnemonic technique is called the "method of loci" (it's a method medical students use to remember body parts). You list the things you need to remember, then visualize yourself walking around a familiar place (like your living room), putting one item on a particular piece of furniture, another item on the next piece, and so on. Then when you need to remember those items, you go through your "living room" to see where each one is. Say, for example, you need to remember the theorists in Chapter 2 of this text. You might put Piaget on the piano, Freud on the sofa, Skinner in the television (a "box"), and so on. (They don't have to be on the object that starts with their name, although that might be an additional mnemonic technique; or you might put them on objects that you associate with their work.) Since you also need to associate the theorists with their theories, you might imagine Piaget is thinking about how to play the piano; Freud has hidden unacceptable thoughts under the sofa; Skinner has been reinforced for sitting so nicely in front of the television, and so forth.

There are many other mnemonic techniques—you might want to check out a book on memory strategies from the library to find some that will work well for you.

Most Important

Remember: professors don't actually "teach" their students. Rather, they facilitate learning so students end up teaching themselves. While professors try really hard to motivate our students, keep them interested, and present information in a way that helps students to understand, the ultimate responsibility for learning rests with the student. Some students have learned despite their professors, others don't learn even with the very best of professors. So, keep your goals in mind, study hard, ask questions, and aim for success.

Life-span development is a fascinating topic. Enjoy your journey through the life span! And remember that you, too, can be an "A" student.

Note: Much of the information in this Study Guide comes from other books' Study Guides for LifeSpan Development, which have been prepared by a number of great instructors, including Tasha R. Howe at CSU, Humboldt and Troianne Grayson at Florida Community College at Jacksonville.

Being Ethical When Working with Real People

In each chapter of this Study Guide you will find suggested Research Activities. Some of these involve working with children, many involve requesting participation by persons (children, adolescents, and/or adults) who are not members of your life-span development class. Professional ethics require that you always have a signed consent form when you are conducting research. A sample form is included below. Whenever you work with persons under the age of 18, obtain written permission from a parent or guardian (even if that is not specifically mentioned in the particular Research Activity). In addition, **always** ask the person assisting you if he or she is willing to help you with your project, despite that person's age. Be sure to tell the parent, guardian, or participant that if he or she begins the activity and later decides not to continue, he or she may quit at any time, without consequences. If the parent, guardian, or participant indicates a reluctance to participate, thank the person and move on to someone else. If, at any point during the project, participants indicate a desire to discontinue participation, stop immediately and thank them for their help up to that point. Participation in research is **always** voluntary; no one should ever be coerced into involvement and, once having begun, participants **always** have the right to discontinue their participation should they so desire.

Further, each institution (college, university, and so on) has its own standards for conducting research. Before engaging in any of the suggested Research Activities, check with your instructor to determine whether you need to obtain approval from your school's Institutional Review Board (IRB). You may need to complete forms and have a review by a Research with Human Participants Committee. If such approval is necessary, plan sufficient time for completing your project, including time for getting your proposal reviewed. It might take several weeks or even months, so do not wait until the last minute and expect to get the tasks completed. (A sample consent form follows on the next page.)

SAMPLE CONSENT FORM

Life-Span Development—Psychology

In partial fulfillment of the requirements of this course, (course name and #) I will need to [**fill in what you will need to do, for example**: *observe a child who is between five and ten years of age. I will need to have this child perform three tasks and answer questions about_____. During the observations I will assess the child's ability to complete various tasks, including:*

- *Discussing whether various items (such as a car or an egg) are alive*
- *Telling me if the child thinks certain shapes look like boys or girls]*

I will compile a summary report based on these observations, and I will submit this report to my professor, _____. My professor and I will be the only two people with access to the information from the observations. The professor will not be given any subject's identity. In my report, I will include information about the child's age and gender, but I will not disclose the child's identity. All information will be held in highest confidentiality and will be destroyed one year after the study is completed. The child's performance on these tasks cannot be used to speculate about the child's potential, and I will make no speculations about the child based on these observations. I will read the preceding statements to the parents of the child I will observe. The information obtained will be used only for class projects or homework. No names will ever be used or released.

Student's Signature: Date:

The preceding statements were read to me. I understand that my child will be observed in the manner described. I agree to allow my child to participate in these observations. I understand that I can withdraw this agreement at any time. If I have any further questions, I understand that I may contact (professor)_____ at (university name)_____, at _____(phone #) .

Child's Name: Age:

Parent's Name Printed:

Parent's Signature: Date:

Chapter 1: Introduction

Learning Goals

1. Discuss the life-span perspective of development.
2. Identify the most important developmental processes, periods, and issues.
3. Describe the main theories of life-span development.
4. Explain how research on life-span development is conducted.

Chapter Outline

THE LIFE-SPAN PERSPECTIVE
    The Importance of Studying Life-Span Development
    Characteristics of the Life-Span Perspective
        Development Is Lifelong
        Development Is Multidimensional
        Development Is Multidirectional
        Development Is Plastic
        Developmental Science Is Multidisciplinary
        Development Is Contextual
        Development Involves Growth, Maintenance, and Regulation of Loss
        Development Is a Co-Construction of Biology, Culture, and the Individual
    Some Contemporary Concerns
        Health and Well-Being
        Parenting and Education
        Sociocultural Contexts and Diversity
        Social Policy

THE NATURE OF DEVELOPMENT
    Biological, Cognitive, and Socioemotional Processes
    Periods of Development
    Conceptions of Age
    Developmental Issues
        Nature and Nurture
        Stability and Change
        Continuity and Discontinuity
        Evaluating the Developmental Issues

THEORIES OF DEVELOPMENT
    Psychoanalytic Theories
        Freud's Theory
        Erikson's Psychosocial Theory
        Evaluating the Psychoanalytic Theories
    Cognitive Theories
        Piaget's Cognitive Developmental Theory
        Vygotsky's Sociocultural Cognitive Theory
        The Information-Processing Theory
        Evaluating the Cognitive Theories
    Behavioral and Social Cognitive Theories

Matching Questions

_____ 1. Theoretical orientation that does not follow any one theoretical approach but rather selects from each theory whatever is considered the best in it.

A. nature-nurture issue

_____ 2. Theory that focuses on five environmental systems: microsystem, mesosystem, exosystem, macrosystem, and chronosystem.

B. psychoanalytic theories

_____ 3. Refers to the debate about whether development is primarily influenced by biological inheritance or by environmental experiences.

C. Ecological Theory

_____ 4. Theories that describe development as primarily unconscious and heavily colored by emotion.

D. normative age-graded influences

_____ 5. These are influences that are similar for individuals in a particular age group.

E. eclectic theoretical orientation

Multiple-Choice Questions

1. For many years, psychology professionals have focused only on the development of young children. In fact, many classes were named Child Development. Professors today are likely to advocate for classes that also include the development of adolescents, adults, and the elderly. These professors are conveying which viewpoint?
   a. life span
   b. storm–stress
   c. tabula rasa
   d. traditional

2. According to Baltes (1987), the life-span perspective includes all of the following views about development EXCEPT which one?
   a. Development is lifelong.
   b. Development is unidirectional.
   c. Development is multidimensional.
   d. Development is plastic.

3. Many older people become wiser with age, yet they perform more poorly than younger adults do on cognitive speed tests. This supports the life-span perspective notion that development is _____.
   a. multidirectional
   b. multidimensional
   c. unidimensional
   d. age-graded

4. The terrorist attacks of 9/11/2001 in the United States would be an example of a _____.
   a. normative age-graded influence
   b. normative history-graded influence
   c. non-normative life event
   d. storm-and-stress event

5. Natalia reached the age of 5 just before her school district's kindergarten entry cutoff date. Therefore, she will attend kindergarten this fall. This is an example of a _____.
   a. normative history-graded influence
   b. non-normative life event
   c. normative age-graded influence
   d. plastic developmental trend

6. Michael's family lives below the national poverty line. The text discusses how low socioeconomic status (SES) can be related to unequal opportunities and obstacles to successful development. All of the following were discussed as obstacles to success that children like Michael might experience EXCEPT which one?
   a. exposure to family turmoil
   b. separation from a parent
   c. high levels of violence
   d. lack of schooling

7. Researchers have raised concerns that as the population of the elderly continues to increase in the twenty-first century, more elderly people will be _____.
   a. taking marriage partners away from younger adults
   b. monopolizing the stock market
   c. continuing to work past retirement age, thereby reducing job opportunities for younger adults
   d. without a support system, because they are less likely to have either a life partner or children

8. _____ processes refer to changes in the individual's thought, intelligence, and language.
   a. Biological
   b. Cognitive
   c. Social
   d. Emotional

9. Which statement concerning the biological, cognitive, and socioemotional processes is TRUE?
   a. Each is distinct from the others.
   b. The cognitive and socioemotional processes are more closely related than are the cognitive and biological.
   c. They are intricately interwoven.
   d. They are more obvious in the early years of life.

10. Jamie and her fiancé, Larry, finished college last year. After living with their parents all their lives, they are now moving in together. They will need to learn to share bathroom time, compromise on grocery items, and spend time together after long days at their new jobs. Which period of development are they probably in?
    a. adolescence
    b. early adulthood
    c. middle adulthood
    d. the young-old

11. Which issue in human development debates the extent to which development is influenced by biological inheritance or environmental experiences?
    a. continuity-discontinuity
    b. stability-instability
    c. nature-nurture
    d. biology-environment

12. In studying changes in the way people think as they age, Dr. Lang notes that a child moves from not being able to think abstractly about the world to being able to do so, which is a qualitative change in processing information. Dr. Lang emphasizes _____.
    a. continuity
    b. discontinuity
    c. stability
    d. nurture

13. In studying child development, Dr. Murphy is intrigued by how motor development seems to unfold according to some blueprint. Dr. Murphy emphasizes _____.
    a. continuity
    b. discontinuity
    c. nature
    d. nurture

14. Social processes are of utmost importance in all of the following theories EXCEPT which one?
a. ethological
b. Freud's
c. Vygotsky's
d. ecological

15. All the following statements about the theories of life-span development are true EXCEPT which one?
a. Each theory contributes an important piece to the life-span puzzle.
b. Although the theories sometimes disagree, much of their information is complementary rather than contradictory.
c. Together the theories let us see the total landscape of life-span development.
d. Although each theory has some value, Bandura's social cognitive theory accounts best for all aspects of life-span development.

16. Erik Erikson's theory emphasize _____.
a. repeated resolutions of unconscious conflicts about sexual energy
b. success in confronting specific conflicts at particular ages in life
c. changes in children's thinking as they mature
d. the influence of sensitive periods in the various stages of biological maturation

17. Which of the following statements is NOT a valid criticism of psychoanalytic theory?
a. The main concepts of psychoanalytic theories have been difficult to test scientifically.
b. The conscious mind is given too much credit for influencing development.
c. Much of the data used to support psychoanalytic theory comes from people's personal recollections.
d. Psychoanalytic theory takes too negative a view of humans.

18. Which of the following statements does NOT represent Vygotsky's view of development?
a. The child's way of knowing is best advanced through internal mechanisms, which are separate from the social environment.
b. The child's cognitive skills can be understood only when they are developmentally analyzed and interpreted.
c. Cognitive skills are mediated by words, language, and forms of discourse, which serve as psychological tools for facilitating and transforming mental activity.
d. Cognitive skills have their origins in social relations and are embedded in a sociocultural backdrop.

19. The information-processing approach to development emphasizes _____.
a. the quality of thinking among children of different ages
b. overcoming certain age-related problems or crises
c. age-appropriate expressions of sexual energy
d. perception, memory, reasoning ability, and problem solving

20. From B. F. Skinner's point of view, behavior is explained by paying attention to _____.
a. external consequences of that behavior
b. the self-produced consequences of that behavior
c. individuals' cognitive interpretations of their environmental experiences
d. the biological processes that determine maturation

21. According to Albert Bandura's social cognitive theory, the three factors that reciprocally influence development involve _____.
a. behavior, the person, and the environment
b. punishment, reward, and reinforcement
c. memory, problem solving, and reasoning
d. cognition, reward, and observation

22. One of the most important applications of ethological theory to human development involves _____.
a. John Bowlby's research demonstrating that critical periods are evident in birds but do not occur in humans
b. John Bowlby's research demonstrating that attachment to a caregiver in the first year of life has important consequences throughout the life span
c. Alan Sroufe's research demonstrating that early attachment is not really that important to the child's social behaviors later in development
d. Mary Salter Ainsworth's research demonstrating a lack of connection between attachment early in life and later life adjustment

23. A common caution for correlational research is that _____.
a. it is difficult to administer
b. correlation does not equal causation
c. correlations do not tell direction of a relationship
d. correlations do not indicate the strength of a relationship

24. The research design that consists only of researchers comparing individuals of different ages at one testing time is _____.
a. cross-sectional
b. longitudinal
c. sequential
d. correlational

25. Effects due to a participant's time of birth or generation, but not to age, are referred to as _____ effects.
a. subjective
b. cohort
c. confounding
d. historical

True/False Questions

1. The life-span approach, as opposed to the traditional approach, emphasizes developmental change throughout adulthood as well as childhood.

2. The average life expectancy of a person born in 2007 is 78 years.

3. The concept of plasticity refers to the capacity for change.

4. The fact that we are living in a technological revolution illustrates the concept of a normative age-graded influence.

5. Ethnicity is a controversial classification of people according to real or imagined biological characteristics such as skin color.

6. Social policy and the welfare of U.S. citizens are rarely influenced by the values held by individual lawmakers.

7. Donald is in poor physical health. When his doctor has him take cognitive tests, the results show that Donald has low intellectual functioning. This is a good illustration of how biological and cognitive processes are bidirectional.

8. Psychoanalysts believe that our behavior is really just a surface manifestation, and that it must be analyzed for its symbolic representation of the deep inner workings of the mind.

9. In Erikson's psychosocial theory, one must solve each crisis or conflict in a completely positive manner, or psychological disorders will develop.

10. When Piaget discussed a child's thinking as qualitatively different in each stage, he meant that the child has a different way of understanding the world, not just that he or she has more information.

11. Information-Processing Theory stresses the importance of stages in cognitive development.

12. One criticism of behavioral and social cognitive theories is the inadequate attention given to developmental changes.

13. Observational research conducted in a laboratory may cause the participants to behave unnaturally

14. Jenny found that the decibel level of fans' voices while people were yelling from the stands at a baseball game was correlated with the number of wins for the team they were yelling for. From this correlation, Jenny can conclude that fan support really is important for helping teams to win.

15. One of the strengths of the longitudinal research design is that it gives us information about how individuals change over time.

Short-Answer Questions

1. Define *development,* and discuss the period it encompasses.

2. Describe how the traditional approach to development differs from the life-span approach.

3. Briefly define biological processes, cognitive processes, and socioemotional processes.

4. Identify and briefly describe the four ways age has been conceptualized.

5. Briefly discuss the nature-nurture controversy.

6. What are two main psychoanalytic theories? List one contribution and one criticism of psychoanalytic theories.

7. Compare and contrast ethological and ecological theories.

8. Explain what is meant by eclectic theoretical orientation. Why is it used in life-span development

research?

9. Describe descriptive, correlational, and experimental types of research.

10. Describe the various ways that researchers study the time span of peoples' lives.

Essay Questions

1. The nature–nurture controversy has been around for a long time. This chapter began with a discussion of the lives of Alice Walker and Ted Kaczynski. If your class were to enter into a debate regarding why Alice became Alice and Ted became Ted, what would you argue? How would you explain Alice's healthy adjustment in adulthood despite a challenging childhood? How would you account for Ted's killing spree despite his promising early potential? Discuss how you think nature and/or nurture comes into play for explaining outcomes such as these. Be sure to incorporate into your answer all you know about biological, cognitive, and socioemotional processes.

2. Your roommate does not allow her 6-year-old child to watch TV, because she thinks violent TV makes children behave aggressively. You're not sure she is correct. For your life-span development class, you decide to design and conduct a research study to test her hypothesis. Outline the variables you would use in this study. Define your independent and dependent variables, experimental and control group(s), whether you would use random assignment and why, what types of measures and methods you would use to collect your data, and so forth. Be sure to include a discussion of any ethical issues that you would need to be particularly aware of while conducting this study. Would you be able to determine causality using your design? Why or why not?

Key to Matching Questions

1. E	2. C	3. A	4. B	5. D

Key to Multiple-Choice Questions

1. A	6. D	11. C	16. B	21. A
2. B	7. D	12. B	17. B	22. B
3. A	8. B	13. C	18. A	23. B
4. B	9. C	14. A	19. D	24. A
5. C	10. B	15. D	20. A	25. B

Key to True/False Questions

1. T	4. F	7. F	10. T	13. T
2. T	5. F	8. T	11. F	14. F
3. T	6. F	9. T	12. T	15. T

Key to Short-Answer Questions

1. Development is the pattern of movement or change that begins at conception and continues through the human life span until death.

2. In the traditional approach, dramatic change occurs in infancy and early childhood, whereas little or no change takes place in adult development. In the life-span approach, developmental change takes

place throughout the human life span.

3. Biological processes involve changes in the individual's physical nature. Cognitive processes involve changes in the individual's thought, intelligence, and language. Socioemotional processes involve changes in the individual's relationships with other people, emotions, and personality.

4. Four conceptualizations of age:
   - Chronological age: the number of years that have elapsed since a person's birth.
   - Biological age: a person's age in terms of biological health.
   - Psychological age: an individual's adaptive capacities compared to those of other individuals of the same chronological age
   - Social age: social roles and expectations related to a person's age.

5. The nature-nurture issue involves the debate about whether development is influenced primarily by maturation (the genetic blueprint or biological inheritance) or by environmental experiences.

6. Two main psychoanalytic theories are Freud's Theory and Erikson's Psychosocial Theory.
   - *Contributions:*
     - Early experiences play an important part in development.
     - Family relationships are a central aspect of development.
     - Unconscious aspects of the mind need to be considered.
     - Erikson's theory acknowledges development during adulthood as well as during childhood.
   - *Criticisms:*
     - Theories are difficult to test scientifically.
     - Data often comes from individual's reconstruction of the past and is of unknown accuracy.
     - Sexual underpinnings of development in Freud's theory are given too much importance.
     - The unconscious mind is given too much credit for influencing development.
     - Images of human beings are too negative.
     - These theories tend to be culture- and gender-biased.

7. Ethological theory holds that behavior is strongly influenced by biology and evolution. Ecological theory puts more emphasis on the environmental contexts in which development occurs and less on biology.

8. An eclectic orientation does not follow any one theoretical approach completely but selects and uses what is considered the best in each theory. No single theory has been able to account for all aspects of life-span development, but each theory has made important contributions to our understanding of development. Different theories contain many ideas that are complimentary and explain different aspects and issues in development.

9. Descriptive research focuses on observing and recording behavior. Correlational research focuses on studying relationships among variables and predictions based on these relationships. Experimental research is the only type of research that examines cause and effect relationships by utilizing randomization and control.

10. The 1) cross-sectional approach involves studying individuals at different ages at the same time to allow for age-group comparisons. This approach is time- and cost-effective; however, it does not allow for information regarding how individuals remain stable or change in specific ways over time. The 2) longitudinal approach studies a group of people over time, to see how the individuals in this

9

group change. This approach allows for researchers to examine the stability or change of individuals over time; however, it is expensive and time consuming, and participants sometimes drop out before the study is over. The 3) sequential approach is a combination of the cross-sectional and longitudinal approaches. This approach is especially effective at studying cohort effects.

Key to Essay Questions

1. The following points should be included in your answer:
    a. an explanation of what nature and nurture are in terms of biological predisposition and environmental influence
    b. a discussion of the interaction between nature and nurture
    c. a discussion the ideas of early theorists as well as of more recent work
    d. a discussion of the many contextual forces that can affect development

2. In this study, you need to consider the ethics of exposing children to violent content if you think it may have a harmful effect on their development. Because of the brief exposure, however, it is likely that this experiment would be considered one of minimal risk to participants. Informed parental consent would be necessary as would consent of any child over age 7 years. Children or parents could cease participation at any time. You would be able to determine causality, because you would use random assignment with a group of children (say, all third graders at a local school) who all vary on their initial levels of aggression. It is not completely random if they all come from the same school, because, for example, that school might be in a violent neighborhood, but it is close. You would randomly assign each child to the violent or nonviolent TV exposure condition, so type of TV viewed would be your independent variable. Then you would measure the children's levels of aggression after viewing, so level of aggression would be your dependent variable. The experimental group would watch something violent, such as professional wrestling. The control group would watch something for the same amount of time that was nonviolent, such as a nature show. Then you would put all the children in a room with various toys, both violent and nonviolent (for instance, toy guns and art supplies), or send them out to a playground for a more naturalistic measurement and see which kids were most aggressive. You could use observational measurements, frequency tallies of specific behaviors, videotaped sessions coded later for aggressive behavior, and so on.

Research Project 1:
Issues in the Media

Review the learning objectives for Chapter 1 and note the issues that Santrock discusses. Then monitor the media (newspapers, talk/news radio, television) for a week, and keep track of when and in what context a specific issue of interest to you is raised. For example, you might keep track of news regarding parenting practices, child development, or crimes that have been committed (and discussion of their perpetrators). Calculate how often the issue is discussed, and note how it was presented (whether reporting was biased, whether it presented in terms of the life-span perspective, whether it was it fully covered, and so forth). What additional information would you need to fully understand the issue (or story presented in the media)? Practice critical thinking whenever viewing media items. Criticize, analyze, and integrate what you hear with what you have learned in your life-span development class. See how these stories or news items can be applied to what you do in your own life. Be ready to discuss your findings in the classroom or online discussion groups.

Research Project 2:
Exploring Professional Journals

Obtain a professional journal article from a journal such as those shown in the chapter (for example, *Child Development*, *Human Development*, *Gerontology*, *Child Abuse and Neglect*, the *Journal of Family Psychology*). You can find journals by going to your university's library's website and looking in their PsycINFO, PsycARTICLES, or Ovid databases. Do a search for any topic that interests you (Freud's lasting contribution to psychology, the impact of the first five years of life, the impact of abuse on children's lives, healthy marriages, treatments for Alzheimer's Disease, and so forth). Many journal articles are available in their full-text format online; just print them out. Others require you to order them through your interlibrary loan (provided you have searched your university's catalog and did not find what you wanted). You may also go to the "BF" or "RC" sections in your library's collection. "BF" and "RC" start most of the call numbers for catalogued items in psychology. Once you find the article you want, evaluate the research in that article using the criteria in the chapter for good research. Be sure that the article is describing an actual research study (you can determine this by reading the abstract or beginning summary of the article). You won't be able to answer the questions below if your article is simply a review of research other people have done (a literature review).

Consider the following:

1. As you read about the research, could you easily determine both the independent and the dependent variables? (Note that there may be more than one of each type.)

2. What theories were emphasized in the introduction? What hypotheses were tested by the research?

3. What did you learn from reading the methods section? Describe the participants and the procedures that were used.

4. What did you learn from reading the results section of this article? What statistical methods were used? Did you understand why those methods were chosen? Which results, if any, did the researchers state were statistically significant? How were (or were not) the graphs, figures, tables, or charts helpful?

5. What did you learn from reading the discussion section of this article? How did the authors interpret the results? Did the authors discuss any limitations of the research? Did they suggest any further study based on their findings?

6. What stumbling blocks, if any, did you encounter in reading and understanding this article? How might the authors have made their paper more clear? If you did have any problems understanding sections of the article, which sections were they? What was the problem with understanding these sections?

7. As you consider the research reported in this article, were there any ethical issues that were raised for you? What were they? How were they (or how could they be) handled?

8. Did this article suggest a research area you might be interested in pursuing? How would you design that research?

Personal Application Project 1:
Consider Your Own Development

Reconstruct your development from as early as you can remember up to the person you are today. Consider the developmental issues of nature–nurture, continuity–discontinuity, and stability–change discussed in Chapter 1. Describe the parts of you (for example, aspects of your personality, your intellect, your values and beliefs, your basic behavior patterns) that you believe result from each of these elements. Use the following chart or devise some other graphic aid to help you visualize which elements have played the strongest role in shaping you.

Aspect of Your Self	Nature–Nurture	Continuity–Discontinuity	Stability–Change
Personality traits (describe)			
Intellect (describe)			
Values and beliefs (describe)			
Behavior patterns (describe)			
Other (describe)			

Personal Application Project 2:
Reflecting on What You Learned by Applying the Theories to Your Own Development

Consider what you read in Chapter 1, and then answer the following questions:

1. Did you realize there were so many theories, or ways, to view and organize the topics in life-span development?

2. Which of the theories seemed most appealing to you? Why?

3. Which theories seemed too complex or confusing? Too weird?

4. Can you use any of the these theories to help you better understand your own or your children's development?

5. Outline some of your characteristics in the following chart. Place theories that you think are relevant to helping you better understand yourself (or your child) in the right-hand column. You might also make note of any theories that would definitely *not* help in explaining each part of your development, and why. This exercise should help you stretch your critical *and* integrative thinking muscles, as well as help you apply text material to your own life in an understandable way. (Remember that this exercise helps you remember complex material for exams!)

Aspect of Yourself	Theory (or Theories) and Explanation of How It Applies (or They Apply)
Personality traits (describe)	
Intellect (describe)	
Values and beliefs (describe)	
Behavior patterns (describe)	
Other (describe)	

Personal Application Project 3:
Designing a Good Research Study to Answer Burning Questions from Your Own Life

PLEASE NOTE: FOR THIS PROJECT YOU ARE ONLY DESIGNING A STUDY. IF YOU WISHED TO ACTUALLY CONDUCT THE STUDY, YOU WOULD NEED TO CHECK WITH YOUR INSTRUCTOR TO SEE IF YOU ARE REQUIRED TO COMPLETE AN INSTITUTIONAL RESEARCH BOARD PROTOCOL.

Think about the mysteries in your own development or experiences with other developing people. Are there questions you have always wondered about that you might be able to answer with a good research study? These are some of the questions students are often interested in:

1. Are boys really more aggressive than girls?

2. Are mothers better listeners than fathers?

3. Do fathers play more with children than mothers?

4. Do husbands get mad less often than wives?

5. Do old people really have bad memories?

Whatever you are wondering about, think about how to design a study to test your hypothesis. Which of the theories in the text might explain the phenomenon you are thinking about? Can you test this theory? Or do you need to perhaps formulate a new theory based on what you find in your study? Try to think about what research methods you would use (case study? survey? observation?). How would you use time in your study: cross-sectionally, longitudinally, or sequentially? Would you ever be able to determine causality using your research design? Why or why not? What ethical problems might arise in working with the participants you have chosen? How would you safeguard them by ensuring an ethically sound study? If you practice this exercise, you are certain to master the section on research methods in the text and really understand it (versus just memorizing definitions or terms).

Internet Projects

Check out the McGraw-Hill website for this text (http://www.mhhe.com/santrockessls). You will find numerous activities there, in particular, quizzes. Also, be patient, because there are many very worthy links on each of the sites, but they do take a little time to access. If you do not go to the links many times, you will not get the full value of the site. Please go to all links.

Please note that all website addresses in this Study Guide have been checked and were correct at the time of publication. However, websites may be discontinued or their addresses may change, so when you try to access a given site, it may no longer be viable. If that occurs, please notify the publisher so that it can make appropriate revisions in future editions of this Study Guide.

Internet Project 1:
Careers in Life-Span Development

The Internet offers many job sites, some general and others more specific to life-span development. The two sites particularly geared toward psychologists are sponsored by the American Psychological Association (APA) and the American Psychological Society (APS). A third site belongs to *The Chronicle of Higher Education*, a publication that is widely read by college faculty and administrators. All three sites (and their print publications) have excellent articles on relevant topics for anyone interested in the social sciences and higher education; they also have job postings. Go to each of these sites and check out the positions listed that are relevant to life-span development.

Graduate Students' Portal: http://www.psychgrad.org
This site organizes the best information on the Web for helping undergraduates do well and also has a large amount of information regarding applying to graduate school and succeeding there.

American Psychological Association: http://www.apa.org
On this site, there is a special "classified ads" link in the student section, and if you look at the books there, you will find one entitled Career Paths in Psychology: Where Your Degree Can Take You.

American Psychological Society: http://www.psychologicalscience.org/
See this site's "employment ads" section.

Chronicle of Higher Education: http://chronicle.com/jobs/
On this site, you can search for jobs by ZIP code.

Internet Project 2:
Psychological Theories

Use http://www.google.com or http://www.dogpile.com (you may also use some of the links to famous theorists listed below) to do a search for your most favorite and least favorite theorist in the chapter. Visit a few of the links that come up for each theorist, and peruse the information provided. Check out the pictures of the person, his/her biography, his/her major writings, and so on. How does the information that you found at these links compare with the information in your text? Was there additional information that was not in the text? Were there additional theories or theories that related to different topics? How much of what you found in the links appeared to be someone's personal opinion as opposed to researched information? How do you judge the credibility of what you found? How helpful was the search? Did reading more about your least favorite theorist make you like him/her any more? Why or why not?

Internet Project 3:
Child Advocacy

There are many different Web sources that deal with the welfare of children. Some are based on empirical research, some are voices of advocacy, some are biased, and others are more balanced. Even on the same site, you might find a mixture. Explore some of these sites, and describe each of them in terms of the type of information provided, the source of the information, how useful it is, how emotionally laden it is, how balanced or biased the site appears to be, and any other comments you might have concerning each site. How research-based is the site? Browse around, and see if there are any research studies cited to support the assertions on the site. Are there any links to full-text professional journal articles? Evaluate the quality of any arguments the site makes, and evaluate the quality of the research used.

Try some of the following:

Children's Defense Fund: http://www.childrensdefense.org
This is the organization headed by Marian Wright Edelman to promote child welfare (discussed in Chapter 1 of the text).

National Coalition for the Homeless: http://www.nationalhomeless.org
The NCH is a major resource on all aspects of homelessness including homeless children.

Child Welfare League of America: http://www.cwla.org
The oldest and largest child welfare organization in the United States, the CWLA is dedicated to promoting the welfare of all children and protecting them from harm.

Child Trauma Academy: http://www.childtrauma.org
The academy is an online classroom devoted to understanding traumatized and maltreated children's

development. There are free online classes for continuing education credits and a wealth of resources for anyone interested in child abuse and traumatized children.

Attachment Parenting International: http://www.attachmentparenting.org
API is an international political movement to bring about world peace through the nurturing of children around the world.

Other Relevant Sites on the Internet

AARP (formerly known as the American Association for Retired Persons): http://www.aarp.org
Explore the website of AARP, an especially powerful organization that educates, lobbies on behalf of, and provides services about and for people age 50 and older.

Children's Defense Fund (CDF): http://www.childrensdefense.org
Headed by Marian Wright Edelman, Children's Defense Fund works to promote child welfare (discussed in Chapter 1 of the text).

George Mason University's Online Resources for Developmental Psychology:
http://classweb.gmu.edu/awinsler/ordp/topic.html
This excellent website is reviewed by experts in the field. It includes a wide array of links for teaching and learning about human development. See especially the students' section.

Society for Research in Child Development (SRCD): http://www.srcd.org
The Society for Research in Child Development promotes multidisciplinary research in human development, fosters the exchange of information among scientists and other professionals of various disciplines, and encourages applications of research findings.

Sigmund Freud: www.freud.org.uk/fmrese.htm
The official site for the Freud Research Centre in London includes Freud's letters, documents, personal art, and photos from when he and his daughter, Anna, fled the Nazi invasion of his native Austria and lived out his remaining years in England.

Erik Erikson: www.erikson.edu/
Erikson is a graduate school for child development studies. The site covers Eric Erikson himself, the history of the school, and the Eriksonian approach, and it also introduces the faculty and programs. www.ship.edu/~cgboeree/erikson.html offers a nice look at Erikson's life and accomplishments, and also summarizes his theories.

Jean Piaget Society: www.piaget.org/
The society's site explores Piaget's theories, offers conferences on cognitive development, has overviews of his life, and explores the cognitive differences in children and adults. www.ship.edu/~cgboeree/piaget.html gives a nice synopsis of the main elements of his theory.

Lev Vygotsky: www.sk.com.br/sk-vygot.html
This site provides a brief overview of Vygotsky's theory of language acquisition and is written in both English and Portuguese. www.humboldt1.com/~cr2/ is Carl Ratner's Institute for Cultural Research and Education. Click on some of the articles, and you can read about Vygotsky's concept of psychological

development, the historical significance of Vygotsky's sociocultural psychology, as well as lots of other info on the theorist.

Albert Bandura: www.emory.edu/EDUCATION/mfp/bandurabio.html
This page contains some nice photos of Bandura's life, covers his biography, outlines his theories, and offers some films for purchase. Bandura is still working at Stanford University.

Chapter 2: Biological Beginnings

Learning Goals

1. Discuss the evolutionary perspective on development.
2. Describe how genes influence human development.
3. Characterize some of the ways that heredity and environment interact to produce individual differences in development.
4. Describe prenatal development.
5. Discuss the birth process.

Chapter Outline

THE EVOLUTIONARY PERSPECTIVE
    Natural Selection and Adaptive Behavior
    Evolutionary Psychology
        Developmental Evolutionary Psychology
        Evolutionary Psychology

THE GENETIC FOUNDATIONS OF DEVELOPMENT
    The Genetic Process
        Mitosis, Meiosis, and Fertilization
        Sources of Variability
    Genetic Principles
        Dominant–Recessive Genes Principle
        Sex-Linked Genes
        Polygenic Inheritance
    Chromosome and Gene-Linked Abnormalities
        Chromosome Abnormalities
            Down Syndrome
            Sex-Linked Chromosome Abnormalities
        Gene-Linked Abnormalities

HEREDITY AND ENVIRONMENT INTERACTION: THE NATURE-NURTURE DEBATE
    Behavior Genetics
    Heredity–Environment Correlations
    The Epigenetic View
    Conclusions about Heredity–Environment Interactions

PRENATAL DEVELOPMENT
    The Course of Prenatal Development
        The Germinal Period
        The Embryonic Period
        The Fetal Period
    Prenatal Tests
    Infertility and Reproductive Technology
    Hazards to Prenatal Development
        General Principles

Prescription and Nonprescription Drugs
Psychoactive Drugs
Caffeine
Alcohol
Nicotine
Cocaine
Methamphetamine
Marijuana
Heroin
Incompatible Blood Types
Maternal Diseases
Maternal Diet and Nutrition
Emotional States and Stress
Maternal Age
Paternal Factors
Environmental Hazards
Prenatal Care
Cultural Beliefs about Pregnancy

BIRTH
The Birth Process
Stages of Birth
Childbirth Setting and Attendants
Methods of Childbirth
Medication
Natural and Prepared Childbirth
Other Nonmedicated Techniques to Reduce Pain
Cesarean Delivery
Low Birth Weight and Preterm Infants
Incidences and Causes of Low Birth Weight
Consequences of Low Birth Weight
Kangaroo Care and Massage Therapy
Bonding
The Postpartum Period
Physical Adjustments
Emotional and Psychological Adjustments

Matching Questions

_____ 1. Chromosomally transmitted form of mental retardation caused by the presence of an extra copy of chromosome

A. teratogen

_____ 2. Period of prenatal development that occurs the first two weeks after conception.

B. Down syndrome

_____ 3. Period of prenatal development in which the embryo undergoes organogenesis.

C. fragile X syndrome

_____ 4. Any agent that can potentially cause a birth defect or negatively alter cognitive and behavioral outcomes.

D. embryonic period

_____ 5. Genetic disorder involving an abnormality in the X chromosome which becomes constricted and often breaks.

E. germinal period

Multiple-Choice Questions

1. Merta believes that, for a species to continue in an environment, it must be able to reproduce and adapt. Merta believes in _____.
a. life-span development
b. polygenetic inheritance
c. natural selection
d. mutation and aggression

2. Fred and Jonathan, who are both 8 years old, love to wrestle and play-fight. According to evolutionary psychology, how could you explain this common activity of young boys in most cultures around the world?
a. Humans have evolved an extended "juvenile" period for complex brain development which results in more aggressive social interactions.
b. Historically men who were competent fighters were more likely to survive and pass their genetic legacy to the next generation, so boys are genetically programmed to be more aggressive.
c. Some characteristics of childhood, such as rough and tumble play, are adaptive early on but not do not prepare us for adulthood when aggression is no longer an adaptive trait.
d. We have evolved "domain-specific" psychological mechanisms that allow boys to show more aggressive behaviors when interacting in same-sex play groups.

3. Francie believes that our physical features and our decision making, aggressive behavior, fears, and mating patterns have been influenced many years ago. According to Buss, this has occurred by _____.
a. environmental shaping
b. instinct
c. social transformation
d. genetics

4. The units of hereditary information that act as a blueprint for cells to reproduce themselves and manufacture the proteins that maintain life are _____.
a. chromosomes
b. DNA
c. genes
d. ribosomes

5. In _____, the number of chromosomes present remains the same, whereas in _____, the number of chromosomes is halved.
a. meiosis, mitosis
b. mitosis, meiosis
c. genotype, phenotype
d. phenotype, genotype

6. Traits that are produced by the interaction between two or more genes are called _____.
a. dominant
b. recessive
c. monogenic
d. polygenic

7. Down syndrome is caused by _____.
a. an extra chromosome
b. alcohol consumption by the mother during pregnancy
c. the mother's poor nutrition
d. an extra X chromosome on the 23rd pair

8. Behavioral geneticists believe that behaviors are determined by _____.
a. only biological factors
b. only environmental factors
c. heredity and environment
d. genetic predisposition

9. If heredity is an important determinant of a specific behavior, what prediction can we make about expression of the behavior in identical twins reared apart compared to its expression in fraternal twins reared apart?
a. Fraternal twins express the behavior more similarly than do identical twins.
b. There is little similarity in the expression of the behavior in either set of twins.
c. Identical twins express the behavior more similarly than do fraternal twins.
d. The behavior is expressed similarly by identical twins and fraternal twins.

10. Children who are highly active, easily distracted, and move very fast frequently elicit adult attempts to quiet them down, punishment for lack of concentration, and angry warnings to slow down. This describes an example of an interaction between _____ and environment.
a. passive genotype
b. active genotype
c. niche-picking genotype
d. evocative genotype

11. Larry and Anita grew up in the same household, went to the same schools, participated in their family's social activities, and observed their parents' dedication to work and community. These experiences constitute Larry and Anita's _____.
a. shared environmental influences
b. nonshared environmental influences
c. niche-picking experiences
d. heritability

12. Which of the following statements regarding how genes work is FALSE?
a. The relative contributions of heredity and environment are not additive in nature (for example you cannot conclude that if 30% of a trait is genetic, then 70 percent must be environmentally influenced)
b. Genetic expression happens at conception, and we carry this genetic legacy with us into the world
c. Genes produce proteins throughout the life span (or do not produce them, depending on our environments)
d. Genes interact bidirectionally with environments

13. A fertilized ovum is called a (an) _____.
a. blastocyst
b. egg
c. embryo
d. zygote

14. The period of prenatal development that occurs in the first two weeks after conception is the _____.
a. fetal period
b. germinal period
c. embryonic period
d. blastocystic period

15. The fetus becomes viable during the _____.
a. germinal period
b. first trimester
c. second trimester
d. third trimester

16. The baby that Marta is carrying is developing fine details to systems that emerged during the embryonic period. Marta's pregnancy is entering the _____.
a. germinal period
b. postembryo period
c. fetal period
d. first trimester

17. Which phrase best defines a teratogen?
a. a life-support system that protects the fetus
b. an agent that stimulates the formation of organs
c. an abnormality in infants of alcoholic mothers
d. an environmental factor that produces birth defects

18. Meri parties and drinks during her pregnancy. Her baby will most likely _____.
a. be physically deformed and below average in intelligence
b. not survive; she will have a miscarriage
c. become a victim of an ectopic pregnancy
d. be born before term and have Down syndrome

19. Marchelle is 6 weeks pregnant. She is ingesting all the following substances. Which one is LEAST likely to be harmful to her baby?
a. multivitamin supplements to compensate for poor diet
b. Accutane for her acne
c. aspirin for her headaches
d. coffee to wake up in the morning

20. Vibeka has used cocaine throughout her pregnancy but believed that her baby was safe from horrible problems such as those found in babies exposed to alcohol in utero. However, research shows that cocaine has many negative effects on the developing baby. In fact, all but which one of the following symptoms are linked to cocaine use during pregnancy.
a. reduced head circumference
b. facial abnormalities
c. poor language development
d. impaired motor skills

21. Which of the following statements most accurately describes the relationship between maternal age and pregnancy outcome?
a. Adolescent mothers are most likely to have retarded children.
b. Artificially inseminated women in their 30s and 40s are more likely to become pregnant than those in their 20s.
c. Mothers over age 30 are most likely to have retarded babies.
d. Adolescent mothers suffer the lowest infant mortality rates of any age group.

22. Amy is afraid to use any drugs during labor because she has heard they can have negative effects on the baby. However, she does not feel she can endure any more pain after 12 hours of labor. Which of the following is NOT a factor that influences the impact of a drug on the fetus?
a. the particular drug
b. the drug dosage
c. individual differences between fetuses
d. the ethnicity of the fetus

23. Which of the following factors is NOT related to preterm birth rates?
a. age of the mother
b. multiple-births
c. high rates of physical activity
d. increased substance abuse

24. Which of the following is NOT one of the benefits of using "kangaroo care" with preterm infants?
a. earlier hospital discharge
b. fewer learning disabilities later on
c. more stable breathing
d. improved milk supply in mothers

25. Marjorie has just had a healthy baby boy, and a relatively easy birth. However, now that she is home with her baby, she is experiencing emotional fluctuations. Which of the following statements is most likely true?
a. Marjorie should get professional counseling immediately for postpartum depression.
b. Marjorie needs to get more education about how to care for her baby and deal with her feelings.
c. Marjorie's husband is not giving her enough support.
d. Marjorie's emotional fluctuations may be due to hormonal changes, fatigue, or the demands of having a new baby.

True/False Questions

1. Evolutionary psychologists argue that if a behavior exists today, it has evolved and continues to exist because it is adaptive for us.

2. Although events inside a cell (considered the gene's environment) can affect genetic expression, events in the human being's environment cannot affect gene expression.

3. Because of complex chromosomal exchanges during meiosis, the zygote formed when sperm and egg meet is not composed of exact copies of the mother's or the father's cells. It is a unique combination of their genes.

4. Women have twice the likelihood of having a sex-linked genetic abnormality, because they have twice as many X chromosomes as men.

5. The genetic abnormality called PKU (phenylketonuria) is a good example of how a person's genetic inheritance for a certain disorder inevitably leads to that disorder's developing later on in the person's life.

6. The epigenetic view sees heredity and environment influencing each other bidirectionally, whereas the heredity—environment correlation view sees only heredity influencing the environment.

7. Wendy and Frank conceived a baby one week ago. That means that cell division has now led to the formation of a trophoblast which will become the placenta.

8. Teratogens such as alcohol and exposure to radiation have devastating effects at all periods of prenatal development. The timing of exposure to harmful influences such as these would not alter their influence on the baby.

9. Some fetuses are genetically more susceptible to the effects of teratogens than are others.

10. The shortest of the three stages of childbirth is the afterbirth stage, when the placenta is expelled.

11. We define low-birthweight infants as those weighing less than 5.5 pounds.

12. Low-birthweight children tend to have learning problems in infancy, but they usually catch up and have no adverse effects once they enter school.

13. Kangaroo care is beneficial for preterm infants and is now being recommended for full-term infants as well.

14. When professionals speak of the postpartum period, they are referring to the period after nine months' gestation when many babies continue their development for a month or two after the average pregnancy has ended.

15. Postpartum depression is a serious problem experienced by over half of new mothers.

Short-Answer Questions

1. What are some basic ideas about human development proposed by evolutionary psychology?

2. Briefly discuss the relationships among human chromosomes, DNA, and genes.

3. Explain the difference between genotype and phenotype.

4. List and describe some chromosomal and gene-linked abnormalities.

5. List three developmental characteristics or events from each of the germinal, embryonic, and fetal periods of prenatal development.

6. Define a teratogen, and identify at least three teratogens.

7. List three paternal factors that can influence prenatal development.

8. List and describe the three main stages of birth.

9. Define low-birth-weight, preterm, and small-for-date infants.

10. Discuss key aspects of mother/newborn bonding.

Essay Questions

1. You are asked to talk to a high school class about potential hazards to prenatal development. The principal of the high school has suggested that you discuss not only alcohol and other drugs but also environmental hazards, maternal diseases, and paternal influences as well. She has asked that you be honest about the different agents that can cause problems, the problems they may cause, and how these problems can be avoided. What would you tell the students about teratogens and prenatal care?

2. One of your friends has recently married and has now confided in you that she is pregnant. She knows you're taking this class in life-span development and asks for your input concerning what she can expect when giving birth, and she wants your suggestions concerning her childbirth options. What would you tell her about the three stages of birth, complications she might expect, options about the use of drugs, and the childbirth strategies that are available to her?

Key to Matching Questions

1. B	2. E	3.D	4. A	5. C

Key to Multiple-Choice Questions

1. C	6. D	11. A	16. C	21. C
2. B	7. A	12. D	17. D	22. D
3. D	8. C	13. D	18. A	23. C
4. C	9. C	14. B	19. A	24. B
5. B	10. D	15. D	20. B	25. A

Key to True/False Questions

1. T	4. F	7. T	10. T	13. T
2. F	5. F	8. F	11. T	14. F
3. T	6. T	9. T	12. F	15. T

Key to Short-Answer Questions

1. The evolutionary process of natural selection applies to behavioral traits as well as physical characteristics. Evolution favors certain behaviors that can increase chances for reproductive success.

2. Each human cell contains 46 chromosomes, threadlike structures that come in 23 pairs with one member of each pair coming from each parent. Chromosomes contain DNA, a complex molecule containing genetic information. Genes, the units of hereditary information, are short segments of DNA. Genes are the blueprints for cell reproduction.

3. Genotype is the person's genetic heritage, the actual genetic material; phenotype is the way an individual's genotype is expressed in observed and measurable characteristics.

4. Some gene or chromosome-linked abnormalities:
    *   *Down Syndrome*
        *   presence of an extra chromosome
        *   characterized by round face, flattened skull, extra fold of skin over eyelids, protruding tongue, short limbs, and retardation of motor and mental abilities
    *   *Klinefelter Syndrome*
        *   presence of an extra X chromosome in males making them XXY instead of XY
        *   characterized by underdeveloped testes and enlarged breasts in males
    *   *Fragile* X Syndrome
        *   abnormality in the X chromosome which becomes constricted and often breaks
        *   characterized by possible mental deficiency, learning disabilities, or short attention spans
    *   *Turner Syndrome*
        *   missing or partially deleted X chromosome in females making them XO
        *   characterized by short stature, webbed neck, and possible infertility
    *   *XYY* Syndrome
        *   presence of an extra Y chromosome in males, making them XYY

5. Key aspects for each period of prenatal development:
   - *Germinal*
     - takes place in first two weeks after conception
     - includes creation of a zygote
     - rapid cell division begins
     - cell differentiation begins
   - *Embryonic*
     - occurs from two to eight weeks after conception
     - zygote attaches to the uterine wall
     - rate of cell differentiation intensifies
     - support systems for cells form
     - organs appear
     - endoderm, ectoderm, and mesoderm develop
     - urogenital system is apparent
     - arm and leg buds emerge
     - four chambers of the heart take place
     - intestinal track develops
   - *Fetal*
     - begins two months after conception and lasts for seven months
     - fetus becomes active, moving limbs, head, and opening and closing mouth
     - face, forehead, eyelids, nose, and chin are distinguishable
     - genitals can be identified as male or female
     - rapid growth and weight gain
     - prenatal reflexes become stronger
     - skin structures form
     - organ function intensifies
     - fatty tissues develop

6. A teratogen is any agent that can cause a birth defect or long-term cognitive/behavioral problems. Teratogens include but are not limited to nicotine, alcohol, heroin, caffeine, toxins (such as lead and various pollutants), cocaine, marijuana, some prescription and nonprescription drugs, infectious diseases, and radiation.

7. Paternal factors that can influence prenatal development include: cocaine (birth defects); nicotine (low birth weight, childhood cancer, and miscarriage); exposure to pollutants and toxins (childhood cancer and miscarriage); and age (Down syndrome, birth defects, dwarfism, and Marfan's syndrome).

8. Descriptions of each stage of birth:
   - *First Stage:*
     - longest of the three stages
     - uterine contractions begin
     - cervix stretches and opens
   - *Second Stage:*
     - lasts an average of 1 ½ hours
     - baby's head starts to move through the cervix and the birth canal
     - baby completely emerges from the mother's body

- *Third Stage (or afterbirth):*
  - shortest of the three stages
  - placenta, umbilical cord, and other membranes are detached and expelled

9. Low-birth-weight infants weigh less than 5 ½ pounds at birth.
   - Preterm infants are those born three weeks or more before pregnancy has reached full term (35 or fewer weeks after conception).
   - Small-for-date infants may be preterm or full term and have a below-normal weight for their gestational age.

10. Bonding is the formation of a connection between parent and newborn. Sometimes hospital conditions can interfere with bonding (pain drugs make the mother drowsy, separation of mother and newborn after delivery, preterm infants may be isolated from the mother, etc.). Some physicians believe that parent and child need to form an emotional attachment shortly after birth in order for optimal development in years to come. The extreme bonding hypothesis that a newborn must have close contact with the mother in the first few days of life to develop optimally is simply not true. Many hospitals offer rooming-in arrangements in which a baby can remain in the mother's room most of the time during its hospital stay.

Key to Essay Questions

1. Answering this question is fairly straightforward if you review the tables and text in the chapter. You could make up a table that lists each teratogen, and its effect on development. Most people don't understand that fathers' behaviors and exposure to toxins also affect babies, so you might stress this to the young men in the audience. Also, over-the-counter drugs and even aspirin can cause problems. So outline the substances and behaviors that should be avoided, and emphasize the extreme importance of regular prenatal care and good health of both the mother and the father. Another important point is that very young mothers tend to have low-birth-weight babies, and these babies tend to have more physical and psychological problems than do babies of women in their 20s. This means trying to avoid having a baby at too young an age.

2. Your friend would need to know about the physiology of pregnancy and birth, so you could discuss the fact that the first stage of birth (labor) is typically 12 to 24 hours long and involves light contractions that steadily grow stronger. Labor leads to dilation (opening) and effacement (thinning) of the cervix so that the baby's head can come through. The second stage of birth usually involves about an hour of pushing the baby out. The third stage of birth is fairly brief and involves expulsion of the placenta and membranes. Each woman experiences labor and birth differently, so there are no generalizations that can be made except that it's painful and that the pain can be managed in various ways. List the different types of drugs mentioned in the chapter, and tell your friend the advantages and disadvantages of each one. Also talk to her about the various nonmedical ways to manage pain, such as breathing techniques and managing the birth environment (see Lamaze, Natural, and Prepared birthing methods). Review the chapter, and add any other pertinent information regarding complications at each stage and of each method.

Research Project 1:
Heritability of Eye Color

PLEASE NOTE: IF YOU NEED TO CONTACT YOUR RELATIVES TO COMPLETE THIS PROJECT, PLEASE CHECK WITH YOUR INSTRUCTOR TO SEE IF YOU NEED TO COMPLETE AN INSTITUTIONAL RESEARCH BOARD PROTOCOL.

To increase your understanding of the concept of heritability (and the dominant–recessive genes principle), collect eye-color data from your own family. (Look only at blood relatives, not relatives by marriage.) Use the following table to record the eye color of all family members, and then answer the following questions.

1. What patterns did you notice for members of your family in terms of eye color?

2. Which eye color seems most prominent?

3. Describe how the dominant–recessive genes principle would explain the patterns you found.

4. Are your observations consistent with what this principle would predict? Explain.

(Note that if there are fewer people of one category of siblings, aunts, uncles, and/or cousins but more of another, you can feel free to change category names—for example, you can change "siblings" to "cousins.")

Totals	Family Information
Number with brown eyes	
Number with blue eyes	
Number with green eyes	
Number with other color (describe)	
Family Member	Eye Color
Self	
Mother	
Father	
Maternal grandmother	
Maternal grandfather	
Paternal grandmother	

Paternal grandfather	
Sibling	
Sibling	
Sibling	
Maternal aunt	
Paternal aunt	
aunt	
Maternal uncle	
Paternal uncle	
uncle	
Maternal cousin	
Maternal cousin	
Paternal cousin	
Paternal cousin	

Research Project 2:
Women's Health Practices

PLEASE NOTE: THIS PROJECT ASKS YOU TO INTERVIEW OTHER WOMEN. PLEASE CHECK WITH YOUR INSTRUCTOR TO SEE IF YOU NEED TO COMPLETE AN INSTITUTIONAL RESEARCH BOARD PROTOCOL BEFORE BEGINNING THIS PROJECT.

The text discusses certain maternal behaviors that are potentially harmful to the unborn child such as smoking and using alcohol and other drugs; it also discusses healthful practices such as good nutrition, safe exercise, and prenatal care. Talk to women you know who are of childbearing age (especially if you know any pregnant women) to see how much they know about what is harmful and healthful for their unborn child; assess the behaviors in which they engage; and for those who smoke, drink, or use other drugs, have them tell you why they do so, whether they will continue to do so when they are pregnant, and what they expect the consequences might be for their child. If they are unaware of the potential harmful effects of teratogens, explain these to them, then ask if they would engage in these practices while pregnant (or if pregnant, ask if they might consider stopping). Compare the responses to see if you can draw any conclusions. What type of campaign might be useful to have women discontinue unhealthy behaviors and engage in healthful ones instead?

Tally the results of your interviews on the chart below. Try to visit with each woman again after you complete the project, and show her the results. At this time, be sure to be able to explain each category—such as the dangers of smoking during pregnancy.

	Aware of Potential Danger	Unaware of Potential Danger	Believes There Is a Critical Period	Problems Caused	Treatment, if Any
Smoking					
Alcohol					
Exercise					
Nutrition					
Prenatal care					
Father smoking					
Fish consumption					

Personal Application Project 1:
Assessing the Risks of Having a Child with Genetic or Chromosomal Abnormalities

Imagine yourself married and planning on starting a family. Review the genetic/chromosomal disorders discussed in the chapter. What are the characteristics of each one, and the factors that put people at risk for having a child with such a disorder? What treatments are available, and how common is each disorder? Are your offspring at risk for any of these disorders? Would you seek genetic testing to reveal either a risk for, or the presence of, each of the disorders in your unborn child? If you found out that your child was going to be born with a disorder, would you consider the possibility of abortion or adoption? What would it be like to raise a child with one of these disorders? Which disorders would be most devastating and which most "acceptable" for you to cope with in a child?

Personal Application Project 2:
How Can This Chapter Help You Understand Your Own Development?

Reflect on your own development, and reconstruct it from as early as you can remember up to today. Consider the theories regarding genetic and environmental influences on development discussed in the chapter, and decide which ones best apply to your own experiences. Feel free to use more than one theory to describe different aspects of your development, or use them as overlapping explanations. Use the following chart.

Aspect of Yourself	Arguments Presented for Influences on This Trait's Development	Describe How the Information Applies to Your Life
Personality traits (describe)		
Intellect (describe)		
Physical characteristics (e.g., height, eye color; describe)		
Physical disorders (e.g., diabetes, Klinefelter syndrome; describe)		
Other (describe)		

On the basis of the information in your chart and in the chapter (and any other information you might have gathered), answer these questions.

1. Does the information in the chapter and in your chart provide you with a better understanding of yourself? In what way?

2. How can you use this information in your own life?

3. In what way (if any) will this information affect your decisions concerning family planning?

4. Was any of this information frightening to you, or did it make you feel less fearful? Explain.

5. What other insights have you gained from preparing this chart?

Internet Projects

Check out the McGraw-Hill website for this text (www.mhhe.com/santrockessls). You will find numerous activities there, and in particular, quizzes. Also, be patient, because there are many very worthy links on each of the sites, but they do take a little time to access. If you do not go to the links many times, you will not get the full value of the site. Please go to all links.

Please note that all website addresses in this Study Guide have been checked and were correct at the time of publication. However, websites may be discontinued or their addresses may change, so when you try to access a given site, it may no longer be viable. If that occurs, please notify the publisher so that it can make appropriate revisions in future editions of this Study Guide.

Internet Project 1:
Biological Beginnings

Use http://www.google.com or http://www.dogpile.com to search for links to websites that discuss topics of interest from the text, such as "behavior genetics," "genetic influences on development," "chromosomal abnormalities," or "DNA." How many of the links referred you to websites that outlined material from professional journal articles? How many were someone's personal opinion? How did the information compare with that in the chapter? Compare the information you got from these different sources of information. What other types of links came up in your search? How helpful was the information you found? Did it help you understand the material in the chapter better?

Internet Project 2:
Prenatal Testing

Go to http://health.howstuffworks.com/prenatal-testing.htm and check out the whole section on how prenatal testing works. What different types of tests did you learn about? Which tests were discussed in the text? Were any tests not presented in the text? When would you use each of these tests, and why would each be used? Select a link that interests you from the end of the article and summarize what you learned from that site.

These sites provide additional information on prenatal testing:

Prenatal Testing and Screening: www.w-cpc.org/pregnancy/testing.html
This page describes and illustrates tests.

Prenatal Testing for Down Syndrome: http://www.ds-health.com/prenatal.htm
This pages describes all the tests done for and how to deal with a Down syndrome diagnosis.

Internet Project 3:
Predicting the Baby's Sex

This is a fun project for predicting whether a child will be a boy or a girl. If you or your partner is pregnant, try this for predicting your own child's sex; otherwise, interview someone you know who is pregnant, using the questions on this website: http://www.childbirth.org/articles/boyorgirl.html. If the parents-to-be already know the sex of the child, see if this prediction agrees with the doctor's prediction. Remember that this quiz is based on old folk tales! Note that there is a lot of other information about pregnancy and childbirth on this site as well.

Internet Project 4:
Preventing FAS

Fetal alcohol syndrome (FAS) is 100% preventable. How? By not consuming alcohol when the baby is being conceived or at any time during pregnancy. Once the damage is done, though, it cannot be undone. There are, however, ways to work with children who have FAS (or the milder FAE [fetal alcohol effects]). Go to the website for the National Organization for Fetal Alcohol Syndrome, www.nofas.org, and research this topic. The website is dedicated to educating people about FAS and related disorders as well as improving the quality of life of families affected by FAS. Try to answer the following questions:

1. What is fetal alcohol syndrome?

2. What are the cognitive and physical characteristics of FAS?

3. What are the major problems encountered by someone with FAS?

4. How does FAS differ from FAE?

5. How do FAS or FAE occur, and how can they be prevented?

6. What information can you find about what it's like to parent or adopt a child with FAS?

7. What population do you think should be targeted to receive FAS information in order to prevent more cases of FAS?

Other Relevant Sites on the Internet

U.S. Department of Energy Office of Science: www.ornl.gov/hgmis
The Office of Science is the founder of the Human Genome Project.

Omics Gateway: http://www.nature.com/omics/index.html
This site by the journal *Nature* presents a variety of sources on genome projects—human and nonhuman—around the world. It has a nice genomics primer, research, and coverage of ethical issues related to gene technology (for example, cloning).
National Center for Biotechnology Information: www.ncbi.nlm.nih.gov
Part of the National Institutes of Health, the center disseminates biomedical information. Look around here to find courses, tutorials, glossaries, and much more.

National Down Syndrome Society: www.ndss.org/
This organization provides comprehensive information about Down syndrome, including education, research, and advocacy.

Human Chromosomal Abnormalities: http://anthro.palomar.edu/abnormal/
This comprehensive site discusses diagnostic tests, research articles, common abnormalities, and sex chromosome abnormalities and gives a tutorial on topics covered.

Literature on Bioethics, Cloning, and Reproductive Technologies: http://ethics.sandiego.edu/Applied/Bioethics/index.asp
The work of Professor Lawrence M. Hinman of the University of San Diego on ethics in reproduction can be accessed here. The site provides good subject matter for discussions of the ethical and legal issues surrounding reproductive technology, including cloning, through videos, lectures, debates, and articles related to religion and gene research.

Embryo Visualization: http://visembryo.com
This site is designed for medical students to learn about prenatal development. It provides excellent graphics of the gestational period with running commentary about each developing organ and body system. It also has links to other sites.

Pregnancy Planning: www.plannedparenthood.org
This website contains a plethora of information about women's health, family issues, and political commentary related to ongoing reproductive health issues and rallies/events.

The Secret Life of the Brain, from PBS: www.pbs.org/wnet/brain/outreach/episodes.html
Episode 1 of this highly acclaimed program provides an amazing video clip on the prenatal brain. The site also provides lesson plans and discussion ideas, for both teachers and students, regarding the brain at all stages of development from prenatal to old age.

Chapter 3: Physical and Cognitive Development in Infancy

Learning Goals

1. Discuss physical growth and development in infancy.
2. Describe infants' motor development.
3. Explain sensory and perceptual development in infancy.
4. Summarize the cognitive processes in Piaget's theory and the stage of sensorimotor development.
5. Describe how infants learn, remember, and conceptualize.
6. Explain language development in infancy.

Chapter Outline

PHYSICAL GROWTH AND DEVELOPMENT IN INFANCY
    Patterns of Growth
    Height and Weight
    The Brain
        The Brain's Development
            Mapping the Brain
            Changes in Neurons
            Changes in Regions of the Brain
        Early Experience and the Brain
    Sleep
        REM Sleep
        SIDS
    Nutrition
        Breast Versus Bottle Feeding
        Nutritional Needs
        A Healthy Start

MOTOR DEVELOPMENT
    The Dynamic Systems View
    Reflexes
    Gross Motor Skills
        The First Year: Milestones and Variations
        Development in the Second Year
    Fine Motor Skills

SENSORY AND PERCEPTUAL DEVELOPMENT
    Exploring Sensory and Perceptual Development
    Visual Perception
        Visual Acuity and Color
        Perceiving Patterns
        Perceptual Constancy
        Depth Perception
    Other Senses
        Hearing
        Touch and Pain

Matching Questions

_____ 1. Sensorimotor substage in which the infant develops the ability to use primitive symbols.

A. fine motor skills

_____ 2. Sensorimotor substage in which the infant becomes more object-oriented, moving beyond preoccupation with the self.

B. secondary circular reactions

_____ 3. Sensorimotor substage in which actions become more outwardly directed, and infants coordinate schemes and act with intentionality.

C. gross motor skills

_____ 4. Motor skills that involve more finely tuned movements such as finger dexterity.

D. internalization of schemes

_____ 5. Motor skills that involve large-muscle activities such as walking. E. coordination of secondary circular reactions

Multiple-Choice Questions

1. Which of the following scenarios best illustrates the basic principle of cephalocaudal development?
   a. an infant first producing an endogenous smile, then an exogenous smile, then a laugh
   b. an infant first being able to raise her head, then sit up, then stand up
   c. an infant obtaining visual skills, then olfactory skills, then auditory skills
   d. an infant cooing, then babbling, then using his first word, then using two-word sentences

2. The proximodistal progression pattern is best illustrated by children's _____.
   a. drawings, which are first done using the entire arm, then eventually using only the wrist and fingers
   b. toileting behavior, which proceeds from urine control to bowel control
   c. head size, which originally accounts for about one-fourth of total body size, then eventually only one-eighth of body size
   d. memory, which proceeds from sensory store to short-term to long-term store

3. Before birth, it appears that _____.
   a. the brain is fully "wired" and ready for action
   b. intrauterine experiences preprogram the brain's development
   c. extrauterine experiences preprogram the brain's development
   d. genes mainly direct how the brain establishes basic wiring patterns

4. If an alien randomly dropped in on ten newborns, it might conclude that humans spend most of their first month of life _____.
   a. eating
   b. crying
   c. playing
   d. sleeping

5. Which of the following statements most accurately portrays the sleep-wake cycle of infants?
   a. Infants sleep less as they grow older.
   b. Newborn sleep is reflexive, whereas infant sleep is intentional.
   c. Infants eventually sleep more during the day than they do at night.
   d. Infants spend less time sleeping than do adults.

6. Since 1992, when the American Academy of Pediatrics began recommending that infants _____, the frequency of sudden infant death syndrome (SIDS) has decreased.
   a. sleep on their stomachs
   b. sleep on their backs
   c. sleep on their sides
   d. do not sleep with their mothers

7. Breast-feeding is superior to formula-feeding for all of the following reasons EXCEPT which one?
   a. Breast-fed infants have a lower risk of becoming obese in childhood.
   b. Bottle-fed infants suffer psychological damage, because they become only weakly attached to their mothers.

c. The incidence of SIDS is lower among breast-fed infants.
d. Formula-fed infants have inferior neurological and cognitive development.

8. Which of the following statements BEST characterizes infant reflexes?
a. Reflexes are simply remnants of early evolutionary processes but serve no purpose now.
b. Reflexes are genetically carried survival mechanisms.
c. Modern infants rely more on learning than on reflexes.
d. All reflexes disappear by the end of infancy.

9. The gross motor skill that infants are likely to exhibit first is _____.
a. standing with support
b. cruising around furniture
c. rolling over
d. sitting without support

10. Was William James correct when he proclaimed that newborns experience a "blooming, buzzing" world of confusion?
a. No
b. Yes
c. There is still controversy over the accuracy of this claim.
d. It depends of the developmental level of the individual newborn.

11. When researchers use the habituation technique to test infant perception, learning, or memory, they may use all but which one of the following measurements?
a. sucking behavior
b. heart and respiration rates
c. number of eye blinks
d. length of looking time

12. What evidence indicates most clearly that a fetus can hear?
a. A newborn moves when a loud noise occurs.
b. Newborns prefer a stranger's voice to their mother's voice.
c. Hearing is more sensitive and better developed among newborns who have been experimentally stimulated before birth.
d. Newborns prefer to hear stories that were read to them in while they were in their mother's womb.

13. Intermodal perception involves _____.
a. integrating information from two or more sensory modalities.
b. unconscious comparisons between sensations and perceptions.
c. the correspondence between new sensory information and memory.
d. applying meaning to sensory information.

14. A cognitive structure in the Piagetian model that helps individuals organize and understand their experiences is _____.
a. a memory
b. an image
c. cognition
d. a scheme

15. An example of Piaget's concept of habit is _____.
a. learning to suck on a nipple and later being able to do it while sleeping
b. accidentally shaking a rattle, which produces a sound, and then purposefully shaking the rattle to produce the sound
c. initially blinking reflexively in response to a bright light, and then blinking when no stimulus is present
d. learning to laugh at people who slip on ice and fall down

16. What mechanism explains how children shift from one stage to another in Piaget's theory?
a. schemes
b. assimilation
c. equilibration
d. organization

17. George shook his rattle, and it made a noise. He then began to repeat this action to make the noise. George is a normal infant in which substage?
a. reflexive
b. first habits and primary circular reactions
c. secondary circular reactions
d. coordination of secondary circular reactions

18. Laurent has problems retrieving a ball that rolled out of reach, so he uses a construction-set stick to hit it. He is in which substage?
a. primary circular reactions
b. secondary circular reactions
c. coordination of secondary circular reactions
d. tertiary circular reactions

19. When Chris was 5 months old and the teddy bear that he had been looking at was covered, he did not search or look for it. Now, however, at 9 months of age, he looks for the bear when it is covered, which indicates the presence of _____.
a. object permanence
b. self-differentiation
c. assimilation
d. schemata

20. Which of the following statements regarding infant memory is FALSE?
a. Two-year-olds can remember events from when they were 6 months old.
b. Most early infant memory is only implicit in nature, not explicit.
c. Infants' early memories are usually explicit in nature, not implicit.
d. Infants' conscious memories are fragile and short-lived.

21. Sarula is 18 years old. She finds it frustrating that she cannot remember anything that happened before she was 3 years old. According to the research on memory, _____.
a. she is "normal," because most adults cannot remember anything from the first 3 years of life
b. her memory is deficient, because it is common for adults to remember back to the time when they were 2 years old or younger
c. she should be concerned, because it appears she is suffering from a rare disorder called infantile amnesia
d. her inability to remember events that occurred before she was 3 years old may be an indicator that she

was sexually molested as an infant

22. Language is most accurately defined as communication with others via a system of _____.
a. images
b. vocalizations
c. symbols
d. words

23. A child's first word is typically uttered at age _____.
a. 3 to 6 months
b. 6 to 9 months
c. 9 to 10 months
d. 10 to 15 months

24. These are gurgling sounds made in the back of the throat that usually express pleasure during interaction with the caregiver.
a. crying
b. cooing
c. babbling
d. gestures

25. All the following are strong pieces of evidence for the importance of environmental influences on language development EXCEPT which one?
a. Children's vocabulary size is related to the talkativeness of their mothers.
b. Children learn the syntax of their native language even if reinforced for incorrect utterances.
c. Children's vocabularies are related to their socioeconomic status.
d. The amount and type of language exposure children have in their homes predict their language skills later on.

True/False Questions

1. Early motor behaviors always develop in a cephalocaudal pattern.

2. By the second year of life, infants' rate of growth increases dramatically.

3. The infant's brain areas do not mature uniformly; some develop earlier than others.

4. Because newborns take several short naps throughout the day, they never fully fall into REM (rapid eye movement) sleep.

5. According to the dynamic systems view, universal milestones such as crawling and walking are caused solely by maturation of the nervous system.

6. The development of gross motor skills requires postural control.

7. Baby Margery heard her father's footsteps on the walkway outside the door and immediately looked at the doorknob in anticipation of its turning. This integrated pattern is called intermodal perception, meaning that information from two or more senses is combined into one experience.

8. Piaget emphasized the importance of environmental stimulation, because children cannot actively construct their own experiences.

9. Because very young infants are only in Piaget's reflex stage, they do not perform complex operations such as assimilation.

10. According to Piaget's theory, simply knowing more information allows a child to progress to the next stage of development.

11. Baby Nina accidentally kicked her crib mirror and found that it has a rattle inside. Now every morning when her father comes into her bedroom, Nina kicks her crib mirror over and over again. This is evidence that she is in the "coordination of secondary circular reactions" stage.

12. Habituation measurements are used to assess infant perception and memory.

13. There is a clear consensus among researchers now that newborns are capable of imitating others.

14. Because babies who are in the cooing stage of language development cannot communicate by speaking, they often use gestures such as pointing.

15. Sylvain is a 2-year-old who calls his cat "kitty" but always says, "What's this?" when he sees another cat. This shows that he is using the overextension principle of language.

Short-Answer Questions

1. What are cephalocaudal and proximodistal patterns?

2. What is the dynamic systems view?

3. Discuss gross motor skill and fine motor skill development during the first year.

4. Define *sensation* and *perception*.

5. What is intermodal perception?

6. List and describe the characteristics of Piaget's stage of sensorimotor development.

7. What is attention, and how is it characterized in infants?

8. Elaborate on the extent to which infants can remember.

9. Discuss how language develops in infancy.

10. Describe some of the biological and environmental influences on language development.

Essay Questions

1. Your classmates are having trouble understanding the dynamic systems view of perceptual-motor development. You have an exam coming up next week, so several of them are getting together to

review their notes. What would you explain to the group regarding this complex theory? Can you make up an original example that would clarify the main tenets of the theory for your classmates? Can you answer the question "How do babies learn to walk?" using a dynamic systems explanation?

2. Your best friend has to fly to another city to look after some personal business. She asks you to care for her 16-month-old baby for a week. You really want to be prepared and know what to expect. Discuss all the things that would be most important for you to understand and remember about the child's language and cognitive capabilities. Also, what can the child NOT do at this age (you should keep your expectations realistic and age-appropriate)?

Key to Matching Questions

| 1. D | 2. B | 3. E | 4. A | 5. C |

Key to Multiple-Choice Questions

1. B	6. B	11. C	16. C	21. A
2. A	7. B	12. D	17. B	22. C
3. D	8. B	13. A	18. D	23. D
4. D	9. C	14. D	19. A	24. B
5. A	10. A	15. C	20. C	25. A

Key to True/False Questions

1. F	4. F	7. T	10. F	13. F
2. F	5. F	8. F	11. F	14. F
3. T	6. T	9. F	12. T	15. F

Key to Short-Answer Questions

1. The cephalocaudal pattern is the sequence in which the greatest growth always occurs at the top—the head—with physical growth in size, weight, and feature differentiation gradually working its way down from top to bottom. The proximodistal pattern is the sequence in which growth starts at the center of the body and moves toward the extremities.

2. Dynamic systems theory seeks to explain how motor behaviors are assembled for perceiving and acting.

3. Gross motor skills involve large-muscle activities. Postural control is the foundation for gross motor skill development. Some milestones for gross motor skill development include holding head erect, lifting head while prone, rolling, sitting with support, sitting independently, crawling, pulling self to standing, standing independently, and walking. Fine motor skills involve more keenly tuned movements. Fine motor skill development begins with crude reaching and grasping movements early in infancy. The palmer grasp involves the infant grasping something with the entire hand. As the infant approaches the first birthday mark, she develops the pincer grip. With the pincer grip, the infant is able to pick up small objects using the thumb and forefinger.

4. Sensation occurs when information interacts with sensory receptors. Perception is the interpretation of

what is sensed.

5. Intermodal perception involves integrating information from two or more sensory modalities such as vision and hearing. Intermodal perception is present in a crude form at birth and develops to adult levels toward the end of their first year.

6. The sensorimotor stage is the first stage of cognitive development in Piaget's theory. It lasts from birth to approximately 2 years of age. Sensorimotor thought is characterized by the infant organizing and coordinating sensations with physical movement. There are six substages for the sensorimotor stage which begins with reflexes and ends with the internalization of schemes. Two noteworthy accomplishments during the sensorimotor stage are object permanence and cause-and-effect relationships.

7. Attention is the focusing of mental resources. In infancy, attention is likely to decrease as a novel stimulus becomes familiar—this is called habituation.

8. We know that even fetuses have some ability to remember, exemplified by a newborn's preference of the mother's voice over a stranger's, or of a familiar story over an unfamiliar one. Two-month-old infants display the ability to retain information about perceptual-motor actions. Some experts, however, argue that consciously trying to recall information does not emerge until sometime during the second half of the first year of life.

9. There are several milestones from birth to two years in the development of infant language. These include crying, cooing, babbling, making the transition from universal linguist to language-specific listener, using gestures, comprehension of words, first word spoken, vocabulary spurt, rapid expansion of understanding words, and two-word utterances.

10. Both biology and environment are necessary for competent language development. Some areas in the left hemisphere of the brain that are key to language processing are Broca's area and Wernicke's area. Chomsky argues that humans are born ready to learn language via the LAD. Environmental influences for language development include parent-child verbal interactions utilizing child-directed speech, recasting, expanding, and labeling.

Key to Essay Questions

1. The dynamic systems view maintains that skills that appear to be solely physical in nature actually develop as a result of complex interactions between biology and environment. Before a baby can learn to walk, she must have motor control, muscular development to control her limbs, motivation to move about, and the ability to understand and react to feedback from the environment (for example, a sharp corner looming ahead or her parent clapping when she takes steps), all of which are possible only because of myelination of the brain's motor cortex. Therefore, motor milestones are really adaptations to one's environment and are the result of complex and changing systems of interaction between maturation of the central nervous system and reinforcements from within and without the child.

2. Keep in mind that children this age may be speaking a few words but have not experienced their "vocabulary spurt," which means that they are not going to be able to have conversations. Your friend's baby has very good receptive language abilities and so will probably understand most of your simple commands and questions regarding everyday events such as feeding and playing. Cognitively, the baby has mastered simple cause-and-effect reasoning and object permanence. She is in Piaget's tertiary

circular reactions stage and so will be fascinated by causing things to happen in her environment. Her interest in novelty and experimentation makes her a "little scientist."

Research Project 1:
Observing Infants' Reflexes and Sensory Abilities

PLEASE NOTE: THIS PROJECT INVOLVES STUDYING OTHER PEOPLE. PLEASE CHECK WITH YOUR INSTRUCTOR TO SEE IF YOU NEED TO COMPLETE AN INSTITUTIONAL RESEARCH BOARD PROTOCOL BEFORE BEGINNING THIS PROJECT.

Obtain the permission of parents you know to observe their infant for half an hour. On the chart below, record the infant's age and your observations of the infant's use of reflexes and sensory modalities. You may want to ask the parents to test some of the infant's reflexes so long as this does not cause any distress for the infant. Carefully explain how to conduct the test. Compare your observations with what you would expect of a child this age, on the basis of what you read in Chapter 5, and research you have done regarding other reflexes. Then answer the questions that follow the chart below.

Child's age (in days or weeks) _____ Child's sex: _____ Female [ ] Male [ ]

Sense	Observed	Expected	Expected Change over Time
Visual (sight)			
Auditory (sound)			
Olfactory (smell)			
Gustatory (taste)			
Tactile (touch)			
Integration of senses			

Reflex	Observed	Expected	Expected Change over Time
Blinking			
Grasping			
Rooting			

Sucking			
Moro			
Tonic neck			
Babinski			
Plantar			

1. How did the infant demonstrate the presence of each sense?

2. What observations indicated that the infant was able to integrate the different senses?

3. Were your observations of this infant's sensory development consistent with your expectations?

4. Which reflexes did you observe? Describe the infant's reflexive behaviors.

5. What additional reflexes did you observe that were not described in the chapter?

6. Were your observations of this infant's reflexes consistent with your expectations after reading Chapter 3 and reading outside sources?

7. What have you learned about the infant's adaptive abilities from observing each child's use of sensory modalities, coordination of senses, and reflexive behaviors?

Research Project 2:
Analyzing Popular Parenting Books

Obtain three parenting books that focus on infants and toddlers. Review the sections on infants' brain development and sensory and motor capabilities. Compare the coverage provided by each book in terms of research cited, depth of coverage, accuracy of coverage (for instance, is it scientific or research-based?), and the exploration of topics not covered in this chapter. On the basis of what you learned in this chapter, which of the three parenting books would you most likely recommend to new parents, and why? What were these books' most obvious inaccuracies? How well did the writers do in terms of disseminating the latest knowledge to the general population?

Research Project 3:
Observing Cognitive and Language Development

1. Engage in a conversation with several children who are under age 2 years. You can do this in the grocery store, at the park, or with children you know. Ask them simple questions such as "Is this your dog?" or make statements such as "That's a big red ball!" and see what they say and do. Parents will usually respond positively to a nice person making conversation with their child, but stop talking to the child immediately if the parents do respond negatively. If you have children of your own, try to talk to them about more things and ask them more questions than you ordinarily do (for example, "Am I

putting on your pajamas right now?" or "Look at how you're pushing that car!") and see what responses you get. Keep mental notes about the types of things children of different ages say and how they respond both linguistically and cognitively. Compare how much they understand with how much they can say.

a. What did you notice about the children's cognitive and language abilities?

b. Are your findings what you would expect for children of each age you observed? (If the parent did not tell you the child's age, you might be able to make an educated guess.)

c. Were you surprised by anything the children did or said?

d. Did it seem that the children could understand more than they could say?

e. What did you learn from observing the interaction?

f. How well do you think the "average" child fits the description of the developmental trajectories outlined in the chapter? Would you make any modifications to the cognitive or language expectations for any of the age periods described in the chapter?

Research Project 4:
Charting Cognitive and Language Development in Infancy

PLEASE NOTE: THIS PROJECT INVOLVES STUDYING OTHER PEOPLE. PLEASE CHECK WITH YOUR INSTRUCTOR TO SEE IF YOU NEED TO COMPLETE AN INSTITUTIONAL RESEARCH BOARD PROTOCOL BEFORE BEGINNING THIS PROJECT.

Describe the components of cognitive development through the first 2 years of life, stating what you would expect to observe on the basis of what you read in the text. Then observe three children of different ages but all under the age of 2 years. Record your observations on the chart below. (Unless you are watching unobtrusively, be sure to get permission from parents and, if possible, from the children.) Finally, answer the questions that follow. Ask parents how much of their children's language use seems to be imitative versus original. (Parents might remark that their child's use of language is "incredible" or "amazing," but get them to be more specific). You might even look for some of the skills identified as part of the Bayley Scales of Infant Development.

Developmental Issue	Age Range	Expected Behavior(s)	Observed Behavior(s)
Simple reflexes			
Primary circular reactions			
Secondary circular reactions			

Coordination of secondary circular reactions			
Tertiary circular reactions			
Internalization of schemes			
Receptive language skills			
Verbalizing skills			
Use of grammar rules			
Imitation			
Deferred imitation			
Memory			

1. How did your expectations compare to what you observed??

2. Did you observe anything that particularly surprised you? Explain.

3. What observations were consistent with Piaget's theory?

4. What observations were inconsistent with Piaget's theory?

5. What observations were consistent with information processing theory?

6. How much did biology or environment influence each thing you observed and recorded in the chart? Or are most skills based on an interaction of these influences?

7. Which theories and research studies appeared to be supported by your observations?

8. What other comments do you have concerning these observations?

Personal Application Project 1: Comparing Babies to Yourself

PLEASE NOTE: THIS PROJECT INVOLVES STUDYING OTHER PEOPLE. PLEASE CHECK WITH YOUR INSTRUCTOR TO SEE IF YOU NEED TO COMPLETE AN INSTITUTIONAL RESEARCH BOARD PROTOCOL BEFORE BEGINNING THIS PROJECT.

Ask as many people as you can if you can hold their babies. (Obviously, you will have better luck with people you know than with strangers.) As you hold each baby, take mental notes about the baby's sensory and motor capabilities. What can the baby see, hear, feel, think, and do? If the baby is old enough to sit up, roll over, or crawl, determine whether you can perceive the dynamic systems view in action with the baby's attempts at locomotion or gross motor control. How does the baby use the environment as feedback for navigating while using physical skills?

After observing several babies, observe yourself doing everyday tasks such as washing dishes, making your bed, brushing your teeth, and walking to your car. Think about how you developed these incredibly complex skills; you used to be capable of only the perceptual and motor skills that you observed in the infants! What specific sensory, perceptual, and motor skills did you employ for each task? Note how smoothly you integrated each movement. This represents life-span development in your own life. Note how many theories and terms from the chapter can be applied to your abilities (hint: intermodal perception). What thoughts and feelings do you have about what you observed in the babies and then in yourself? Given the vast difference between babies' physical skills and yours, can you now appreciate the rapid changes in the fascinating and complex period of infant development?

Personal Application Project 2:
Analyzing Memories of Your Own Infancy

If you have the opportunity, talk to your parents about the day you were born (or the day someone else was born). Ask them to describe their observations of you (or the other baby you are discussing). Were they surprised at how much/how little you could see, hear, touch, and do? Ask them about their memories of you learning to crawl, to walk, and so on. Did they think that you were a fragile child with few capabilities? Or were they amazed at all the sensory, perceptual, and motor skills you had early on? Compare their answers with the information in the chapter. On the basis of the research presented in the chapter, can you readily spot any inaccuracies in their recollections (for example, they swear that you said your first word at the age of 4 months)? How much do they seem to know about what babies can and cannot do at various ages? Did they tell you anything that really surprised you? How much do you think the general population understands about the material in this chapter?

Personal Application Project 3:
Consider Your Own Development

This may be difficult, but give it a try. Now that you have learned about infantile amnesia, you might understand why you cannot remember your early life, so you will have to rely on input from older adults who were around at the time you were a baby. Ask your relatives about your developmental milestones during the first 2 years of your life. Be sure to include cognitive milestones (such as Piaget's six substages, if possible), imitation, memory, and language development. If they kept a baby book, use it to confirm their memories. You can also use old, dated photos or home movies to solve the puzzle regarding when you were

able to do certain things. On the basis of these recollections, indicate how consistent your early development was with what the theorists would predict. Use the chart below to help you.

Developmental Milestone	Your Development	Comments

Piaget's sensorimotor substages (describe)		
Other cognitive milestones (describe)		
Language development (describe)		
Memory development/other (describe)		

Internet Projects

Check out the McGraw-Hill website for this text (www.mhhe.com/santrockessls). You will find numerous activities there, in particular, quizzes. Also, be patient, because there are many very worthy links on each of the sites, but they do take a little time to access. If you do not go to the links many times, you will not get the full value of the site. Please go to all links.

Please note that all website addresses in this Study Guide have been checked and were correct at the time of publication. However, websites may be discontinued or their addresses may change, so when you try to access a given site, it may no longer be viable. If that occurs, please notify the publisher so that it can make appropriate revisions in future editions of this Study Guide.

Internet Project 1:
Views on Breast-Feeding

People tend to have very strong opinions about breast-feeding. What do you think? Is breast-feeding a natural or a learned behavior? If they are able, should all mothers do it? Do humans automatically desire to breast-feed, and, if so, do they know how to do it? Or do they need help? How do you feel about breast-feeding? How do you feel when you see a mother nursing her baby in public? Why do you think you have those feelings? See the website for La Leche League at www.lalecheleague.org. When the home page comes up, how do you feel about the picture of the woman breast-feeding her baby? On the basis of information you read on the website, can you answer some of the questions posed here more fully? Did the website change or confirm any of your views? Did anything on the site surprise you? Explain your answers.

Internet Project 2:
Analyzing Parenting Websites
Use www.Google.com or www.Dogpile.com to search for links to websites relating to parenting infants

and toddlers. Look for topics on each site such as "what to expect from your 1-year-old" or "reflexes in the newborn" or anything related to the material in the textbook chapter. Analyze the content of at least three sites in relation to what you learned in this chapter regarding infants' brain, perceptual, motor, and sensory development. Which topics do all the sites cover? Which topics are unique to one or two sites? Why do you think they differ? Who sponsors each site? Are there researchers involved in the material on the site, or does the site refer to any scientific studies? Is the site more pop psychology than scientific psychology? Are there any errors in the material presented? On the basis of what you learned in this textbook chapter, which parenting site would you recommend to new parents, and why?

Internet Project 3:
Language Development in Infancy

PLEASE NOTE: THIS PROJECT INVOLVES STUDYING OTHER PEOPLE. PLEASE CHECK WITH YOUR INSTRUCTOR TO SEE IF YOU NEED TO COMPLETE AN INSTITUTIONAL RESEARCH BOARD PROTOCOL BEFORE BEGINNING THIS PROJECT.

Two particularly interesting web sites are www.parentingme.com/language.htm and http://childdevelopmentinfo.com/development/language_development.shtml. The former provides in-depth information concerning language development; the latter presents a chart of language development. Compare the information from the two sites, and then compare that information with the text. As you observe young children, can you apply what you are learning from all these sources (text and Internet sites)? Is there a good fit between what you observe and the information you gather from these sources? Describe any discrepancies you notice. What information is present in one resource and absent in another? Why do you think this is?

Internet Project 4:
Stimulating Cognitive and Linguistic Development

The text offers several studies that demonstrate the importance of interactions between the baby and others (parents, siblings, other adults, other children) for maximal development. (One thing to watch out for, though, is overstimulation—take your cue from the baby). Check out the information about early learning and cognitive development on the Zero to Three sites (http://zerotothree.org). Go through all the sections on the site and pay particular attention to http://zerotothree.org/magic (the Magic of Everyday Moments section) regarding infant stimulation in everyday contexts.

1. How does the information on this site augment what you learned from the text?

2. Was there anything that particularly surprised you?

3. What information did you already know? What was new to you?

4. How will this information help you interact effectively with young children?

5. How will this information help you interact effectively with parents of young children?

6. What concerns might there be about overstimulating children? How would you address those concerns?

7. If you were to design a program that provided the optimal experience for children—to encourage their

cognitive (and linguistic) development while helping them learn to enjoy learning—what would that program look like?

Other Relevant Sites on the Internet

Zero to Three Project: http://www.zerotothree.org/site/PageServer
The Zero to Three project website discusses all aspects of early childhood development including how the brain develops within a context of human relationships.

Child Trauma Academy: http://www.childtrauma.org
This site focuses on the effects of trauma, violence, and abuse on children's brain development. It discusses the important work of Dr. Bruce Perry and provides free online classes on brain development for continuing education credits.

Development Home Page: http://alpha.furman.edu/~einstein/general/development/development.htm
This site, sponsored by the Mellon Foundation, presents concise articles and graphics of different aspects of prenatal and infant development. Click on "Infant Reflexes" to see drawings of babies exhibiting each reflex.

The Senses and Your 1- to 3-Month-Old: http://kidshealth.org/parent/growth/senses/sense13m.html
This KidsHealth.org for Parents section covers infant sensory capabilities by age and tells parents when they should be concerned about developmental abnormalities.

Reducing the Risk of SIDS: www.sids.org/nprevent.htm
This section of the American SIDS Institute website provides very clear, simple precautions that have been shown to greatly reduce the risk of sudden infant death syndrome.

iParenting.com: http://iparenting.com
This comprehensive site describes itself as an Internet community for parents. It includes parents' diaries, chat rooms, articles on hundreds of topics, and advice from experts.

Baby Sign Language for Hearing Parents and Children: www.topbabypages.com/babysign.html
This site is a great resource for the current trend of teaching babies sign language. Advocates suggest that we help babies communicate in any way we can, and that sign language skills coming before verbal language is possible. There are lots of books, discussion boards, and research studies presented on this topic.

The Jean Piaget Society: http://piaget.org
This master site for information on Piaget's ideas and life covers conferences, research papers, theories, and so on relating to the "nature of the developmental construction of human knowledge." It also focuses on the developmental applications of Piaget's ideas to education and parenting.

Noam Chomsky: www.chomsky.info/
Originator of the language acquisition device, Chomsky is a world-renowned political commentator, author, and activist. To view all the information about the fascinating ideas and work of this MIT linguistics professor, be prepared spend at least 30 minutes on this site. It includes his biography, a bibliography of his work, his debates, audio and video selections, and thought-provoking commentary on the September 11, 2001 terrorist attacks and the U.S. war in Iraq.

Chapter 4: Socioemotional Development in Infancy

Learning Goals

1. Discuss emotional and personality development in infancy.
2. Describe attachment and explain how it develops in infancy.
3. Explain how social contexts influence infant development.

Chapter Outline

EMOTIONAL AND PERSONALITY DEVELOPMENT
    Emotional Development
        What are Emotions?
        Biological and Environmental Influences
        Early Emotions
        Emotional Expression and Social Relationships
            Crying
            Smiling
            Fear
        Social Referencing
        Emotional Regulation and Coping
    Temperament
        Describing and Classifying Temperament
            Chess and Thomas's Classification
            Kagan's Behavioral Inhibition
            Effortful Control (Self-Regulation)
        Biological Foundations and Experience
            Biological Influences
            Gender, Culture, and Temperament
        Goodness of Fit and Parenting
    Personality Development
        Trust
        The Developing Sense of Self
        Independence

ATTACHMENT
    What is Attachment?
    Individual Differences in Attachment
        Interpreting Differences in Attachment
    Caregiving Styles and Attachment

SOCIAL CONTEXTS
    The Family
        The Transition to Parenthood
        Reciprocal Socialization
        Maternal and Paternal Caregiving
    Child Care
        Parental Leave

Variations in Child Care
National Longitudinal Study of Child Care

Matching Questions

_____ 1. Refers to the match between a child's temperament and the environmental demands with which the child must cope.

A. reciprocal socialization

_____ 2. Sudden appearance of loud crying without preliminary moaning, followed by breath holding.

B. insecure disorganized babies

_____ 3. Babies who show insecurity by being confused and disoriented.

C. anger cry

_____ 4. Socialization that is bidirectional; children socialize parents, just as parents socialize children.

D. goodness of fit

_____ 5. A cry similar to the basic cry, with more excess air forced through the vocal cords.

E. pain cry

Multiple-Choice Questions

1. _____ is a feeling or affect that occurs when a person is in a state or an interaction that is important to him or her.
   a. Emotion
   b. Personality
   c. Attachment
   d. Bonding

2. Which of the following emotions appears in the first six months of life?
   a. jealousy
   b. disgust
   c. guilt
   d. embarrassment

3. One-year-old Brendan feels very proud when he can stack ten blocks to build a tall tower. His feeling of pride is a _____.
   a. facial expression
   b. primary emotion
   c. basic emotion
   d. self-conscious emotion

4. Which emotion develops first in the following list of emotions?
   a. guilt
   b. contempt
   c. surprise
   d. shame

5. What is the name of the cry that has a rhythmic pattern consisting of first a cry, then a brief silence, then a short inspiratory whistle that is somewhat higher-pitched than the main cry, and then a brief rest before the pattern repeats?
a. basic cry
b. anger cry
c. pain cry
d. colicky cry

6. An external stimulus may result in the infant having a(n) _____.
a. social smile
b. internal smile
c. reflexive smile
d. universal smile

7. Which of the following situations is most likely to produce stranger anxiety in an infant?
a. sitting on the mother's lap
b. meeting a stranger in a research laboratory
c. meeting a stranger in the infant's home
d. encountering a stranger who smiles

8. Temperament is best defined as _____.
a. the way an individual reacts to a special person in the environment
b. an individual's general behavioral style
c. the emotions experienced by infants and children
d. the reaction displayed by a parent when a child engages in an unwanted activity

9. Chess and Thomas believe _____ to be the most typical temperament for a child.
a. easy
b. positive approach
c. difficult
d. slow-to-warm-up

10. _____ influence(s) temperament, but the degree of influence depends on _____.
a. Heredity; environmental experiences
b. The positive approach; emotionality
c. Affectivity; situational experiences
d. Environment; long-term experiences

11. Joseph has just started looking in the mirror and saying, "Joseph!" This indicates that a sense of self is developing. How old is he?
a. 9 months
b. 12 months
c. 18 months
d. 24 months

12. According to Erik Erikson, children develop an excessive sense of shame and a sense of doubt about their abilities under all the following circumstances EXCEPT when _____.
a. impatient parents do things children can do for themselves
b. children are consistently overprotected
c. accidents the children have had or caused are criticized
d. children are allowed to express their negative emotions

13. The research of Harry Harlow and Robert Zimmerman (1959) found that the critical element in the attachment process is _____.
a. oral satisfaction
b. contact comfort
c. feeding the infant
d. synchronous interaction

14. Mary Ainsworth believes that attachment _____.
a. varies from one child to another, even within the same family
b. depends on the mother's love and concern for the welfare of her child
c. stems from the consistency of parental responses during the child-care routine
d. provides the key basis from which siblings relate to each other

15. A baby with this type of attachment shows strong patterns of avoidance and resistance or displays certain specified behaviors, such as extreme fearfulness around the caregiver, in the Strange Situation.
a. secure
b. avoidant
c. resistant
d. disorganized

16. You are asked to baby-sit your niece, Tara, for the evening. When you are in the room with her parents, Tara is happy. However, when they go into the bedroom to finish getting dressed, she cries. Tara is not comforted when you pick her up, but then her mother comes back out and picks her up. The baby is immediately calmed. Tara is exhibiting signs of a(n) _____ attachment.
a. secure
b. avoidant
c. resistant
d. disorganized

17. Jerome Kagan has emphasized the importance of _____ as a determinant of social competence.
a. bonding
b. temperament
c. peer responsiveness
d. learning

18. All the following statements are criticisms of attachment theories EXCEPT which one?
a. Genetics and temperament have not been accounted for and may play more of a role in development than the nature of the attachment does.
b. The role of multiple social agents and changing social contexts has been largely ignored in the study of attachment.
c. Cultural variations show different patterns of attachment.
d. The relationship between the parent and the infant is not emphasized enough.

19. Which one of these patterns has NOT been found in research on the relationship between parenting styles and attachment security?
a. Caregivers of avoidant babies tend to be unavailable or rejecting.
b. Caregivers of resistant babies tend to be inconsistent in their responding.
c. Caregivers of disorganized babies tend to have dirty, disorganized homes that lead to a feeling of chaos and instability.
d. Caregivers of secure babies tend to be warm and responsive to their children's needs.

20. Reciprocal socialization is best defined in which of the following ways?
a. Children are products of their parents' socialization techniques.
b. Parents are products of their children's socialization techniques.
c. Socialization is bidirectional.
d. The interactions that children have with people, other than their parents, determine how they will be socialized.

21. _____ involves parental behavior that supports children's efforts, allowing them to be more skillful than they would be if they were to rely only on their own abilities.
a. Reciprocal socialization
b. Scaffolding
c. Parental investment
d. Secure attachment

22. Concerning mother-infant and father-infant interactions, _____.
a. fathers' interactions are more likely to include play
b. fathers' interactions are more likely to center on child-care activities
c. fathers are less able than mothers are to act sensitively and responsively with their infants
d. no big differences are seen in mothers' and fathers' interactions with infants in today's "typical" American family.

23. In his research concerning the effects of child care on children, Kagan has found in the experimental program at Harvard that _____.
a. child care had long-term, detrimental effects on children
b. child care had no observed adverse effects
c. child care facilitated development
d. the effects of child care are dependent on the length and type of care given

24. A longitudinal study by the National Institute of Child Health and Human Development (NICHHD) assessed the child-care experiences of children and their development and found all the following statements to be true EXCEPT which one?
a. Infants from low-income families are more likely to receive low-quality child care than are their higher-income counterparts.
b. Child care does not adversely affect the security of infants' attachments to their mothers.
c. High quality of child care is linked to fewer child problems.
d. Children reared in the exclusive care of their mothers have higher cognitive abilities.

25. On the basis of what you learned in this chapter, which one of the following characteristics would you NOT look for in a child-care program?
a. caregivers who provide positive talk
b. a low teacher-to-child ratio
c. a combination of both indoor and outdoor scheduled activities
d. programs that involve language development activities

True/False Questions

1. It is very difficult for blind children who have never seen a person smile to experience the emotions of joy and happiness.

2. The initial phase of infant attachment to parents is based on early emotional interchanges, whether positive or negative.

3. Sensitive, responsive parents are essential for helping an infant grow emotionally.

4. Developmentalists suggest that parents not jump up and soothe crying infants because doing so just reinforces their crying and leads to higher levels of crying in the future.

5. Before 6 months of age, stranger anxiety is fairly mild, but by 8 months it has reached its peak and begins to decline, and by 1 year of age, it is usually gone.

6. Although separation anxiety tends to peak at age 15 months in most children from the United States, research has found that it does not exist in most other cultures.

7. Kagan's research has shown that because it is a biological trait, children's behavioral inhibition rarely, if ever, becomes more moderate.

8. Rashmi is high on the temperamental quality called "effortful control," so we would expect that she is easily agitated and intensely emotional.

9. Research shows that children may learn to modify their temperament to a certain degree.

10. Feeding is the crucial element in the attachment process. Without being fed consistently by the caregiver, an infant will not attach to that caregiver.

11. In the third phase of the attachment process, infants have increased motor abilities and so actively seek contact with their caregivers. This is when specific attachments start forming.

12. For an infant to be classified as insecure-disorganized, there must be certain behaviors present such as extreme fearfulness of the caregiver, avoidance, and/or resistance.

13. Research consistently shows that infant attachment history provides a powerful predictor of adult attachment patterns.

14. When states enact policies that improve child-care worker training and reduce child-staff ratios, we see higher cognitive and social competence in children.

15. Extensive child-care experiences tend to weaken the influence of families on children.

Short-Answer Questions

1. Explain the nature of an infant's emotions and how they develop.

2. Describe some of the different cries infants have.

3. Explain what is meant by temperament, and describe the three basic types of temperament?

4. What is meant by goodness of fit?

5. Describe the major conflicts experienced by infants and toddlers that Erikson believed were central in shaping personality. According to Erikson, how does the resolution of these conflicts promote development?

6. According to Sanson and Rothbart, what are the best parenting strategies to use in relation to children's temperament?

7. Define attachment, and discuss several different theories of attachment.

8. Describe some individual variations in attachment assessed by the Strange Situation. Discuss how caregiving styles are related to attachment classifications.

9. What is reciprocal socialization, and why is it important?

10. How can child care influence infant development?

Essay Questions

1. Your sister, Sheri, and her husband work for the same internationally based company that has branches in 50 countries and on every continent. Sheri has confided in you that she would like to have children, but that she would rather work than stay at home all the time with the children while they are growing up (which makes her feel guilty). Sheri says her husband also wants children, and that he is willing to stay home with them for a while so Sheri could continue working, but he is concerned about the loss of income if he does not work for several months. They both would like to spend some time staying home with their children but would also want to put them into child care for a significant period of time. Assuming that you think Sheri and her husband would be good parents, what information would you give them about where in the world they might want to live to maximize their ability for both of them to have time with their newborn children? What would you advise them about placing their children in child care? What would you tell them about the characteristics of high-quality child care and some of the long-term effects of child care on children's development?

2. The local PTA chapter has asked you to talk to its parents and teachers about working with young children. They have specifically asked you to address the idea of attachment—what it is, the research supporting a notion of attachment, the different forms of attachment, and how to help a child develop secure attachment—and the different types of temperament, including how to deal effectively with children according to their temperamental styles. What will you tell these parents and teachers? Give examples they can relate to. Be as specific as possible.

Key to Matching Questions

1. D	2. E	3. B	4. A	5. C

Key to Multiple-Choice Questions

1. A	6. A	11. C	16. A	21. B
2. B	7. B	12. D	17. B	22. A
3. D	8. B	13. B	18. D	23. D
4. C	9. A	14. A	19. C	24. B
5. A	10. A	15. D	20. C	25. C

Key to True/False Questions

1. F	4. F	7. F	10. F	13. F
2. F	5. F	8. F	11. T	14. T
3. T	6. F	9. T	12. T	15. F

Key to Short-Answer Questions

1. Emotion is a feeling that occurs when a person is in a state or an interaction that is important to them. It is believed that emotions, especially facial expressions of emotions, have a biological basis. Infants display surprise, interest, joy, anger, sadness, fear, and disgust during the first 6 months of life. After that, self-conscious or other-conscious emotions emerge, such as empathy, embarrassment, pride, shame, and guilt. Emotions are important for the development of social relationships.

2. The basic cry is a rhythmic pattern that usually consists of a cry, followed by a briefer silence, then a shorter whistle that is somewhat higher in pitch than the main cry, then another brief rest before the next cry. The anger cry is a variation of the basic cry, but more excess air is forced through the vocal cords. The pain cry is a sudden, long, initial cry followed by breath holding. No preliminary moaning is present prior to the cry.

3. *Temperament* is defined as an individual's behavioral style and characteristic way of responding. Temperament has a strong biological component, and aspects of it are apparent shortly after birth. Chess and Thomas identified three basic clusters of temperament: easy, difficult, and slow-to-warm-up. An easy-temperament child is generally in a positive mood, quickly establishes regular routines in infancy, and adapts easily to new experiences. The difficult-temperament child reacts negatively and cries frequently, engages in irregular daily routines, and is slow to accept change. The slow-to-warm-up temperament child has a low activity level, is somewhat negative, and displays a low intensity of mood.

4. Goodness of fit refers to the match between a child's temperament and the environmental demands the child must cope with. Some temperament characteristics are more challenging for parents to cope with than others, which can lead to negative parent-child interactions if the parent is not aware of this danger and prepared to cope with it. It is important for parents/caregivers to be sensitive to the individual characteristics of the child, to be flexible in responding to these characteristics, and to avoid applying negative labels to the child. This type of parenting will help promote a positive goodness of fit.

5. Erikson stated that the first year of life is characterized by the trust-versus-mistrust conflict in which infants who are cared for in a consistently nurturant manner develop trust. In the second year of life, toddlers experience a crisis between autonomy and shame/doubt. When toddlers experience pride in their accomplishments, they will develop a sense of independence.

6. Some temperament characteristics are more challenging for parents to cope with than others. Sanson and Rothbart have suggested some best-parenting strategies to assist in these circumstances. These strategies include attention to and respect for individuality; structuring the child's environment; and programs for parents with difficult-temperament children.

7. Attachment is defined as a close emotional bond between two people. Three theorists of attachment discussed in the text include Freud, Erikson, and Bowlby. Freud believed that infants become attached to the person or object that provides oral satisfaction, but he was wrong, as Harlow's research demonstrated. Erikson emphasized that during the first year of life, physical comfort and sensitive care are critical for an infant to establish a sense of basic trust. This basic trust is the foundation for attachment. Bowlby also stressed the importance of caregiver responsiveness during the first year. He added the idea that both infants and caregivers are biologically primed to form attachments, and that an infant's primary attachment develops through a series of four phases.

8. Attachment can be secure or insecure and can be assessed in infants by using the Strange Situation. Securely attached babies use their caregiver as a secure base from which to explore the environment and display positive interactions with their caregiver. There are three types of insecure attachments: avoidant, resistant, and disorganized. An avoidant baby actively avoids his or her caregiver. A resistant baby oscillates between clinging to his or her caregiver, and resisting closeness to the caregiver. A disorganized baby often appears dazed and confused. Babies may also demonstrate strong patterns of avoidance of, resistance to, or fearfulness of the caregiver.

   Caregiving styles are correlated to different attachment styles. Securely attached infants have sensitive and responsive caregivers. Avoidant infants have caregivers that tend to be unavailable and rejecting. Resistant babies have caregivers that tend to be inconsistent and out of synch in their interactions. Disorganized babies often have caregivers who are neglectful (sometimes because of depression) or abusive.

9. *Reciprocal socialization* is defined a socialization that is bidirectional. This means that parents socialize their children, but children also socialize their parents. One aspect of reciprocal socialization is mutual synchrony in which each person's behavior depends on the partner's previous behavior. In infancy, you can see this mutual synchrony in eye contact, mutual regulation, and synchronization. A form of reciprocal socialization is scaffolding in which parents time interactions in such a way that the infant experiences turn-taking with the parent. This is important because infants who have these scaffolding experiences with their parents are more likely to engage in turn-taking with peers when they are older.

10. Child care during the first year of life can have long-lasting negative effects. For example, such children in child care can have poorer cognitive outcomes than children who stay at home with a caregiver. Or, such children can experience higher rates of illness and more behavioral problems. However, several factors influence whether or not child care will have these negative effects. For example, if the caregiver works less than 30 hours a week, if the caregiver is responsive and comforting in caregiving, and if the child care is of high quality, negative effects will be minimized.

Key to Essay Questions

1. You would need to explore the maternity and paternity leave policies of different countries around the world, including the United States, which presently does not have a paternity leave policy, and also discuss the various child-care policies around the world. (Sweden, of course, comes to mind as an excellent example of a country that provides paid leave to both parents during the first year of a child's life.) You would also need to discuss the benefits and problems that could arise from having only one or both parents involved in early child rearing, and of placement of infants and young children into child-care facilities. The issue of child care for both infants and young children should be discussed, including the different types of child care that exist in the United States and abroad, the effects of child care on children as shown by the research to date, and how widely the quality of day care varies. Give tips from the chapter for determining what defines high-quality day care. As for the issue of feeling guilty, sometimes it is not an option (either financially or emotionally) for the mother or other caregiver to stay home with the children, so you would want to address this issue as well.

2. Define *attachment*, then look at the various research studies that have explored attachment, including the research of Harry and Margaret Harlow and Robert Zimmerman with rhesus monkeys, and Ainsworth's Strange Situation research. Talk about the different types of attachment that Ainsworth described, and discuss ways to promote secure attachment so children will feel safe to explore new environments and take on new challenges (be sure to include Erikson's stage of trust versus mistrust in your discussion). Then look at the work by Chess and Thomas on temperament, discussing the three types they describe (note that only 65% of children can be clearly designated as one of the three types), as well as the factors that Rothbart and Bates suggest (for example, positive affect and approach). Finally, using the guidelines in the chapter, provide some strategies for the parents and teachers to use to work most effectively with children's different temperaments.

Research Project 1:
Observing Developmental Periods

PLEASE NOTE: THIS PROJECT INVOLVES STUDYING OTHER PEOPLE. PLEASE CHECK WITH YOUR INSTRUCTOR TO SEE IF YOU NEED TO COMPLETE AN INSTITUTIONAL RESEARCH BOARD PROTOCOL BEFORE BEGINNING THIS PROJECT.

Bearing in mind the three temperaments described by Thomas and Chess (that is, easy, difficult, slow-to-warm-up) and the three temperament classifications of affect, approach, and control suggested by Rothbart and Bates, observe six different infants at a child-care center, friend's home, the park, and so on, and, using the chart below, describe which category(ies) each child fits. Indicate each child's sex and age in months, and state the specific behaviors that justify this categorization.

	Child 1 Sex: Age:	Child 2 Sex: Age:	Child 3 Sex: Age:	Child 4 Sex: Age:	Child 5 Sex: Age:	Child 6 Sex: Age:
Temperament style						
Affect						
Approach						
Control						
Behaviors observed to justify classification						

1. How easy was it to classify each child?

2. What effect do you believe the child's age or sex had on that child's behavior?

3. If you were able to observe the child interacting with parents or other adults, describe the nature of the interactions and what effect you believe it had on the child's behavior.

4. Does Kagan's emphasis on behavioral inhibition help you in understanding any of the children you observed? How so?

5. Describe what you would include in your own system for classifying temperament.

6. On the basis of your observations, what advice would you give to parents who want to maximize the positive and minimize the negative aspects of their children's temperaments?

Research Project 2:
Parental Leave and Child Care

In a group with other students in your class, prepare a chart that compares parental leave policies around the world, different types of child-care facilities, and research indications about the effects that parental leave and various forms of child care can have on the developing child. Using the findings of the NICHHD study, and after comparing and contrasting each of these variables, write a paper that presents a policy statement concerning what you believe would be the best possible situation in the United States to ensure optimal development of our next generation. You may wish to go a step further and write a letter, based on your findings, to your elected officials in Washington and in your home state. Report to the class whether you received any response to your letter, what the response was, and how it relates to the information in this chapter.

Personal Application Project 1:
Reflecting on What You Learned

Consider what you read in Chapter 4; then answer the following questions:

1. What information in this chapter did you already know?

2. What information in this chapter was totally new to you?

3. How can you use that new information in your own life?

4. What information in this chapter was different from what you previously believed?

5. How do you account for the differences between what you believed and what you learned in the chapter?

6. What is the most important thing you learned from reading this chapter?

7. What's your opinion of the level of importance our early experiences have for our later developmental outcomes?

Personal Application Project 2:
Comparing Temperaments

PLEASE NOTE: THIS PROJECT INVOLVES STUDYING OTHER PEOPLE. PLEASE CHECK WITH YOUR INSTRUCTOR TO SEE IF YOU NEED TO COMPLETE AN INSTITUTIONAL RESEARCH BOARD PROTOCOL BEFORE BEGINNING THIS PROJECT.

A common question among siblings is "Did we really grow up in the same family?" This puzzle originates each child's unique temperament, which in turn affects the child's experiences and perceptions. Observe your own family (or, if you have no siblings, look at a parent and his or her siblings, or a friend who is not an only child) and consider the temperament of each child in the family (if it's one of your parents, for purposes of this exercise, consider him or her as a child of his or her own family). Using the chart below, indicate the temperament type and the different characteristics of each individual included. Add siblings as needed. Then answer the questions below.

	Temperament Type	Positive Affect/Approach	Negative Affectivity	Effortful Control
Self				
Sibling 1				

Sibling 2				
Sibling 3				
Sibling 4				

1. How similar are you (or your parent or your friend) to the siblings listed?

2. Do you have similar or dissimilar temperaments? In what ways are you similar or dissimilar?

3. Do your dissimilarities complement one another or create conflict?

4. How can you use this information to improve your relationships with your siblings?

5. Were you or any of your siblings difficult to categorize? (Note that not everyone is easily described using the Chess and Thomas labels.)

6. What do you think would be the best way to categorize a child's temperament? Describe your "labels" and the characteristics each would have.

7. What have you learned about yourself and your (or another person's) family by looking at temperament?

Internet Projects

Check out the McGraw-Hill website for this text (www.mhhe.com/santrockessls). You will find numerous activities there, in particular, quizzes. Also, be patient, because there are many very worthy links on each of the sites, but they do take a little time to access. If you do not go to the links many times, you will not get the full value of the site. Please go to all links.

Please note that all website addresses in this Study Guide have been checked and were correct at the time of publication. However, websites may be discontinued or their addresses may change, so when you try to access a given site, it may no longer be viable. If that occurs, please notify the publisher so that it can make appropriate revisions in future editions of this Study Guide.

Internet Project 1:
Child-Care Guidelines

Go to www.naeyc.org, which is the website for the National Association for the Education of Young Children. This organization provides information and resources to promote the delivery of high-quality child-care services to children and families. After reviewing the guidelines for high-quality care and the various pages on the site, compare them with the characteristics of high-quality day care that are outlined in the text. What differences do you find? If you were to design your own child-care facility, what would you take from each of these sets of guidelines? View the information provided on the other links of this site. You may also check www.nccic.org (the National Child Care Information Center) for the minimum standards of care in your home state. This site also provides guidelines for tribal child-care centers. You may be interested in comparing the standards for these children to the standards outlined in the text.

Internet Project 2:
Analyzing Temperament and Attachment

Go to www.temperament.com and take the adult temperament questionnaire. Then go to http://www.yourpersonality.net/affect/ and take the attachment styles personality test.

1. Do you think these self-assessments are accurate?

2. Are these assessments scientific or more intuitive in nature?

3. Do the questions asked seem to relate to the material and research presented in the chapter about temperament and attachment?

4. What is the relationship between the different temperamental styles and the quality of one's attachment relationships? (Use the chapter in the text and the websites to help you answer this question.)

5. How is understanding temperament and attachment important in your own personal life? Give several examples of how this knowledge could help you and others you know.

Other Relevant Sites on the Internet

Cascade Center for Family Growth: www.attach-bond.com
This site offers assistance to parents and children in developing healthy attachment and addresses issues of both healthy attachment and attachment disorders.

Attachment Parenting International: http://attachmentparenting.org
This is the official website for the attachment parenting movement. Read all the information on the site, and see if it overlaps with the scientific material on attachment described in the text. Some people feel that attachment parenting is an extreme and distorted form of what Bowlby had in mind. Others feel it is the only way to parent if we are to ever have world peace.

Attachment Disorder Site: http://attachmentdisorder.net
Read about many aspects of attachment problems at the Attachment Disorder Site. The Attachment and Bonding Center of Pennsylvania, at www.abcofpa.net/, also has some interesting information about the importance of attachments for psychological health.

Child Welfare Links: www.childwelfare.com/kids/cwlinks.htm
This tremendous storehouse is chock-full of links to almost every child welfare and developmental site in the United States.

Collaborative for Academic, Social, and Emotional Learning: http://www.casel.org
The CASEL website provides information on "how schools, families, and communities can work together to nurture social, emotional, and academic growth of all children."

Administration for Children and Families (Department of Health and Human Services): www.acf.dhhs.gov/
There are plenty of links here and information concerning child care, child welfare, and agencies to assist children, parents, and families. This is an excellent site.

Developmental Psychology—Temperament: www.psy.pdx.edu/PsiCafe/Areas/Developmental/Temperament
This section of the Psi Cafe site (a psychological resources site) discusses what temperament is and how it is measured; gives links to research labs around the United States that study temperament; and has online surveys, book recommendations, and links about parenting.

Chapter 5: Physical and Cognitive Development in Early Childhood

Learning Goals

1. Identify physical changes in early childhood.
2. Describe three views of the cognitive changes that occur in early childhood.
3. Summarize how language develops in early childhood.
4. Evaluate different approaches to early childhood education.

Chapter Outline

PHYSICAL CHANGES
    Body Growth and Change
        Height and Weight
        The Brain
    Motor Development
        Gross Motor Skills
        Fine Motor Skills
        Handedness
    Nutrition
        Overweight Young Children
        Malnutrition
    Illness and Death
        The United States
        The State of Illness and Health of the World's Children

COGNITIVE CHANGES
    Piaget's Preoperational Stage
        The Symbolic Function Substage
        The Intuitive Thought Substage
        Centration and the Limits of Preoperational Thought
    Vygotsky's Theory
        The Zone of Proximal Development and Scaffolding
        Language and Thought
        Teaching Strategies Based on Vygotsky's Theory
        Evaluating Vygotsky's Theory
    Information Processing
        Attention
        Memory
            Short-Term Memory
            How Accurate Are Young Children's Long-Term Memories?
        The Young Child's Theory of Mind
            2 to 3 Years of Age
            4 to 5 Years of Age
            Beyond Age 5

LANGUAGE DEVELOPMENT
    Understanding Phonology and Morphology
    Changes in Syntax and Semantics
    Advances in Pragmatics

EARLY CHILDHOOD EDUCATION
    Variations in Early Childhood Education
        The Child-Centered Kindergarten
        The Montessori Approach
        Developmentally Appropriate and Inappropriate Education
    Education for Children Who Are Disadvantaged
    Controversies in Early Childhood Education

Matching Questions

_____ 1. Education that involves the whole child by considering both the child's physical, cognitive, and social development and the child's needs, interests, and learning styles.

A. developmentally appropriate practice

_____ 2. Educational philosophy in which children are given considerable freedom and spontaneity in choosing activities and are allowed to move from one activity to another as they desire.

B. Montessori approach

_____ 3. Government-funded program designed to provide children from low-income families the opportunity to acquire the skills and experiences important for school success.

C. zone of proximal development

_____ 4. Education that focuses on the typical developmental patterns of children and the uniqueness of each child.

D. Project Head Start

_____ 5. Vygotsky's term for tasks too difficult for children to master alone but that can be mastered with assistance.

E. child-centered kindergarten

Multiple-Choice Questions

1. As preschool children grow older, the percentage of increase in height and weight _____ with each additional year.
a. increases
b. decreases
c. doubles
d. varies

2. The changes in brain development that occur in early childhood enable children to do ALL BUT WHICH ONE of the following?
a. think abstractly
b. plan their actions
c. attend to stimuli more effectively

d. make large advances in language development

3. Myelination improves the efficiency of the central nervous system in the same way that _____.
a. talking to an infant speeds the baby's ability to produce a first word
b. reducing the distance between two children playing catch reduces the time it takes for a baseball to travel from one child to the other
c. the ingestion of certain chemicals (for example, steroids) can improve overall muscle development
d. the insulation around an electrical extension cord improves its efficiency

4. An example of fine motor skills is _____.
a. bouncing a ball
b. walking a straight line
c. sorting blocks
d. writing your name

5. _____ seems to be the strongest influence of handedness in children.
a. Genetic inheritance
b. Socialization
c. Modeling
d. Positive reinforcement

6. If your child is overweight, what can you do to help him the most?
a. Give him snacks only when he has been good.
b. Put him on a low-carbohydrate diet.
c. Encourage him to get more exercise.
d. Punish him when you find him eating snacks.

7. A young child who gains the ability to mentally represent an object that is not currently present is in the _____.
a. symbolic function substage
b. intuitive thought substage
c. tertiary circular reactions substage
d. preoperational substage

8. Three-year-old Henry tripped on an uneven sidewalk and ran crying to his mother, saying, "The sidewalk made me fall on purpose!" Henry is demonstrating _____.
a. animism
b. egocentrism
c. centration
d. conservation

9. When her father asked Kim how she concluded that two apples and two apples make five apples, she believed her answer was correct and confidently replied, "I know it, because I know it!" Kim is in which substage of development?
a. primary circular reactions
b. tertiary circular reactions
c. symbolic function
d. intuitive thought

10. A child's lack of ability to conserve is often the result of _____.
a. egocentrism
b. centration
c. concentration
d. animism

11. Professor Rosen showed 4-year-old Clarence two balls of clay that were the same size. As he watched, she rolled one of the balls into a snake shape, neither adding nor taking away any clay. When asked if both the ball and the "snake" had the same amount of clay, Clarence responded that the snake had more. This demonstrates Clarence's _____.
a. imagination
b. inability to reverse actions mentally
c. shape preferences
d. mature conservation abilities

12. According to Gelman's research, children fail conservation tasks because they _____.
a. cannot think about more than one aspect of a task
b. do not notice important features of the tasks
c. cannot mentally reverse the sequence of actions in the tasks
d. do not understand why researchers are testing them

13. Which of the following questions is typical of the preoperational child?
a. "How many different piles of toys can I make from my toys?"
b. "How much is two plus two?"
c. "Where does the moon go when it's light out?"
d. "Do you see the same thing I do, Daddy?"

14. Lev Vygotsky argued that some tasks are too difficult for children to handle alone but can be done with the help of someone more skilled. Such tasks _____.
a. fall into the zone of proximal development
b. are difficult because they are not salient to the child
c. are best taught by having the child work with classmates who are also having difficulty
d. will be frustrating for the child and should be left to a time when the child can more easily accomplish them

15. Lev Vygotsky's beliefs about language and thought can be summed up by which one of the following statements?
a. Children who engage in high levels of private speech are usually socially incompetent.
b. Children use internal speech earlier than they use external speech.
c. Inner speech, or thought, has external or social origins.
d. Language and thought initially develop together and then become independent.

16. Vygotsky believed that a child's cognitive development while in the classroom was influenced by _____.
a. a child's interactions with a teacher and more skilled classmates
b. watching educational programs on television
c. the traditions of a child's ethnic group

d. the use of computers to teach math concepts

17. In a class of mixed age-group toddlers and preschoolers, one must remember that a toddler does not have the ability to _____.
a. use language to communicate
b. habituate to repeated stimulation
c. concentrate on an activity for long periods of time
d. pay attention in class

18. Jamal is 5 years old. His mother has noticed that his attention capabilities have really changed in the past year or so. She has probably seen ALL BUT WHICH ONE of these changes in his attentional abilities?
a. the ability to control attention and pay attention to TV for longer periods
b. the ability to attend to relevant instead of salient aspects of a task
c. the ability to systematically attend to details of pictures
d. the ability to direct attention to what the teacher is saying for the entire school day

19. All of the following factors have been found to account for differences in memory performance between younger and older children EXCEPT which one?
a. use of rehearsal
b. speed and efficiency of processing
c. use of strategies
d. increased intelligence

20. Evidence that children understand the rules of their language includes all of the following abilities EXCEPT which one?
a. adjusting speech style to match the situation
b. application of rules to nonsense words
c. correct word order placement
d. identifying the names of objects they have never previously seen

21. Pragmatics deals with _____.
a. the appropriate use of language in different contexts
b. the way words are combined to form acceptable phrases and sentences
c. the units of meaning involved in word formation
d. overgeneralization of language rules

22. Joseph is attending a child-centered kindergarten, so we would expect to see all of these characteristics EXCEPT which one?
a. instruction organized around Joseph's needs, interests, and learning style
b. an emphasis on the process of what Joseph is learning
c. an emphasis on what Joseph learned
d. play as an important aspect of Joseph's development

23. An instructor who uses developmentally appropriate methods for teaching the alphabet might engage in all of the following activities EXCEPT which one?
a. have the children recite the alphabet three times a day every day
b. use music to teach the alphabet

c. use animal names and shapes to teach the alphabet
d. use the sandbox to let children draw the letters of the alphabet

24. Developmentally appropriate practice must be both _____ appropriate and _____ appropriate.
a. content; economically
b. gender; context
c. age; individual
d. socially; emotionally

25. Project Head Start was designed to _____.
a. provide low-income children a chance to acquire skills that would help them succeed at school
b. assess the advantages and disadvantages of preschool educational programs
c. give children a head start on kindergarten work during preschool
d. determine the feasibility of starting formal education at an earlier age

True/False Questions

1. During the preschool period, the brain increases in size because of increases in the number and size of nerve endings within and between brain areas.

2. Research has shown that children's cognitive development can be directly linked to certain brain structures and specific neurotransmitters.

3. Although what children eat does affect their body shape and growth, there is no evidence that it affects children's susceptibility to developing diseases.

4. Children as young as 5 years of age are now at risk for obesity-related diseases such as diabetes.

5. When children are in the preoperational period of Piaget's theory, they cannot mentally think about things without acting them out.

6. A child is exhibiting centration when she reports that witches are real and are hiding in her closet.

7. Research has found that once a child can perform conservation of number, he can automatically transfer that skill and perform conservation of mass, volume, area, and so on.

8. In Vygotsky's zone of proximal development, the lower level of the zone is where the child can solve problems independently.

9. Mrs. Vargas is scaffolding Hector's learning of a brand new task. To scaffold correctly, she will first start with direct instruction. As Hector gets the hang of the task, she will slowly give less and less guidance.

10. For Vygotsky, private speech is immature and egocentric, but for Piaget, it serves as a valuable tool of thought.

11. In both Piaget's and Vygotsky's theories, teachers serve as facilitators and guides rather than as

directors of the learning experience.

12. While children's memories about peripheral details are quite suggestible, they tend to accurately remember the central aspects of an event.

13. In general, when trying to remember things, young children tend to be fairly good at using strategies such as rehearsal and organization.

14. When a child is 2 to 3 years old, they are likely to understand desires but do not yet have the capacity to grasp differences in perceptions and emotions.

15. Critics of the Montessori approach to early childhood education believe that there is too much focus on imaginative play and not enough emphasis on intellectual activities.

Short-Answer Questions

1. How does the body grow and change in early childhood?

2. Describe changes that take place in motor development.

3. What are some concerns about malnutrition during early childhood?

4. List some causes of illness and death among young children in the United States.

5. List and describe what characterizes Piaget's stage of preoperational thought.

6. Elaborate on Vygotsky's theory of children's cognitive development.

7. Explain some important ways that young children process information.

8. Elaborate on how the grasp of language's rule systems changes in early childhood.

9. What efforts are being made to educate young children who are disadvantaged?

What are some controversial issues related to early childhood education?

10. Essay Questions

1. You are stuck in the middle of an argument among your three best friends concerning cognitive development during early childhood. One of them thinks that Piaget had the best explanations of how children develop, the second believes that Vygotsky has the most plausible theory, and the third says that Gelman and information processing offer the best explanations and has criticisms of (especially) Piaget's theory. Discuss all three of these theories, and state which you think makes the most sense and why.

2. Your cousin has told you that she is going to enroll her child in a preschool. She considers you a wise person, especially now that you are taking this class in life-span development. What would you suggest to her in terms of finding the best type of preschool for her child? Outline the general practices of the

different early childhood education programs presented in the chapter, and evaluate which type you think she should look for and explain why it is better than the others.

Key to Matching Questions

1. E	2. B	3. D	4. A	5. C

Key to Multiple-Choice Questions

1. B	6. C	11. B	16. A	21. A
2. A	7. A	12. B	17. D	22. C
3. D	8. A	13. C	18. A	23. A
4. D	9. D	14. A	19. D	24. C
5. A	10. B	15. C	20. D	25. A

Key to True/False Questions

1. T	4. T	7. F	10. F	13. T
2. T	5. F	8. T	11. T	14. F
3. F	6. F	9. T	12. F	15. F

Key to the Short-Answer Questions

1. The average child's height increases 2 ½ inches per year during early childhood. The average child gains 5 to 7 pounds per year during this period as well. Brain growth during early childhood is due to increases in myelination and the size/number of dendrites. The frontal lobes of the brain experience the greatest growth.

2. Both gross and fine motor skills increase during early childhood. Typical gross motor activities include hopping, running, and skipping. Building blocks and puzzles are activities that help children improve fine motor skills during early childhood.

3. Iron deficiency is one of the most common nutritional problems in early childhood which can lead to chronic fatigue. Malnutrition is of particular concern for low-income families, where children may lack adequate intake of iron, vitamins, and protein. WIC is one program that works to improve the nutrition of children in America.

4. The United States has a relatively high rate for under-5 mortality. Factors such as inadequate health care and poverty are possible causes for this high rate. Motor vehicle accidents are the leading cause of death in early childhood, followed by cancer and cardiovascular disease. Other accidental causes of death include poisoning, drowning, and falls. The increase in motor skills coupled with an increase in adventurousness can have disasterous outcomes if parental monitoring is lacking. One major cause of childhood illness is parental smoking. Children who live in a home where there is second-hand smoke are much more likely to develop wheezing, asthma, respiratory illness, and low levels of vitamin C in their blood then children who live in a smoke-free home. Another cause of childhood illness is lead

poisoning. Lead poisoning can lead to lower intelligence and poor academic performance as well as attention deficit hyperactivity disorder.

5. Preoperational thought involves being able to think about the world with symbols, emerging reasoning, and the formation of stable concepts. Egocentrism, animism, centration, and a lack of conservation both characterize and limit thinking at this stage. This is also a stage of curiosity and constant questions.

6. Vygotsky's theory of cognitive development is considered a social constructivist approach. This means that children develop cognitively through social interactions. Cognitive development is assisted through activities in their zone of proximal development, scaffolding, and language.

7. Attention and short-term memory are two areas of information processing that improve during early childhood. Children also have a nascent theory of mind.

8. During early childhood, children become more sensitive to the phonemes of their spoken language. They begin to understand and apply the morphological, syntactical, and pragmatic rules of their language. Vocabulary expands substantially during early childhood.

9. The Head Start program is one way that the United States is trying to educate preschool children from disadvantaged backgrounds. The Head Start programs, and programs like that, allow children to be prepared for entry into the school system.

10. One controversy related to early childhood education is the curricula approach. Not everyone advocates for a child-centered, constructivist educational approach. Although such an approach is developmentally appropriate, some argue for an instructivist, academic approach. Another controversy is whether or not preschool is necessary for later academic success. If a parent has the time, skills, and commitment to educate their young child; they can do so as effectively as a preschool.

Key to Essay Questions

1. To answer this question, you will need to explain the three cognitive approaches that describe development at this point in time: Piaget, Vygotsky, and information processing. This will involve a discussion of the various facets of the two substages (symbolic function and intuitive thought) of the preoperational stage (for example, animism, egocentrism), how Piaget arrived at his ideas, and how they have been supported; then address the criticisms of Piaget's findings (for instance, problems with his research designs, the fact that children demonstrate certain abilities earlier than he suggested); then contrast Piaget's theory with that of Vygotsky, which states that development is embedded within the sociocultural context (be sure to discuss the zone of proximal development and scaffolding); then compare those theories with the information-processing approach concerning attention, memory, and children's theory of mind. After presenting these three perspectives, state which makes most sense to you (or whether all three are needed together), and explain the rationale for your choice.

2. There are many issues to address here, including the educational applications of Vygotsky's theory (for example, use of scaffolding), the various types of early childhood education programs (for instance, child-centered kindergarten, the Montessori approach, the Reggio Emilia technique, Project Head Start for educationally disadvantaged children, and so on), developmentally appropriate and inappropriate practices (for example, providing experiences in all developmental areas rather than narrowly focusing

on cognitive development), nonsexist education; and a discussion of what factors predict a successful early education program. Also note Elkind's position that young children do need early education, whether by parents who are willing and able to provide it or by competent preschools. Evaluate what is in the chapter so that you can use your critical thinking skills and provide your cousin with the best information possible in choosing a good preschool.

Research Project 1:
Designing a Developmentally Appropriate Preschool Curriculum

PLEASE NOTE: THIS PROJECT INVOLVES STUDYING OTHER PEOPLE. PLEASE CHECK WITH YOUR INSTRUCTOR TO SEE IF YOU NEED TO COMPLETE AN INSTITUTIONAL RESEARCH BOARD PROTOCOL BEFORE BEGINNING THIS PROJECT.

Visit two local preschools, and take notes about whether they are developmentally appropriate, whether they have positive teacher-child interactions, and so forth. You will need to record observations regarding such things as the décor, children's artwork being displayed, the schedule they abide by, and the curriculum (or lack thereof) that they use. Talk to one of the teachers or to the director and ask him or her to summarize the mission of the preschool and what the school's goals are for the children there. Do you think the preschools fit under a Piagetian, Vygotskyan, Montessori, Reggio Emilia, or other type of program? Is it a combination of many approaches? Considering everything you have learned in this chapter concerning developmentally appropriate and inappropriate practices and creating an atmosphere that will optimize children's learning abilities while minimizing stress, reflect on what was developmentally appropriate or not in the programs you visited. If you could give the directors advice about their programs, what would you specifically include? What would you specifically omit? Describe your dream preschool, explaining the kinds of personnel, activities, curriculum, and physical environment you would want, and why you think these would be important. Which theories would you consider to be most relevant when designing this curriculum? How are they important, and how would they be incorporated into your design? Remember that this dream preschool is one where you would not have any reservations about leaving your own child.

Research Project 2:
Early Childhood Memory

PLEASE NOTE: THIS PROJECT INVOLVES STUDYING OTHER PEOPLE. PLEASE CHECK WITH YOUR INSTRUCTOR TO SEE IF YOU NEED TO COMPLETE AN INSTITUTIONAL RESEARCH BOARD PROTOCOL BEFORE BEGINNING THIS PROJECT.

This project will assist you in understanding memory changes for young children. First, get permission from the parents of three children of the same sex, ages 3 to 5, 6 to 8, and 11 to 13 years; then ensure that the children are willing to help you with this project. Using the number sets in the chart below, ask the children (separately) to listen as you read the number set. Tell them you will begin each set by saying "Start" and end by saying "Go," at which time they should write down the numbers of each set in the order they were read. Read the numbers clearly, with 4 seconds between each number in the set. Record their answers in the chart below, then answer the questions that follow. After you have finished, ask the children how they were able to remember the numbers that they did remember, and what they thought were the reasons they did not remember all the numbers. Remember that you are working with only one child from each age group. DO NOT make any comparisons of the children to the parents, because this could lead to misunderstandings. Each child is different, may have different abilities, and could have different background experiences. By using one child from each of the three age groups you will get informal impressions, but do not confuse them with a true research project.

Number Set	Child 1 Age: Sex:	Child 2 Age: Sex:	Child 3 Age: Sex:
2-6			
7-4-9			
8-1-7-2			
5-3-0-9-4			
6-1-8-3-9-2			
9-2-4-3-5-7-1			
4-3-7-9-5-1-2-8			
3-9-4-6-5-1-8-0-2			

1. Based on the text, what did you expect to find in terms of each child's ability to remember these numbers? Were your findings consistent with your expectations?

2. What strategies (for example, rehearsal), if any, did each child use to try to remember these numbers? Were these behaviors consistent with what you read in the text? If so, explain how; if not, explain how they were not consistent.

3. What reasons did the children give for their ability to remember or not remember? Were these reasons consistent with the literature on cognitive development? Explain how they were or were not consistent.

4. On the basis of your observations of these children, which theory do you think best explains cognitive development for these age groups?

5. What similarities did you notice among the children in the way they performed? What differences did you notice?

Personal Application Project 1:
The Best Teachers

Analyze your own learning experiences. If you can remember, think back to your early childhood education experiences, all the way up to the present, in your college classes. Who were your best teachers and your worst teachers? What made them so? Now that you know about the different theories of cognitive development and different methods of education, how would you characterize your own learning? Did you do best and enjoy your class/school the most when there was a more Vygotskyan approach, with lots of scaffolding and collaborative learning? Or do you feel more positively about those experiences that were Piagetian, where students were allowed to discover learning on their own? What theoretical approaches do you think your best teachers came from? What approaches characterized your worst learning experiences? Do you find certain approaches typical of one discipline (for example, science versus literature classes), or do they just vary by teacher? Were your earliest experiences developmentally appropriate or inappropriate? Write a paper summarizing your responses to these questions, and describe your own theory of the best way to educate students like you. Incorporate the theories and research on educational practices in the chapter, including the information-processing approach, and integrate your personal learning history to illustrate your points.

Personal Application Project 2:
Favorite Toys

Ask your parents what your favorite toys were when you were a young child. Pick one of your favorite toys, and analyze it from a developmental perspective. What developmental skills did this toy utilize? What aspects of development are targeted by this toy? Are there features of this toy that make it particularly valuable from a developmental perspective? Write a short paper examining the developmental value of your favorite childhood toy.

Internet Projects

Check out the McGraw-Hill website for this text (www.mhhe.com/santrockessls). You will find numerous activities there, in particular, quizzes. Also, be patient, because there are many very worthy links on each of the sites, but they do take a little time to access. If you do not go to the links many times, you will not get the full value of the site. Please go to all links.

Please note that all website addresses in this Study Guide have been checked and were correct at the time of publication. However, websites may be discontinued or their addresses may change, so when you try to access a given site, it may no longer be viable. If that occurs, please notify the publisher so that it can make appropriate revisions in future editions of this Study Guide.

Internet Project 1:
Poverty in Childhood

THIS WOULD BE BEST AS A GROUP PROJECT, BECAUSE IT ALLOWS FOR BRAINSTORMING AND INTERACTION AMONG MEMBERS OF THE GROUP.

The chapter addresses some issues of poverty in childhood, particularly in the sections on illness and health and early education. Go to www.nccp.org (the website for the National Center for Children in Poverty). How does that information augment what you learned in the chapter? What are the consequences of living in poverty for the children involved? What are the societal consequences of having any children living in poverty, and of having 20% of our children living below the poverty level? For this activity, pretend your own community has an even higher rate of children living below the poverty level. Your group has been asked to make a presentation to the county/city health council concerning ways to help these children. Combining what you have learned from the chapter with information you gather from this website (and any other sources), develop your presentation.

Internet Project 2:
The Theorist versus the Person and Constructing a Better Theory

Based on this chapter, which theory did you like best, Piaget's or Vygotsky's? You can see the basic ways in which they differ by examining the figure in the text. If you do not already have an opinion about which theory makes more sense to you, check out www.kolar.org/vygotsky to learn more about the man and his work. See the photo archive link to view his various looks as well as other photographs relevant to his life. Then examine www.piaget.org to view the website for the Jean Piaget Society. Click on his picture to see his biography and some great photos. To really understand these two theorists, read as much as possible from each of these two sites, and take notes on which person/theorist you like best and why. Then answer the following four questions:

1. Did seeing pictures of these men change your feelings or ideas about them? Explain.

2. Did reading their biographical sketches add anything to your understanding of each man and his ideas? For example, when you read something about their own childhood or adulthood development, did that give you any insights into how they developed their theories? Explain.

3. What would a theory of cognitive development look like if we combined the best aspects of Piaget and Vygotsky's work? Would it help us to have a better understanding of how children think and learn? Outline the tenets of this new theory.

4. Does incorporating the ideas of the information-processing theorists enrich our new picture of children's cognitive development? What are its most valuable contributions?

Other Relevant Sites on the Internet

Child Nutrition, Health, and Physical Activity: www.fns.usda.gov/cnd/
This is the site for the U.S. Department of Agriculture's Food and Nutrition Service which provides current information about children's nutrition. Follow all the links to the information here.

American Academy of Pediatrics: www.aap.org/
Here you will find a great deal of information regarding physical and mental health topics related to children and adolescents.

Children's Safety Network: www.childrenssafetynetwork.org/
National Injury and Violence Prevention Resource Center offers safety tips. CSN works with maternal and child health (MCH), public health, and other injury prevention practitioners to:
- provide technical assistance and information
- facilitate the implementation and evaluation of injury prevention programs
- conduct analytical and policy activities that improve injury and violence prevention

Administration for Children & Families in the Department of Health and Human Services: http://www.acf.hhs.gov/
This organization's site offers links and information concerning child care, child welfare, and agencies to assist children, parents, and families.

Handedness—all these sites have appealing information regarding handedness in children and adults:
- http://toddlerstoday.com/resources/articles/lefthand.htm for basic information
- www.indiana.edu/~primate/brain.html for a discussion of brain lateralization and hand preference

Chapter 6: Socioemotional Development in Early Childhood

Learning Goals

1. Discuss emotional and personality development in early childhood.
2. Explain how families can influence young children's development.
3. Describe the roles of peers, play, and television in young children's development.

Chapter Outline

EMOTIONAL AND PERSONALITY DEVELOPMENT
- The Self
  - Initiative Versus Guilt
  - Self-Understanding and Understanding Others
- Emotional Development
  - Self-Conscious Emotions
  - Young Children's Emotional Language and Understanding of Emotion
  - Emotion-Coaching and Emotion-Dismissing Parents
  - Regulation of Emotion and Peer Relations
- Moral Development
  - Moral Feelings
  - Moral Reasoning
  - Moral Behavior
- Gender
  - Social Influences
    - Social Theories of Gender
    - Parental Influences
    - Peer Influences
  - Cognitive Influences

FAMILIES
- Parenting
  - Baumrind's Parenting Styles
  - Parenting Styles in Context
  - Punishment
  - Coparenting
- Child Maltreatment
  - Types of Child Maltreatment
  - The Context of Abuse
  - Developmental Consequences of Abuse
- Sibling Relationships and Birth Order
  - Birth Order
- The Changing Family in a Changing Society
  - Working Parents
  - Children in Divorced Families
  - Gay Male and Lesbian Parents

PEER RELATIONS, PLAY, AND TELEVISION
Peer Relations
Play
   Play's Functions
Television
   Effects of Television on Children's Aggression
   Effects of Television on Children's Prosocial Behavior

Matching Questions

_____ 1. Play that involves interaction with peers.

A. practice play

_____ 2. Play that involves repetition of behavior when new skills are being learned or when physical or mental mastery and coordination of skills are required for games or sports.

B. sensorimotor play

_____ 3. Play in which the child transforms the physical environment into a symbol.

C. constructive play

_____ 4. Play that combines sensorimotor and repetitive activity with symbolic representation of ideas. Play that occurs when children engage in self-regulated creation of a product or a problem solution.

D. social play

_____ 5. Behavior engaged in by infants to derive pleasure from exercising their existing schemas.

E. pretense/symbolic play

Multiple-Choice Questions

1. Olivia's parents openly value Olivia's participation in family conversations. Although she frequently misunderstands the topic, they answer her questions, help her to join in, or simply enjoy her sometimes fantastic ideas. According to Erik Erikson, these parents are encouraging _____.
a. initiative
b. conscience
c. identification
d. self-concept

2. Preschoolers most often describe themselves in terms of their _____.
a. thoughts
b. physical characteristics
c. emotions
d. relationships to other people

3. Emotional development in 4- to 5-year-olds is characterized by all the following factors EXCEPT which one?
a. ability to reflect on emotions
b. ability to understand that similar situations can elicit different emotions in different people
c. ability to teach younger children how to manage their own emotions
d. awareness of managing emotions in order to meet social standards

4. Cesar has "emotion-coaching" parents. Therefore, compared to children in emotion-dismissing families, he is likely to have many advantages in his development. Which of the following would NOT be one of those advantages?
a. He may be better able to soothe himself when upset.
b. He may be better at focusing his attention.
c. He may have fewer behavior problems.
d. He may be better able to mask his negative emotions.

5. A major distinction between autonomous morality and heteronomous morality is that autonomous moral thinkers focus on the _____.
a. consequences of behavior
b. intentions of someone who breaks a rule
c. way a specific behavior makes them feel
d. rewards moral behavior will bring

6. Piaget believed that the social understanding of autonomous children comes about through _____.
a. parental modeling
b. what they learn in their cultural settings
c. biological maturation
d. the mutual give-and-take of peer relations

7. Emory's work indicates that when children are rewarded for behavior that is consistent with laws and social conventions, they are likely to repeat that behavior. This is the _____.
a. Piagetian view of development
b. social cognitive view of development
c. Freudian view of development
d. gender identification view of development

8. If a person has the capacity for empathy, one can assume that he/she has the cognitive ability of _____.
a. conservation
b. logical reasoning
c. decentration
d. perspective taking

9. Gender identity refers to the _____.
a. biological dimension of being male or female
b. social and psychological dimensions of being male or female
c. sense of being male or female
d. set of expectations that prescribe how males or females should think, act, or feel

10. Which of the following is the most accurate characterization social cognitive theory with respect to gender-role development?
a. It assumes that children automatically adopt the characteristics of their parents.
b. It assumes that rewards directly shape gender-role development.
c. It assumes that children must experience a psychosocial conflict to shape gender development.
d. It assumes that anatomy is destiny in forming gendered behavior.

11. In terms of parental influences on their children's gender development, _____.
a. fathers are more consistently given responsibility for physical care
b. mothers are more likely to engage in playful interaction
c. mothers are more likely to be given responsibility for ensuring that their children conform to cultural norms
d. fathers are more involved in socializing their sons than their daughters

12. Dr. Van Cleef argues that children do not have to perceive gender constancy before they begin to understand gender stereotypes. She states that gender typing can occur when children can understand social information regarding what is appropriate for males and females in their culture. Children are then motivated to act in the ways that conform to what they have seen around them and believe to be correct. Dr. Van Cleef is a _____ theorist.
a. cognitive developmental
b. psychoanalytic
c. gender schema
d. Piagetian

13. According to gender schema theory, children are _____ to perceive the world and to act in accordance with their developing schemas.
a. externally motivated
b. lacking the ability
c. genetically predispositioned
d. internally motivated

14. All the following are characteristics of children of authoritarian parents EXCEPT which one?
a. They fail to initiate activity.
b. They have weak communication skills.
c. They are anxious about social comparison.
d. They lack self-control.

15. Mr. Williams brought 3-year old Tanesha to day care. He explained to the teacher that Tanesha was rather sleepy this morning, because she did not go to bed until 2 A.M. The teacher asked why, and Mr. Williams replied, "Oh, we don't like to put limits on our children—they need to experience life to the fullest. We play games, and she goes to sleep when she gets tired." It sounds as if Mr. Williams is _____.
a. an authoritarian parent
b. an authoritative parent
c. a neglectful parent
d. an indulgent parent

16. All the following statements regarding spanking are true EXCEPT which one?
a. Spanking provides children with an out-of-control model for handling stress.
b. Spanking can instill fear, rage, or avoidance in children.
c. Spanking is related to higher levels of moral reasoning in children.
d. Spanking teaches children what not to do but does not provide discussion regarding desired behaviors.

17. Spanking that can be classified as abuse is typically caused by _____.
a. a raging parent who becomes so aroused when they are punishing a child that they lose control
b. an overwhelmed parent who lacks the emotional or social knowledge to implement more effective parenting strategies
c. an alcoholic parent who cannot differentiate between punishment and abuse
d. an authoritarian parent who demands strict obedience to their rules

18. "Child maltreatment" is preferred by developmentalists today instead of "child abuse" because

_____.
a. "child abuse" is a legal term, not a psychological term
b. they believe that changing the term is likely to reduce the incidence of abuse
c. the term "maltreatment" includes several different conditions, not just abuse
d. they want to be able to differentiate the two in terms of severity

19. Which type of abuse is almost always present when other forms of abuse are identified?
a. physical
b. neglect
c. sexual
d. emotional

20. The research on the effects of divorce on children suggests that _____.
a. most children in divorced families do not develop major adjustment problems
b. strong-willed children are better able to cope with their parents' divorce
c. children who are very mature often take divorce the hardest because of their deeper understanding of the issues
d. generally speaking, it is better for the children if parents remain in a marriage, even if there is a great deal of conflict, because children need two parents at home

21. Joel is growing up with homosexual parents: two fathers. On the basis of the research in the chapter, what can we expect for Joel?
a. He will be more likely to be homosexual himself.
b. He will be unpopular and teased mercilessly by his peers.
c. He will be more likely to develop a major depressive disorder than other children will.
d. He will be likely to have adjustment problems if his parents use a neglectful parenting style.

22. It is more common for low-income families than middle- or upper-income families to _____.
a. use a conversational, less directive style with their children
b. use physical punishment with their children
c. use a democratic style in which children are seen as equals
d. encourage their children's initiative and delay of gratification

23. One of the most important functions of the peer group is to _____.
a. foster love and understanding
b. act as a surrogate for the parents
c. teach the importance of friendship
d. teach about the world outside the family

24. Practice play differs from sensorimotor play in that practice play _____.
a. is most common in the infancy stage of development
b. involves coordination of skills
c. revolves around the use of symbols
d. is done for its own sake

25. Research concerning children's TV watching shows that _____.
a. children should not be allowed to watch television unless supervised by an adult
b. there is no relationship between watching violence on television and aggressive behavior
c. children who watch violence on television get it out of their systems and are less likely to fight
d. children who view violence on television are more likely to engage in aggressive behavior

True/False Questions

1. During the period of initiative versus guilt, children begin to increase the size of their social world and explore new experiences.

2. Young children's self-descriptions are typically negative and limited due to their lack of social experiences.

3. The heteronomous moral reasoner believes in "immanent justice," the idea that any time he or she does something bad; the deed will always be met with punishment, even if no one saw the transgression.

4. Piaget argued that parents are the main source of children's advancements in their moral reasoning.

5. In social role theory, power and status differentials throughout history are used to explain current gender differences found in most societies.

6. Fathers are likely to treat boys and girls similarly, whereas mothers are likely to treat sons and daughters very differently.

7. Girls tend to be much more constricted by gender-role expectations than are boys.

8. Physical punishment is harmful for all children, regardless of what ethnic background they come from or where they live.

9. Although spanking has some consequences for children's development, it remains one of the most effective parenting techniques.

10. We cannot assume that all children would benefit from receiving extra time and attention from stay-at-home parents.

11. The nature of parents' work can have an important impact on a child's development.

12. Research shows that children who have no siblings tend to be spoiled and self-centered.

13. Lower SES parents tend to spend more time talking with their children and are less directive.

14. Children find play very entertaining and fun, but it serves no real developmental purpose.

15. Television can have a negative influence on children because it often presents them with unrealistic and stereotypical views of the world.

Short-Answer Questions

1. Describe the development of a child's conception of "self" during early childhood.

2. Explain the changes that take place in emotional development in early childhood.

3. According to Piaget, what is moral reasoning like during early childhood?

4. Explain what is meant by gender identity and gender roles.

5. What are some theories of social influences on gender differences?

6. Explain the four parenting styles proposed by Baumrind and the child outcomes associated with each.

7. Discuss some forms of child maltreatment.

8. Describe how sibling relationships influence children's development.

9. Discuss the effects of divorce on children's development.

10. What are some reasons that play is important for children?

Essay Questions

1. Your friend's daughter wears nothing but pink, plays only with dolls and other stereotypically "girl" toys, and hates to play outside or get dirty. Your friend tells you that she just can't figure out how she got that way. Given the research evidence in the chapter, what would you tell your friend regarding possible explanations for such gender-typical behavior and preferences?

2. Your next-door neighbor comes to you for advice. She confides in you that her husband has been repeatedly unfaithful. His behavior has been erratic in that she never knows if or when he'll be home, he does not participate in the children's school and extracurricular activities, and the two of them spend most of their time together either arguing or in icy silence. She has suggested that they see a marriage counselor, but he says he is perfectly happy with the way things are. She tells you that she is considering leaving him and asks you what the effect might be on her children if she divorces him. She has heard that even in the worst of relationships, it is better for the couple to stay together "for the sake of the children." Short of giving her legal advice (other than "see an attorney to learn what you can do

and what your rights are"), what can you tell her about the effects of divorce on children, and how she can minimize the trauma to her children in the event of a divorce?

Key to Matching Questions

1. D	2. A	3. E	4. C	5. B

Key to Multiple-Choice Questions

1. A	6. D	11. D	16. C	21. D
2. B	7. B	12. C	17. A	22. B
3. C	8. D	13. D	18. C	23. D
4. D	9. C	14. D	19. D	24. B
5. B	10. B	15. D	20. A	25. D

Key to True/False Questions

1. T	4. F	7. F	10. T	13. F
2. F	5. F	8. T	11. T	14. F
3. T	6. F	9. F	12. F	15. T

Key to Short-Answer Questions

1. Erikson proposed that early childhood is the time when children struggle with initiative versus guilt. The young child's self-understanding also progresses to describing him/herself primarily through body characteristics, material possessions, and physical activities.

2. Toddlers increasingly experience self-conscious emotions. By mid-early childhood, children increase the vocabulary they use to describe emotions and develop an understanding of the causes and effects of emotions. By the end of early childhood, children are able to reflect on emotions and understand that a single event can evoke different emotions in different people.

3. Piaget thought that children exhibit heteronomous morality in early childhood. This type of moral reasoning involves thinking of rules and justice as unchangeable properties of the world, out of the control of other people.

4. Gender identity is the awareness of being a male or a female. This usually develops by the age of three. The term *gender role* refers to the set of expectations about how males and females are supposed to behave, think, and feel. Knowledge of these gender roles and conformity to the expectations inherent in them increase during early childhood.

5. The text discusses three main social theories of gender: social role theory, psychoanalytic theory, and social cognitive theory. Social role theory proposes that gender differences result from the contrasting

roles of men and women. Psychoanalytic theory proposes that gender differences develop through repressing attraction to the opposite-sex parent and identification with the same-sex parent. Social cognitive theory proposes that gender differences occur through the observation and imitation of gender behavior and through the rewards and punishments children experience for gender-appropriate and gender-inappropriate behavior.

6. The four parenting styles Baumrind proposed are authoritarian, authoritative, neglectful, and indulgent. These styles vary the dimensions of degree of parental control and degree of affection. Authoritarian parenting involves a high degree of control and minimal affection. Children with authoritarian parents often exhibit self-doubt, low initiative, and are unhappy. Authoritative parenting involves a moderate degree of parental control and optimal levels of affection. This is the parenting style associated with the best outcomes for children such as displaying self-control, good social skills, and coping well with stress. Neglectful parenting involves a low degree of both parental control and affection. Children of neglectful parents exhibit low self-esteem, immaturity, and may engage in delinquent behavior in adolescence. Indulgent parenting involves a low degree of parental control but high levels of affection. Children of indulgent parents may always expect to get their way, have difficulties in peer relations, and be domineering.

7. Some of the forms that child maltreatment can take include physical abuse, child neglect, sexual abuse, and emotional abuse. Physical abuse is described as the infliction of physical injury through physical actions. Child neglect is described as the failure to provide for the child's basic needs (physical, educational, or emotional). Sexual abuse is defined as any sexual contact or acts, exhibitionism, or exposure to pornographic materials. Emotional abuse includes acts or omissions that have caused, or could cause, serious behavioral, cognitive, or emotional problems. Within these parameters, emotional abuse includes verbal abuse and psychological abuse.

8. Sibling relationships involve both negative and positive interactions. Positive interactions can include teaching, playing, sharing, and helping. Siblings may have a stronger socializing influence than do parents.

9. Children of divorce tend to experience greater academic difficulties; to exhibit more externalized and internalized problems; to have a higher likelihood of dropping out of school; to have low self-esteem; to have less competent intimate relationships; to be less socially responsible; to engage in sex at an early age; to take drugs; and to be less securely attached as an adult than children with intact families.

10. Play is essential for a child to be healthy. Play is a safe environment for children to work through life's anxieties and conflicts. Play is a good forum to dispose of excess energy or pent-up stress. Play encourages cognitive development and social skill development. Play also encourages exploratory behavior and is, in itself, a pleasurable way to spend time.

Key to Essay Questions

1. You should tell your friend that biological sex is determined by genes, hormones, and so on. You could point out that evolutionary arguments suggest that her daughter's behavior is highly adaptive for finding a mate in the future. However, most psychologists would argue that the behavior her daughter is exhibiting is likely learned. Discuss the research findings on the differential treatment that boys and girls receive from fathers and the work that shows how peers greatly socialize children to follow traditional gender roles, and present some of the theories of gender-role development to illustrate the

many ways in which one can view the development of gendered behavior. For example, you might discuss gender schema theory, and how children form schemas regarding what their culture presents as acceptable behavior for girls. From this theoretical perspective, her daughter is probably internalizing the values she sees in her home and culture.

2. You need to discuss how children adjust to divorce (although more children from divorced families have adjustment problems than do children from nondivorced families, most children competently cope with their parents' divorce), the factors involved in children's risk and vulnerability (for example, adjustment prior to divorce, temperament, gender, age), and change in socioeconomic status. Because she specifically asked whether they should "stay together for the sake of the children," you will need to address the research in that regard. It would be particularly important also to discuss with her the guidelines for communicating with young children about divorce (for instance, explaining the separation, explaining that it is not the children's fault). Incorporating other relevant topics would also make for an excellent essay (for example, the role of warm/responsive parenting and positive discipline).

Research Project 1:
Sibling Birth Order

PLEASE NOTE: THIS PROJECT INVOLVES STUDYING OTHER PEOPLE. PLEASE CHECK WITH YOUR INSTRUCTOR TO SEE IF YOU NEED TO COMPLETE AN INSTITUTIONAL RESEARCH BOARD PROTOCOL BEFORE BEGINNING THIS PROJECT.

The text provides interesting findings concerning the effects of birth order on later development but notes that these effects may be overemphasized. Using the chart below as a starting point, track as many of your friends and relatives as you practically can, indicating each person's birth order (for example, only child, firstborn of six, second of four), sex, personal characteristics (those indicated in the text and others), and job title/position; add other information that you believe is relevant. Then answer the questions that follow.

Person	Birth Order	Sex	Characteristics	Job Title/ Position	Other

1. In looking at your data overall and understanding that there will be individual differences, do you find that your observations are consistent with what you might expect from the research described? Explain your response.

2. In terms of the material discussed in this chapter, what patterns did you notice when comparing people of similar birth order?

3. In terms of the material discussed in this chapter, what differences did you notice when comparing people of similar birth order?

4. What might you conclude about the effects of birth order on the basis of your observations (for example, did you find that there really are consistent effects of birth order, or did you find that the effects have been overemphasized)?

Research Project 2:
Parental Guidelines for Children's Television Viewing

PLEASE NOTE: THIS PROJECT INVOLVES STUDYING OTHER PEOPLE. PLEASE CHECK WITH YOUR INSTRUCTOR TO SEE IF YOU NEED TO COMPLETE AN INSTITUTIONAL RESEARCH BOARD PROTOCOL BEFORE BEGINNING THIS PROJECT.

Interview three parents of young children regarding their child's television watching habits. Ask the parents how much television the child watches, and whether it is mainly a solitary activity or whether the parent sits down and watches/discusses the shows with the child. Ask the parents if they have any rules regarding how much or what types of shows the child can watch and why those rules exist. Discuss their philosophies regarding the influence of television on children's development. Do they feel it has any particularly good or bad effects on children? On the basis of the answers you received, do you believe that parents, in general, understand, care, or know about the issues and research findings discussed in the text regarding television's effects on children?

Apply the life-span developmental concepts in this chapter to devise guidelines that would assist parents in using television as a positive influence on their children's lives. Consider the different roles that television plays, the types of influence that it has on children, the characteristics of children who are attracted to specific types of programs, how the amount of television watching may affect children, and how parents can most effectively use television as a positive factor for their children's socioemotional development. Suggest how parents might interact with their children to discuss what they view on television.

Personal Application Project 1:
Are You a Stereotype or a Modern Marvel? Examine the Development of Your Gender Role

Think about your own personality traits, characteristics, behaviors, attitudes, and preferences and the activities you most often engage in. Are they stereotypically masculine or feminine? Are you the quintessential macho man or the epitome of a traditional woman? Or are you more like a sensitive man of the twenty-first century (a metrosexual, perhaps?) or an energetic, assertive woman who always mindfully pursues what she wants? Most of us fall somewhere between these extremes. But how did we get that way? Think about the way your parents discussed (or did not discuss) what was proper for boys and girls? How much did they encourage you to adopt traditional behaviors, or did they support nontraditional pursuits? What about your peer group? Did they allow any gender-role transgressions, or did you have to stick to what was "normal"? Is your culture very traditional or fairly modern? What about your religious background? Does it allow women to be equal with men? Or are women supposed to allow men to make most of the decisions?

Apply the research in the chapter to your own gender-role development. What were the most important biological and environmental influences? Incorporate a discussion of the theories and research in the chapter into your own life analysis.

Personal Application Project 2:
Consider Your Own Development (Your Parents' Parenting Style)

As discussed in the text, Diana Baumrind describes four primary styles of parenting: authoritative, authoritarian, neglectful, and indulgent. Of course, none of us is perfectly consistent, and often two parents in the same family unit may have different parenting styles. Further, as discussed in the text, parents may shift their style and become less controlling as their children grow up. Consider your own parents and the style(s) they used with you and your siblings. (They may have used different styles of parenting for each child—this is not a really cut-and-dried typology.) Using the chart below, indicate which style was used primarily by each of your parents, with examples, that would indicate to you that this was, indeed, the style that parent used; then indicate what other styles might have been used and the situations that elicited that style. Also indicate the style(s) used for your siblings, and any changes in parenting style as you got older. After filling in the chart, answer the questions that follow.

Parent and (Your Age)	Primary Style with You	Other Style(s) with You	Primary Style with Siblings
Mother (toddler)			
Mother (preschooler)			
Mother (middle and late childhood)			
Mother (adolescent)			
Father (toddler)			
Father (preschooler)			

Father (middle and late childhood)			
Father (adolescent)			

1. Which primary parenting style did each of your parents use with you? Which other style(s) did they use? When?

2. How consistent were your parents in terms of their parenting style? If they were not consistent, what do you think accounted for the lack of consistency?

3. Did both of your parents use the same parenting style?

4. If your parents used different styles, how do you think that affected you?

5. Did they change parenting styles as you got older? If yes, in what way?

6. If you can, describe the various parenting styles to your parents, and ask them which style they think they used as you were growing up. Is this consistent with your assessment?

7. How do you think these parenting styles affected your development? Do you see current traits, behaviors, or characteristics in yourself that either confirm or contradict the research findings in the chapter?

8. How much do you think your own temperament or behaviors elicited the type of parenting styles that your parents used with you? Can you answer this question regarding your siblings as well?

9. Can you see any connections between the parenting styles used by your parents and current similarities or differences between your siblings and you in terms of behaviors, traits, attitudes, and so on?

10. If you or your siblings have children, will you use your parents' parenting styles, or have you and/or your siblings chosen to use other parenting styles? Why or why not?

Internet Projects

Check out the McGraw-Hill website for this text (www.mhhe.com/santrockessls). You will find numerous activities there, in particular, quizzes. Also, be patient, because there are many very worthy links on each of the sites, but they do take a little time to access. If you do not go to the links many times, you will not get the full value of the site. Please go to all links.

Please note that all website addresses in this Study Guide have been checked and were correct at the time of publication. However, websites may be discontinued or their addresses may change, so when you try to access a given site, it may no longer be viable. If that occurs, please notify the publisher so that it can make appropriate revisions in future editions of this Study Guide.

Internet Project 1:
Exploring Your Own Interests

Using a search engine (for example, www.google.com or www.dogpile.com) and search for terms of interest to you in this chapter (such as "children and divorce," "gay and lesbian parents," "corporal punishment of children,"). Look at three of the sites that come up, and spend about 15 minutes browsing through each. Take notes on items that mesh well with the material in the text, as well as information that seems to contradict what you read in the text. What new material did you find that should be included in the text? Is the material mainly scientific in nature or just someone's opinion? Who sponsors the site? Is there something really interesting that you want to learn more about? If so, click on any accompanying links that give you a more in-depth analysis of your desired topic. Write a brief paper on this topic, incorporating what you learned from the chapter with your own experience of the topic and the Internet material. Discuss any controversies that exist as well as the latest research. End your paper with any lingering questions that were unanswered by any of the sources.

Internet Project 2:
The Scientists and the Victims (Exploring Child Abuse and Neglect)

See the U.S. Department of Health and Human Services' website for the Child Welfare Information Gateway, at www.childwelfare.gov. This is the official website for all things related to child maltreatment. It includes how to detect signs of abuse, what the consequences of maltreatment are for its victims, how to report suspected abuse, relevant conferences and professional workshops, and links to resources and research. It also has all information available in Spanish. Spend about 30 minutes browsing this site and taking notes regarding the information that most interests you.

Then search for more information on the topics that most interested you, using either www.google.com or www.dogpile.com. See what sites come up when you do this general search. View several sites for your topic and evaluate the information on sites developed mainly by and for victims of maltreatment versus the sites developed by and for professionals (scientists, clinicians, politicians, and so on). How do the sites compare? Does one seem to have more of an emotional tone than another? Was the information provided on the sites by or for victims accurate? Or was it based on personal experience with no reference to research on the topic? Evaluate the quality of information out there for victims, professionals, families of victims, and students like you who want to learn about maltreatment. What would you say are the three best sites you visited, and why?

Other Relevant Sites on the Internet

Gender Roles & Stereotypes: www.tolerance.org/parents/kidsarticle.jsp?p=0&ar=8
This page is from the Southern Poverty Law Center's section of "tolerance.org." The site is great for helping parents to talk to children about gender-role stereotypes. It provides activities and discussion topics and helps parents to use images in the media as discussion starters for talking to kids about accepting different types of people.

ParentKidsRight: www.parentkidsright.com/pt-gender.html
Dr. Marilyn Heins's site for parenting kids gives some very useful information about gender roles and parenting.

"With More Equity, More Sweat":
www.washingtonpost.com/wp-srv/national/longterm/gender/gender1.htm
This fascinating article in the Washington Post concerns current gender issues in the workplace and family.

Adult Consequences of Childhood Parenting Styles:
http://ourworld.compuserve.com/homepages/hstein/adult.htm
Psychoanalyst Alfred Adler's Institute in San Francisco uses a typology different from Baumrind's for classifying parenting styles which you might find intriguing. It covers the adult consequences for children parented with the various styles in his system.

Parenting Style and Its Correlates: www.athealth.com/Practitioner/ceduc/parentingstyles.html
Part of the Health.com website, which has vast amounts of material on physical and mental health, this excellent article summarizes Baumrind's parenting styles and the effects of using each one. It also covers ethnic differences.

Positive Discipline and Child Guidance:
http://muextension.missouri.edu/xplor/hesguide/humanrel/gh6119.htm
Parents and teachers can find useful solutions for discipline problems on this page sponsored by the University of Missouri's Extension program. It provides information regarding research references, workshops, and books. It also has several activities and worksheets to print out.

Prevent Child Abuse America: www.preventchildabuse.org
This is the official site for Prevent Child Abuse America, the largest nonprofit organization dedicated to raising awareness and preventing maltreatment.

Adults & Children Together Against Violence: www.actagainstviolence.org
The American Psychological Association's early violence prevention program has a lot of great free resources for parents, teachers, and social service providers that can be downloaded for use in workshops, trainings, the classroom, or at home. There is a special section on the impact of media violence on children and provides numerous links.

Movie Mom's Reviews: http://movies.yahoo.com/moviemom/
Movie Mom reviews every movie that comes out and evaluates content in terms of violence, sexist imagery and characters, racism and the portrayal of ethnic minorities, the portrayal of differently abled people, harsh language, sex/mature themes, and so on. Movie Mom is accurate and insightful in her analysis of the age-appropriateness of each movie.

Chapter 7: Physical and Cognitive Development in Middle and Late Childhood

Learning Goals

1. Describe physical changes and health in middle and late childhood.
2. Explain the various types of disabilities and discuss issues in educating children with disabilities.
3. Explain cognitive changes in middle and late childhood.
4. Describe key features of language development in middle and late childhood.

Chapter Outline

PHYSICAL CHANGES AND HEALTH
    Body Growth and Change
    Motor Development
    Exercise
    Health, Illness, and Disease
        Accidents and Injuries
        Cancer
        Cardiovascular Disease
        Overweight Children

CHILDREN WITH DISABILITIES
    Learning Disabilities
    Attention Deficit Hyperactivity Disorder (ADHD)
    Educational Issues

COGNITIVE CHANGES
    Piaget's Cognitive Developmental Theory
        The Concrete Operational Stage
        Evaluating Piaget's Concrete Operational Stage
    Information Processing
        Memory
            Knowledge and Expertise
            Strategies
            Fuzzy Trace Theory
        Thinking
            Critical Thinking
            Creative Thinking
        Metacognition
    Intelligence
        The Binet Tests
        The Wechsler Scales
        Types of Intelligence
            Sternberg's Triarchic Theory
            Gardner's Eight Frames of Mind
            Evaluating the Multiple-Intelligence Approaches
            Culture and Intelligence
    Interpreting Differences in IQ Scores

The Influence of Genetics
Environmental Influences
Group Differences
Creating Culture-Fair Tests
Using Intelligence Tests
Extremes of Intelligence
Mental Retardation
Giftedness

LANGUAGE DEVELOPMENT
Vocabulary and Grammar
Metalinguistic Awareness
Reading
Bilingualism and Second Language Learning

Matching Questions

_____ 1. Retardation involving no evidence of organic brain damage, but the individual's IQ is between 50 and 70.

A. mental retardation

_____ 2. Includes three components: minimum IQ level; a significant difficulty in a school-related area; and exclusion of severe emotional disorders, second-language background, sensory disabilities, and/or specific neurological deficits.

B. cultural-familial retardation

_____ 3. Condition of limited mental ability in which an individual has a low IQ, usually below 70 on a traditional test of intelligence, and has difficulty adapting to everyday life.

C. learning disability

_____ 4. Category of learning disabilities involving a severe impairment in the ability to read and spell.

D. dyslexia

_____ 5. Having above-average intelligence (an IQ of 130 or higher) and/or superior talent for something.

E. gifted

Multiple-Choice Questions

1. The period of middle and late childhood involves _____.
a. slow, consistent growth
b. rapid, consistent growth
c. rapid spurts of growth
d. moderate growth with occasional spurts

2. Which pattern best portrays changes in gross and fine motor skills in the elementary school years?
a. Boys outperform girls in fine motor skills.
b. Girls outperform boys in fine motor skills.
c. Girls outperform boys in gross motor skills.

d. There are no sex differences in the development of gross and fine motor skills.

3. All the following factors were discussed as negative consequences of childhood obesity EXCEPT which one?
a. increased blood pressure
b. problems in peer relations
c. increased incidence of leukemia
d. increased blood cholesterol levels

4. Nine-year-old Fernando has had a weight problem since he was an infant. One of the best strategies he could use to lose weight would be _____.
a. stomach surgery
b. wiring his mouth closed to reduce food intake
c. a high-protein, low-carbohydrate diet
d. exercise and a moderate reduction in calories

5. The most frequent disability among schoolchildren in the United States is _____.
a. visual impairment
b. learning disabilities
c. mental retardation.
d. speech handicaps

6. _____ refers to tendency for boys to be more likely to be referred by teachers for learning disabilities due to troublesome behavior.
a. Dyslexia
b. Gender disparity
c. Referral bias
d. Individualized assessment

7. Which of the following characteristics may be displayed by a child with ADHD?
a. inattention
b. hyperactivity
c. impulsivity
d. all of the above

8. According to Piaget, mental actions, which are reversible, are called _____.
a. strategies
b. symbolic thought
c. abstractions
d. operations

9. Taylor understands that he can be his father's son, his grandmother's grandson, and his favorite uncle's nephew all at the same time. Taylor is in the _____.
a. sensorimotor stage
b. preoperational stage
c. concrete operational stage
d. formal operational stage

10. Joshua is participating in an experiment on cognitive development. The experimenter shows Joshua 10

pennies, each touching the other, in a straight row. The experimenter makes another identical row of pennies next to it. He asks Joshua if one row has more or if they have the same number of pennies. Joshua says they have the same. The experimenter then spreads out the pennies in one row so that the row is very long. He asks Joshua if either row has more or if they have the same number of pennies. Joshua says they still both have the same, because even though one looks longer, the number cannot change. He states that if you put the pennies back together, the row would look the same as before. Joshua is exhibiting _____.

a. preoperational thought
b. seriation
c. magical thinking
d. conservation

11. Which of the following statements is NOT a criticism usually leveled against Piaget's ideas?
a. Not all aspects of a cognitive stage develop at the same time.
b. Changing the tasks that measure cognitive development changes the skills children can exhibit.
c. Children can be trained to do tasks that they should not be able to do given the cognitive stage they are in.
d. Some of the skills he identified actually appear much later in elementary school children than Piaget suggested.

12. _____ involves thinking reflectively and productively, as well as evaluating the evidence.
a. Creative thinking
b. Critical thinking
c. Use of strategies
d. Abstract learning

13. Jasper is participating in a memory experiment. He is asked to remember a long list of different fruit names. He pictures the oversized fruit bowl at his grandmother's house, imagines himself picking through the fruit in the bowl, and eating each item he is asked to memorize. Jasper is using the strategy called _____.
a. rehearsal
b. critical thinking
c. elaboration
d. metacognition

14. Aaron is aware of his thinking and understands that he uses certain strategies to help him remember. These skills demonstrate _____.
a. memory
b. cognition
c. metacognition
d. abstract reasoning

15. Dr. Gonzalez is one of the best surgeons in his state. According to Gardner's frames of mind, Dr. Gonzalez is strong in _____ intelligence.
a. spatial
b. naturalist
c. interpersonal
d. bodily-kinesthetic

16. When one has the ability to adapt to and learn from life's everyday experiences, possesses problem-solving skills, and has verbal ability, the person is said to have _____.
a. creativity
b. intelligence
c. metacognition
d. wisdom

17. Indira grew up in poverty and first learned to care for herself and her younger brother by selling newspapers and developing street smarts. Although she never went to school, she has become successful in business. In terms of Robert Sternberg's triarchic theory, Indira has _____.
a. analytical intelligence
b. creative intelligence
c. practical intelligence
d. stereotype threat

18. Ariadne is an architect. According to Howard Gardner's theory of intelligence, Ariadne has _____.
a. spatial intelligence
b. mathematical intelligence
c. kinesthetic intelligence
d. naturalist intelligence

19. Many of the early intelligence tests favored urban, middle-income, White individuals. These tests are considered to be _____.
a. culture-fair
b. culture-biased
c. culturally differentiating
d. normative

20. It is very difficult—in fact, almost impossible—to design a universal, culture-fair intelligence test because _____.
a. we cannot establish norms for the different populations of people who take the test
b. languages are so different that some languages cannot express what other languages can
c. most tests tend to reflect what the dominant culture thinks is important
d. we are beginning to doubt that IQ tests actually measure intelligence

21. IQ tests are valuable because _____.
a. the scores on an IQ test may reinforce stereotypes
b. they are the sole reliable indicator of a person's competence
c. they pinpoint the areas where a student needs additional academic help
d. they can be used as a tool to help understand individual differences

22. Research on the causes of mental retardation suggests that _____.
a. the causes are primarily organic
b. environment is more important than biology
c. most retardation is due to genetic factors
d. both biological and environmental factors are involved

23. Santara is a gifted student. She is likely to have all the following characteristics EXCEPT which one?

a. high levels of maturity
b. a high likelihood of emotional problems or mental disorders
c. positive family relationships
d. a passion to master

24. Ms. Kumin believes that, in early reading instruction, children should be presented with materials in their complete form such as stories and poems. Ms. Kumin supports the _____.
a. whole-language approach
b. basic-skills-and-phonetics approach
c. balanced approach
d. classical approach

25. Research has shown that bilingualism _____.
a. has a negative effect on children's cognitive development
b. has a positive effect on children's cognitive development
c. confuses children in regard to language development
d. results in bilingual children's scoring lower than monolingual children on intelligence tests

True/False Questions

1. Jamie can now aim a hammer, tie her shoes, and fasten her clothes. These fine motor skills have developed because of the myelination of her central nervous system which occurs in middle and late childhood.

2. Owing to better medical technology, the incidence of cancer in children is decreasing.

3. Elementary school children are more fatigued by long periods of sitting than by engaging in physical activity.

4. Although ADHD can be devastating for children diagnosed with the disorder, most children grow out of it by the end of adolescence.

5. Although medication is widely prescribed for children with ADHD, research shows that the most effective treatment involves medication in combination with behavior management.

6. In regard to education for children with disabilities, the term "inclusion" means that these children should be included in regular classrooms whenever possible, such as during physical education or art classes.

7. Research has found considerable cross-cultural support for the timing of the cognitive milestones proposed by Piaget.

8. Dr. Shin asks a Piagetian scholar how he can best help his son, Zao, quickly advance in his cognitive development. However, Piagetian scholars would recommend against any attempt to do this as children should advance when they are mature enough to naturally do so.

9. Recent evaluations of Piaget's theory have emphasized that Piaget overestimated what children can do at each stage yet greatly underestimated the sophisticated level of thought exhibited by most adults.

10. Young children tend to overestimate their memory abilities, but children in middle and late childhood have more realistic evaluations of their memory skills.

11. Vonda scores very highly on traditional intelligence tests, and her academic strengths are valued in conventional school programs. This shows that she is high on Sternberg's practical type of intelligence.

12. Bobby has mentally retarded parents, and, as a preschooler, he also scored within the mentally retarded range on IQ tests. However, with participation in an intensive intervention program, Bobby's IQ is now within the normal range. This illustrates that even highly heritable traits can be modified by environmental influences.

13. Even though ethnic differences in IQ have been found, when minorities are given equal opportunities, educational interventions, or more enriched homes, the ethnic differences in IQ scores become minimal.

14. In evaluations of the whole-language approach versus the phonics approach to reading, research confirmed that phonics is the best approach when teaching children to read, but that whole-language has benefits as well.

15. Research shows that bilingualism gets in the way of cognitive development because students spend too much cognitive energy on keeping their two languages straight.

Short-Answer Questions

1. Describe some of the changes in body growth and proportion in middle and late childhood.

2. Explain how children's motor skills develop in middle and late childhood.

3. Give examples to illustrate the role exercise plays in children's lives.

4. List some of the characteristics of health, illness, and disease in middle and late childhood.

5. How do you differentiate a child with a learning disability?

6. Describe the behavior of children with attention deficit hyperactivity disorder, and explain the typical treatment given to these children.

7. Characterize Piaget's stage of concrete operational thought.

8. Explain how children process information in middle and late childhood.

9. What is meant by intelligence?

10. Explain Sternberg's triarchic theory of intelligence.

Essay Questions

1. You are very excited that your university class has assigned you to do your student teaching internship with your favorite elementary school teacher. While helping you to prepare for a positive experience,

Mr. Cano has asked you for your ideas on creating a healthy, holistic atmosphere for his students. He wants you to address their physical, emotional, and cognitive needs but also wants a special emphasis on teaching children to read. Bearing in mind all of the developmental issues you have studied in this chapter, what would you present to Mr. Cano before being in the classroom with the children?

2. Your roommates are arguing about whose ideas were more appropriate for application to education—Piaget's, Gardner's, or Sternberg's. Your roommates do agree that intelligence tests are biased and should not be used. Because you are taking this class in life-span development, they turn to you to determine the merits of Piaget's, Gardner's, and Sternberg's theories. What would you tell them? Also, which theory more readily lends itself to useful applications? Do you agree with your roommates' stand on intelligence tests? Why or why not?

Key to Matching Questions

1. B	2. C	3. A	4. D	5. E

Key to Multiple-Choice Questions

1. A	6. C	11. B	16. B	21. D
2. B	7. D	12. B	17. C	22. D
3. C	8. D	13. C	18. A	23. B
4. D	9. C	14. C	19. B	24. A
5. B	10. D	15. D	20. C	25. B

Key to True/False Questions

1. T	4. F	7. F	10. T	13. T
2. F	5. T	8. T	11. F	14. T
3. T	6. T	9. F	12. T	15. F

Key to Short-Answer Questions

1. There is slow, consistent growth during middle and late childhood. Muscle mass and strength gradually increase. The most noticeable changes in body growth and proportion are decreases in head circumference, waist circumference, and leg length in relation to height.

2. Motor skills become smoother, more coordinated, and more controlled owing to increased myelination of the CNS. Fine motor skills, such as handwriting, also improve.

3. Children's lives at this time should be activity-oriented and very active. Most American children do not get enough exercise. Exercise can be improved through school programs, community activities, and family interactions.

4. Middle and late childhood are typically times of excellent health. Motor vehicle accidents near the

child's home or school are the leading cause of severe injury and death for this age group. The second leading cause of death is cancer. Cardiovascular disease is not very common during childhood, but one can identify the precursors for adulthood disease. There has also been an increase in childhood obesity which can lead to serious health problems down the road.

5. Approximately 10% of all American children receive special education or other related services. Of this 10%, over 40% of these children are classified with one or more learning disabilities. In order to be classified as having a learning disability, the child must meet the following criteria: exceed a minimum IQ level; have a significant difficulty in a school-related area; and not have any severe emotional disorders, second-language background, sensory disabilities, or specific neurological deficits.

6. Attention Deficit Hyperactivity Disorder (ADHD) is characterized by trouble in one or more of these areas: inattention, hyperactivity, and impulsivity. Behavioral problems associated with ADHD include low frustration tolerance, immaturity, clumsiness, poor peer relations, and repudiating discipline. Treatments include taking a stimulant medication and behavior management.

7. The concrete operational stage is Piaget's third stage in cognitive development. It typically emerges around age 7 and lasts until around age 11 (although Piaget believed some people never go beyond this stage). Concrete operational thought is characterized by children being able to reason and think logically, provided this reasoning and thought can be applied to real and concrete examples. Skills that emerge during this stage include classification, seriation, and transitivity.

8. There are many improvements in information processing during middle and late childhood. Long-term memory increases owing to increased knowledge and increased strategy use (elaboration is one particular strategy that improves). Children can also develop expertise in certain subjects or activities during middle and late childhood. Finally, critical thinking and metacognition also improve during middle and late childhood.

9. Intelligence is defined as problem-solving skills and the ability to learn from and adapt to life's everyday experiences.

10. Sternberg's theory argues that intelligence comes in three forms: analytic, creative, and practical. Analytic intelligence refers to the ability to analyze, judge, evaluate, compare, and contrast. Creative intelligence refers to the ability to create, design, invent, originate, and imagine. Practical intelligence refers to the ability to use, apply, implement, and put ideas into practice. This means that individuals can be intelligent in different ways.

Key to Essay Questions

1. Your answer should encompass the entire chapter, including physical changes in the skeletal and muscular systems and increased motor skills (gross and fine) and how they relate to proper diet and the need to exercise, as well as the positive and negative consequences of participating in sports and sensitivity to various issues of children's disabilities (for example,, learning disabilities, ADHD) and socioeconomic issues. Then move on to the developmental changes in children's cognitive abilities (they are now in the concrete operational stage), addressing application of Piaget's theory to education and what information-processing theory says about development during this period (for instance, memory, metacognition, critical thinking). Then address the issues of intelligence, creativity, language development, and the debate on teaching reading using the whole-language approach or the basic-skills-and-phonetics approach. After addressing all these developmental issues, suggest how you

would use this information to assist in creating a model classroom with a developmentally appropriate curriculum to achieve optimal outcomes for all the students. You might also want to include the benefits of bilingualism and a discussion of how it would be appropriate for children at this age to start to learn a second language if they do not come from a bilingual home.

2. You need to lay out the theories of Piaget, Gardner, and Sternberg; discuss what Piaget said about children's abilities in the concrete operational stage, and how that information can be applied to education (for example, assuming the constructivist approach, children need to be actively involved in seeking solutions for themselves) and the criticisms of his theory (for instance, some cognitive abilities emerge earlier than he thought). Then you should address Sternberg's triarchic theory of intelligence with its three separate components, and explain how each of those can be incorporated into the teaching/learning process, discussing what he believes is important in teaching (such as balanced instruction related to the three types of intelligence in addition to traditional memorization). Do the same with Gardner's multiple intelligences. Outline some of the unique aspects of his theory and what the main contributions are. Bringing in any of the other theories you wish to consider, state which approach you think works best, and explain your rationale. Then move on to the concerns about use of intelligence tests (understanding why Binet and Simon developed them in the first place, you can understand their use as a general predictor for how well a student may be expected to perform, but discuss the many issues of bias, inability to create a truly culture-free test, and other misuses) and develop a clear argument presenting the safeguards, limitations, and cautions that you believe are necessary for these tests to be used effectively.

Research Project 1:
Fine and Gross Motor Activity

PLEASE NOTE: THIS PROJECT INVOLVES STUDYING OTHER PEOPLE. PLEASE CHECK WITH YOUR INSTRUCTOR TO SEE IF YOU NEED TO COMPLETE AN INSTITUTIONAL RESEARCH BOARD PROTOCOL BEFORE BEGINNING THIS PROJECT.

This is a way to see developmental changes in fine and gross motor activity over time. After obtaining written parental permission and the permission of the children with whom you will be working, have five children from five different age groups (ranging from 4 through 12) write (or print, as appropriate) their first name and their age and draw a picture of themselves. (Note that only one chart is provided below. Be sure to make four more copies before using this one.) Compare the handwriting and the drawings in terms of what you have learned so far. Then answer the questions below. Be sure that you do not compare the children's work in the children's presence and that the names, ages, and other data about the children remain confidential.

Name:	Age:

Self-portrait:

1. What similarities and what differences did you notice in how the children held their writing/drawing utensil (pencil, crayon, and so on)?

2. In terms of the material discussed in this chapter, what patterns of development did you notice when comparing the writing and drawing of the children?

3. Were your observations consistent with what you might expect from the research described? Explain your response.

4. What might you conclude about development of these skills based on your observations?

Research Project 2:
Children with Disabilities

PLEASE NOTE: THIS PROJECT INVOLVES STUDYING OTHER PEOPLE. PLEASE CHECK WITH YOUR INSTRUCTOR TO SEE IF YOU NEED TO COMPLETE AN INSTITUTIONAL RESEARCH BOARD PROTOCOL BEFORE BEGINNING THIS PROJECT.

Interview three teachers who teach children in the middle childhood period (between 6 and 12 years of age). Ask the teachers how they approach children with disabilities, both those with physical handicaps and those with learning and behavioral issues. Ask the teachers whether they endorse inclusion or whether they prefer mainstreaming children into regular classrooms for some periods of the day but not for the entire day. Ask them how they feel about the growing rates of learning and behavioral problem diagnoses. Do they believe that these increases in diagnoses are accurate, are due to biases, or are due to something else? How do they feel about children taking medication for their problems? Do they think children are overmedicated, or do they see real benefits in the classroom when children take medications? What do these teachers know about the policies outlined in IDEA? How do these policies affect their teaching? What strategies do they use with children with disabilities that they might not use with typical children in their classrooms? Compare the answers the three teachers gave you to the material in the text regarding children with learning disabilities and ADHD. How knowledgeable were the teachers? How sympathetic were they toward children with these problems? Write up an analysis of your findings in relation to the material in the chapter. Make some suggestions for types of training that might improve teachers' attitudes toward, interactions with, and/or teaching techniques used with atypical students.

Personal Application Project 1:
Your Experiences with Sports, Exercise, and Health

Think back to your own experiences with physical education classes, organized sports, casual neighborhood sports, physical play with friends, and your general overall physical health as a child in the middle childhood period. Outline the activities you participated in, how often, with whom, how hard you practiced, and so on. Then think about whether these experiences were beneficial to you and how. Did they help with your overall physical health? Did they help you develop social skills? Cognitive abilities? Do you still engage in any of the physical tasks that you started in middle childhood? Write up a brief analysis of your own physical developmental history. What were the costs and benefits involved in engaging in these activities? How did you feel about the experiences then, and how do you feel about them now? Incorporate the material in the text regarding competitive sports and the general information regarding children's physical health today to help you with your analysis. Do you think children today could benefit by hearing your story? Is there anything they could learn about how to have a healthier lifestyle? Or could you, as a child, have benefited from learning the material in the chapter? Discuss these issues in light of the research presented in the text on children's current health trends.

Personal Application Project 2:
Sternberg's Triarchic Theory

Think about your own intellectual growth over the years. Consider the three components of Sternberg's triarchic theory of intelligence and use the chart below to indicate what evidence you have concerning your strengths and challenges in each of these categories as you have developed. Then answer the questions that follow.

	Analytical	Creative	Practical
Early childhood			
Middle to late childhood			
Adolescence			
Present time			
Comments			

1. What area of intelligence are you strongest in? What are you weakest in?

2. What do you think most influenced your intelligence profile? Your genes? Environmental experiences? Both? Explain how you think you developed into a person who is very strong on some or all of the three aspects in Sternberg's intelligence typology.

3. How does your charted intelligence profile make you feel about the education you received as a child? Do you think more could have been done to help you develop the other areas of your intellectual profile? Did your teachers seem to recognize that there was more than one type of intelligence?

4. Write a brief analysis of your responses to these questions and integrate some of the material in the text regarding the importance of intelligence testing, general versus specific intelligences, Gardner's frames of mind, ethnic and socioeconomic status considerations, and any other information that you think would be helpful in gaining a comprehensive understanding of how the material in the text relates to your own intellectual development.

Internet Projects

Check out the McGraw-Hill website for this text (www.mhhe.com/santrockessls). You will find numerous activities there, in particular, quizzes. Also, be patient, because there are many very worthy links on each of the sites, but they do take a little time to access. If you do not go to the links many times, you will not get the full value of the site. Please go to all links.

Please note that all website addresses in this Study Guide have been checked and were correct at the time of publication. However, websites may be discontinued or their addresses may change, so when you try to access a given site, it may no longer be viable. If that occurs, please notify the publisher so that it can make appropriate revisions in future editions of this Study Guide.

Internet Project 1:
How Intelligent Are the Intelligence Tests?

Have some fun with this project. Go to www.queendom.com/tests/iq/index.html and select the Classical Intelligence Test-R. Take the test (it takes about 30 to 45 minutes, depending on how quickly you read, how many interruptions you have, and how fast your modem is) and see what it tells you your IQ is. Please do NOT take this too seriously—if you continue studying psychology, you will spend a lot of time taking classes on how to administer and assess tests, so do this just for fun. And it can give you some idea about the verbal, spatial, and mathematical nature of a classic intelligence test. After completing the test, answer the following questions.

1. How accurate do you think this test is?

2. What parts were most challenging for you?

3. There are several questions on the test that ask you to determine which of five words does not fit. What are the different classifications that you can think of for those questions? Can you think of other ways that the words could be classified so that an answer other than the one that the test writers consider correct might be correct (although they do not tell you what the "correct" answers are)?

4. Note in the Adventures for the Mind section the question of whether parents should test their children's IQ. Consider what you learned in the chapter, what you gained from this website, and answer the questions in that box.

5. To what degree do you think this test is culturally biased?

6. What problems might someone from another culture have taking a test like this?

7. How might you put the results of a test like this to good use?

Try the other tests at this website. A relatively new area of interest is in emotional intelligence, so you might want to look at that as well. You might also want to try the Culture-Fair IQ Test to see if you think it really is culture-fair.

Internet Project 2:
Evaluating Bilingual Education

Visit the website for the National Association for Bilingual Education (NABE) at www.nabe.org. This organization is concerned with the education of language-minority students in the United States. Read several of the pages, such as the legislation/policy link, conferences available, products and publications, and the organization's recent activities. Take notes regarding areas of interest to you, things you disagree with, things that are consistent with information in the text chapter, and so forth. You may also want to visit some of the interesting links they provide, such as one for the National Council of La Raza, a political group.

Next, go to the website for the Center for Research on Education, Diversity & Excellence (www.crede.ucsc.edu). This is a federally funded program out of the University of California, Santa Cruz. The program focuses on the improvement of education for students who may be facing challenges caused by language or cultural barriers, race, geographic location, or poverty. Read the center's philosophy statement and its standards for effective pedagogy. Take notes on those and the other sections of the website. Note particularly where the material confirms what was in the chapter, expands on it in more detail, or perhaps disagrees with it.

Write a brief analysis of the content of the two websites. How do you feel about bilingual education after reading the sites and the material in the text? Did you have a certain attitude about bilingual education before reading this material? Have your ideas changed or have your views become stronger? Explain. Address the direction in which you think the United States should move because its ethnic minority and immigrant populations are growing exponentially. How should Americans educate children from language-minority homes? What should some major considerations be that perhaps are not being widely addressed in schools?

Other Relevant Sites on the Internet

Child Nutrition and Health: www.fns.usda.gov/cnd/
The website of the U.S. Department of Agriculture's Food and Nutrition Service has information on school meals and national policies for child nutrition.

Child Care Nutrition Resource System: www.nal.usda.gov/childcare/
This site provides recipes, resources, and information on how to provide nutritious meals for children. It also discusses food sanitation and safety and has several links.

Physical Development in Middle Childhood: www.fractaldomains.com/devpsych/midchildphys.htm
This site summarizes middle childhood physical development, talks in depth about obesity in children, and takes viewers on a virtual field trip.

Middle Childhood Cognitive Development: www.fractaldomains.com/devpsych/midchildcog.htm
This funny site analyzes the information in most developmental textbooks regarding Piaget's ideas about middle childhood. It also discusses metacognition.

Jean Piaget Society: www.piaget.org
Here you will find Piaget's biography, photos, and theoretical information. The site discusses the current happenings of the society, conferences, research, and more.

Intelligence Testing: http://iqtest.com
This site offers viewers a brief intelligence test. It is not an official or a scientific test, but it is still fun to take. Especially impressive is the developer's use of the "two cautions" at the start of the test. There is also a history of IQ testing. Check it out and see what you think. Compare it with the material in the text regarding culture-fair and culture-biased testing.

Human Intelligence: http://www.indiana.edu/~intell/
This site provides a comprehensive overview of intelligence testing. It features information on historical influences as well as current controversies.

Chapter 8: Socioemotional Development in Middle and Late Childhood

Learning Goals

1. Discuss emotional and personality development in middle and late childhood.
2. Describe parent-child issues and societal changes in families.
3. Identify changes in peer relationships in middle and late childhood.
4. Characterize contemporary approaches to student learning and sociocultural aspects of student achievement.

Chapter Outline

EMOTIONAL AND PERSONALITY DEVELOPMENT
    The Self
        The Development of Self-Understanding
        Self-Esteem and Self-Concept
        Increasing Children's Self-Esteem
        Self-Efficacy
        Self-Regulation
        Industry Versus Inferiority
    Emotional Development
        Developmental Changes
        Coping with Stress
    Moral Development
        The Kohlberg Stages
        Influences on Kohlberg Stages
        Kohlberg's Critics
            Moral Thought and Moral Behavior
            Culture and Moral Reasoning
            Families and Moral Development
            Gender and the Care Perspective
        Prosocial Behavior
    Gender
        Gender Stereotypes
        Gender Similarities and Differences
            Physical Development
            Cognitive Development
            Socioemotional Development
        Gender-Role Classification
        Gender in Context

FAMILIES
    Parent-Child Images
    Stepfamilies
    Latchkey Children

PEERS
    Friends

Peer Status
Social Cognition
Bullying

SCHOOLS
Contemporary Approaches to Student Learning
Constructivist and Direct Instruction Approaches
Accountability
Socioeconomic Status and Ethnicity
Educating Students from Low-Income Backgrounds
Ethnicity in Schools
Cross-Cultural Comparisons of Achievement

Matching Questions

_____ 1. Lowest level in Kohlberg's theory of moral development. The individual's moral reasoning is controlled primarily by rewards and punishment

A. conventional reasoning

_____ 2. Highest level in Kohlberg's theory of moral development. At this level, the individual recognizes alternative moral courses, explores the options, and then decides on a personal moral code.

B. postconventional reasoning

_____ 3. Kohlberg's stage of moral development where individuals reason that values, rights, and principles undergird or transcend the law.

C. social contract or utility and individual rights

_____ 4. Intermediate level in Kohlberg's theory of moral development. At this level, individuals abide by certain standards, but they are the standards of others such as parents or the laws of society.

D. preconventional reasoning

_____ 5. Kohlberg's stage of moral development where moral judgments are based on understanding the social order, law, justice, and duty.

E. social systems morality

Multiple-Choice Questions

1. As a normal third-grader, Nora is likely to define herself in ALL BUT WHICH ONE of the following terms?
a. her feelings
b. her eye color
c. her religious beliefs
d. how she compares with other third-graders

2. Global evaluations of the self refer to _____.
   a. self-esteem
   b. self-perception
   c. self-concept
   d. self-efficacy

3. The text suggests that to increase a child's self-esteem, one should _____.
   a. set high goals with a need to succeed
   b. identify the causes of low self-esteem and the domains of competence important to the self
   c. provide emotional support and social approval
   d. encourage achievement and effective coping

4. Amara is a single mother. She decides to enroll 8-year-old Aslam in a local Boys' Club program. In doing so, Amara is attempting to raise her son's self-esteem through _____.
   a. achievement
   b. coping
   c. emotional support
   d. identifying areas of competence

5. During the elementary school years, we should see ALL BUT WHICH ONE of the following emotional developments taking place?
   a. improved ability to mask emotions
   b. increased ability to understand complex emotions
   c. increased understanding of events that lead to emotional reactions
   d. improved ability to engage in emotion-laden conversations with opposite-sex peers

6. Children in the middle and late childhood period of development are also in Erikson's psychosocial stage of _____.
   a. trust versus mistrust
   b. autonomy versus shame and doubt
   c. initiative versus guilt
   d. industry versus inferiority

7. All the following statements are recommendations for helping children cope with stress EXCEPT for which one?
   a. Protect children from re-exposure to frightening situations and reminders of the trauma.
   b. Avoid talking about the event.
   c. Encourage children to talk about any disturbing or confusing feelings.
   d. Help children make sense of what happened.

8. Kohlberg's theory of moral development in 27 diverse cultures around the world has _____.
   a. provided no universal research support for this theory
   b. provided research support for the universality of the first four stages
   c. provided research support for the universality of all six stages
   d. found conflicting research results in terms of the theory's universality

9. Kohlberg's highest stages of moral reasoning emphasize _____.
a. communal equity and collective happiness
b. the sacredness of all life forms
c. individual rights and abstract principles of justice
d. preventing suffering and the role of compassion

10. Gilligan's (1996) research found that as girls reach adolescence, they _____.
a. apply care-based reasoning in making moral decisions
b. adopt a justice perspective of morality
c. increasingly silence their "distinctive voice"
d. become more outspoken about their inner feelings

11. Hector became a police officer, because he believes that members of society prosper from understanding social order, law, justice, and duty. On what moral level does he reason?
a. postconventional
b. conventional.
c. heteronomous
d. autonomous

12. Tate is interviewed while participating in a protest. Tate states that she has the right to express her opinion, as does anyone else, and that the protest increases her personal power. Which moral level does Tate's statement reflect?
a. postconventional
b. conventional
c. unconventional
d. preconventional

13. Research on prosocial moral behavior has found that _____.
a. prosocial behavior is more prevalent in adolescence than in childhood
b. moral reasoning and moral behavior always correspond
c. girls are more likely to show moral reasoning, but not moral behavior
d. children in the United States show more prosocial behavior than those in other cultures

14. The notion that boys should be independent, aggressive, and powerful is a _____.
a. gender bias
b. gender indentification
c. gender stereotype
d. gender role

15. Investigators continue to find gender differences in _____.
a. physical aggressiveness
b. verbal skills
c. cognitive abilities
d. suggestibility

16. The term "androgyny" refers to a gender role that is _____.
a. highly masculine
b. highly feminine
c. both highly masculine and highly feminine
d. neither masculine nor feminine

17. The parent-child issue that will most likely emerge around age seven is _____.
a. getting dressed
b. getting the chores done
c. attention-seeking behavior
d. bedtime

18. The gradual process in which some control is transferred from the parent to the child is called _____.
a. autonomy
b. industry
c. coregulation
d. reciprocal socialization

19. Marlene, a single parent, works full time. Her daughter, Beth, is an after-school latchkey child. Research suggests that to minimize the negative effect on her 11-year-old daughter, Marlene should _____.
a. encourage Beth to make friends with whom she can hang out after school
b. use authoritative parenting and monitor Beth's activities
c. explain the importance of independence and provide at-home responsibilities so that Beth learns independent living
d. hire a baby-sitter

20. Children are likely to be popular with their peers if they do all the following things EXCEPT which one?
a. give out lots of reinforcement
b. listen carefully to what others have to say
c. try to please others, even if it means compromising themselves
d. exhibit self-confidence

21. Samantha has few friends at school. The other children do not actively dislike her but pay little attention to her, and no one invites her to visit in their home. Samantha is probably a _____.
a. rejected child
b. neglected child
c. latchkey child
d. controversial child

22. To reduce bullying, the text suggests doing all the following things EXCEPT which one?
a. get older peers to serve as monitors for bullying and intervene when they see it taking place
b. suspend bullies from school for victimizing other children
c. form friendship groups for children who are regularly bullied by peers
d. incorporate the antibullying message into community activities where the children are involved

23. Kozol's research found that many inner-city schools _____.
a. are receiving funds to increase the quality of education for inner-city youth
b. have done an excellent job of integrating students from diverse backgrounds
c. do not provide adequate opportunities for children to learn effectively
d. are where older teachers about to retire get placed

24. Santrock suggests teachers use ALL BUT WHICH ONE of the following strategies to improve relations between ethnically diverse students?
a. Turn the class into a jigsaw classroom.
b. Teach students the harmful effects of segregation.
c. Encourage students to engage in perspective taking.
d. Be a competent cultural mediator.

25. In Stevenson's research comparing students in the United States with students in Asian countries, he found that _____.
a. students in the United States scored higher on math than did students in Taiwan
b. American teachers spent more of their time teaching math than did the Asian teachers
c. students in the United States spent more time in school than did their Asian counterparts
d. Asian parents were more likely than American parents to believe achievement in math was due to effort and training

True/False Questions

1. During middle and late childhood, children increasingly define themselves in terms of external characteristics such as appearance.

2. Elijah is proud of how well he can build things out of construction toys. However, he is disappointed that he cannot kick a soccer ball very well. These are example of his developing self-concept.

3. People with high self-esteem are prone to being both aggressive bullies and helping other children who are being bullied.

4. Self-esteem refers to domain-specific evaluations of oneself.

5. When Rosa Parks, an African American woman, refused to give up her bus seat to a White person, this sparked a component of the civil rights movement (a bus boycott by African Americans). Ms. Parks risked her own personal safety to follow her conscience. This would be an example of Kohlberg's fourth stage of moral development: social systems morality.

6. Kohlberg believed that parents had relatively little effect on children's moral development.

7. Parents play a large role in influencing children's sharing behaviors, but children pay virtually no attention to their peers' bids for sharing.

8. It is important to foster prosocial behavior early on because research shows that it is stable from early childhood to early adulthood.

9. In studies of prosocial behavior, research shows that although males and females are equally kind and considerate, females show significantly greater levels of sharing than do males.

10. Research has suggested that androgynous individuals might be better adjusted than people who score high in either masculinity or femininity. However, more recent studies suggest that the best gender role to exhibit really depends on the context in which one finds him- or herself.

11. Research shows that establishing a new stepfamily while the child is experiencing puberty may be especially difficult.

12. Research shows that conflict-ridden friendships are excellent for children's development in that the children learn to sacrifice their own needs for the desires of another.

13. Bullies tend to be very lonely and have difficulty making friends.

14. Being aggressive and rejected by peers leads to extensive difficulties in social relationships.

15. Constructivist teachers tend to construct high expectations for students and provide lots of direction and control over their students' activities.

Short-Answer Questions

1. Elaborate on changes that take place in the self and in emotions during middle and late childhood.

2. What is Kohlberg's theory of moral development? Discuss how it has been criticized.

3. Discuss the development of prosocial behavior and altruism during middle and late childhood.

4. Discuss some of the important parent-child issues in middle and late childhood.

5. Describe some of the societal changes in families that influence children's development.

6. Explain how children's peer status influences their development.

7. Discuss how social cognition is involved with children's peer relations.

8. Elaborate on the nature of bullying.

9. Elaborate on how socioeconomic status and ethnicity influence schooling.

10. Describe some cultural comparisons of achievement.

Essay Questions

1. You are helping your new neighbor find an excellent school for his third-grade child. The family just moved to the United States from another country and is concerned about how their child will do. The child speaks rudimentary English but is not fluent. Using the information in the text on controversies in contemporary approaches to student learning and assessment, describe what would be the ideal classroom for this child and why. Would it include direct instruction, constructivist approaches, or both? Would you be concerned with accountability? What kinds of cultural and socioeconomic issues would you be sure your friend took into consideration while looking at schools? Incorporate the

information on self-esteem issues as well. What concerns would you have, and how might the family and school address them?

2. You have decided to open a day-care center for elementary school children to provide an optimum environment for them between the hours that school lets out and the time their parents finish working. You have already talked to some of the parents, and although they may not tell you that their child has problems, each has been quite open about some of the other children's problems, including low self-esteem, difficulties establishing friendships, and even bullying. The parents have also asked if you would be willing to help their children (not to mention the others!) develop in a morally appropriate manner, but they come from different religious perspectives, so they want to keep religion out of the picture in your center. Further, it appears that all five peer statuses are represented among the population of children who you anticipate will be enrolled (popular, average, neglected, rejected, and controversial). How would you help all these children have the best possible growth experience in your day-care facility? How would you assist them in developing a healthy sense of self-esteem, altruism, and a solid foundation for moral development?

Key to Matching Questions

1. D	2. B	3. C	4. A	5. E

Key to Multiple-Choice Questions

1. B	6. D	11. B	16. C	21. B
2. A	7. B	12. D	17. B	22. B
3. A	8. B	13. A	18. C	23. C
4. C	9. C	14. C	19. B	24. B
5. D	10. A	15. A	20. C	25. D

Key to True/False Questions

1. F	4. F	7. F	10. T	13. F
2. T	5. F	8. F	11. T	14. T
3. T	6. T	9. F	12. F	15. F

Key to Short-Answer Questions

1. The internal self, the social self, and the socially comparative self become more prominent in middle and late childhood. Emotional changes include increased understanding of complex emotions, detecting that more than one emotion can be experienced in a particular situation, taking into account the circumstances that led up to an emotional reaction, improvements in the ability to suppress and conceal negative emotions, and using self-initiated strategies to redirect feelings.

2. Kohlberg's theory of moral development involves three levels, each with two stages. The highest levels of moral development are achieved by very few. There are many influences on progressing through the

stages of moral development, including cognitive development, imitation and cognitive conflict, peer relations, and perspective taking. Criticisms of Kohlberg's theory include Gilligan's argument for the care perspective to play a larger role in understanding moral behavior and development. Other criticisms focus on the ability to predict moral behavior from moral reasoning and the influence of the family on moral development.

3. Prosocial behavior in the elementary school years is marked by the emergences of children expressing objective ideas about fairness.

4. Some new parent-child issues that appear during the middle and late childhood years are these: Should children have to complete chores, and, if yes, for what compensation? How can one help children learn to entertain themselves? How can one monitor children's lives outside the family? During this period, coregulation emerges, so that control is shared by the child and the parents.

5. Two key societal changes in families that can affect child development are stepfamilies and latchkey children. Children in stepfamilies, as in divorce, show more adjustment problems than do children in intact families. The problems can include academic problems and lower self-esteem. Latchkey children are often given more responsibility than they are ready to handle and may engage in delinquent behavior owing to lack of proper supervision.

6. Peer status can be related to several developmental outcomes. For example, rejected children often have more serious adjustment problems than do other peer-status children, even neglected children. Rejected children may disengage in the classroom environment, avoid school, and report higher levels of loneliness than other children. If rejected children also have aggression problems, the outcomes are even more severe including delinquent behavior or dropping out of school during adolescence.

7. Social cognition is defined as the thoughts about social matters. Social cognition about peers becomes more important during middle and late childhood for understanding peer relationships. Social cognition is involved in the ability for children to get along with peers, because it helps them in the following ways: knowing what goals to pursue in ambiguous situations; initiating and maintaining a social bond; and developing friendships following scripts.

8. Bullying can be defined as verbal or physical behavior intended to disturb someone less powerful. Boys and younger middle school students are the most likely targets of bullying. The victims of bullying report difficulty in making friends and loneliness. Bullies tend to have low grades, smoke, and drink alcohol. The effects of bullying can be far reaching, including headaches, sleeping problems, physical ailments, and depression in the victims of bullying.

9. The effects of socioeconomic status (SES) and ethnicity are entwined as many U.S. schools are segregated. Many schools in poorer neighborhoods lack the quality school environment found in other more financially secure neighborhoods. Many poor or ethnic minority students lack role models that more advantaged students have. Ethnic minority and poor students may also experience low expectations in their schools, neighborhoods, or homes.

10. American children are more achievement-oriented than are children in many other countries, but they are focused on in-born ability and perform more poorly in math and science than do children in many other nations. Children from many Asian countries believe that academic achievement is more dependent on effort than on in-born ability, work harder for longer periods of time, and have more involved parents than American children do.

Key to Essay Questions

1. This child would probably benefit most from a constructivist-based classroom that did not rely heavily on national academic standards for its daily practices. Helping the child to construct her own learning experiences through art, music, storytelling, problem solving, group projects, and drama will increase her self-esteem while facing a new culture. At the same time, this approach will also teach her English, math, and social studies skills. A teacher who is aware of the disadvantages faced by ethnic minority and language-minority children in school would be beneficial. This type of teacher would take extra care to incorporate the child into the classroom community through activities such as jigsaw learning. Your essay should incorporate material from the text for how to improve children's peer relations, self-esteem, and transition to school. Also worthy of consideration are elements of Comer's ideas, Kozol's ideas, or the ideas of both on education reform.

2. You need to describe the five peer statuses, explain the stages of moral development and development of altruism, and describe how these can be facilitated in children. You also need to address self-esteem building and the various domains where a child can learn to acquire skills, plus how to incorporate the less socially competent students (for example, rejected) into supportive peer groups. Finally, you need to address the issues concerning bullying both in terms of reducing (and hopefully eliminating) the behavior and helping the victimized children learn not to be bullied.

Research Project 1:
Asking Children about Peer Status

PLEASE NOTE: THIS PROJECT INVOLVES STUDYING OTHER PEOPLE. PLEASE CHECK WITH YOUR INSTRUCTOR TO SEE IF YOU NEED TO COMPLETE AN INSTITUTIONAL RESEARCH BOARD PROTOCOL BEFORE BEGINNING THIS PROJECT.

Interview three children in the middle to late childhood period (around 6 to 12 years). Be sure to get their parents' permission first, and the children's consent as well. Ask each child to describe the classmate who is most liked by everyone (most popular), and have the child explain why he or she thinks this classmate is so popular. Then have each child describe the child who is least liked in his or her class. What characteristics does this classmate have that make him or her so unpopular or rejected? Is there a class or school bully? Does your interviewee know anything about this bully's family? What about the bully's performance in school? Popularity or friendship status? After interviewing all three children, compare their answers. Do certain characteristics, traits, and behaviors clearly distinguish popular children from rejected children? Rejected children from bullies? Popular children from bullies? Compare the answers you received to the material provided in the text. Do your young interviewees confirm the material in the text regarding the characteristics of popular, rejected, and bullying children? Did anything the children said seem particularly insightful? Would you add anything to the discussion in the text about children's peer relationships and friendships? Does anything in the text seem incorrect?

Research Project 2:
Helping the Challenged Child

Consider the problems of the rejected, neglected, and controversial children discussed in this chapter as well as the problem of bullying. If you understand that these children may become the bane of society in years to come, you can see that it would benefit us all to have some early intervention. Design a program that looks at the underlying factors that lead to these children adopting their respective behaviors, then present appropriate interventions to teach them to interact effectively with other children and with adults. This will need to include development of friendships, perspective taking, altruism, and morality. Ask members of a school or community group what they already do about children with peer problems. Are they already doing much of what you would suggest? If there are things that you think might be helpful to them, present your ideas to your professor for critique and streamlining, then present them to a local school or community group to see if the group would be willing to put your plan into action.

1. When designing this program, what do you believe are the underlying factors that will lead a child to attain a status of rejected, neglected, or controversial, or to become a bully?

2. Would the same types of interventions help all of these children? If not, what will work for each?

3. Considering their current level of development (ignoring their peer status) and current research, what could reasonably be expected from these children in terms of perspective taking, altruism, and moral development?

4. How can you teach these children to develop friendships, perspective taking, altruism, or morality, or to become more assertive or less aggressive?

Personal Application Project 1:
Consider Your Own Moral Development

Think about your own moral code. What kinds of things do you feel are always wrong? Or do you feel that everything is relative, and that a judgment of morality is based on such things as contextual factors, intentions, and goals of the actor? Looking at Kohlberg's stages, do you see yourself as being above level four (the level most adults in the United States attain)? If so, what do you think led to such a high level of moral reasoning? Did religion, family, culture, personality, personal experience, and other factors play important roles? How so? Did you have any experiences earlier in life where you acted immorally and decided not to do such things again? If you are at level four or below, what do you think has to happen for you to reach a higher level? Do you need more life experience? Better role models? A better grasp on your culture, religion, or family values? Analyze your own moral development, and describe yourself as you progressed through each stage. Does Kohlberg's theory make sense for your developmental journey? Or do you have problems with this theory, for example, the criticisms outlined in the text? Did you grow up in a family, religion, or culture that emphasized other types of morality than just those related to justice? Describe your journey of moral development, its most important influences, and how you think you might be able to progress to higher levels.

Personal Application Project 2:
Gender Roles

PLEASE NOTE: THIS PROJECT INVOLVES STUDYING OTHER PEOPLE. PLEASE CHECK WITH YOUR INSTRUCTOR TO SEE IF YOU NEED TO COMPLETE AN INSTITUTIONAL RESEARCH BOARD PROTOCOL BEFORE BEGINNING THIS PROJECT.

Over two or three days' time, listen to people speak, and note whether their language seems gender biased. (You may be so used to hearing gender-biased language, that it may take a while to pick up on it.) Listen for such things as use of male pronouns to represent all people or to represent high-ranking professions, or female pronouns used in more low-status contexts. Listen, too, for the way people address each other—are women and children more likely than men to be called "dear," "sweetie," or "honey," even by people they do not know? What effect do you think this has on an individual's self-esteem, self-perceptions, and attitudes about gender roles? What effect does it have on your attitudes? How do people in your family feel about the roles women and men should play? What are your current gender-role beliefs?

The text discusses femininity, masculinity, and androgyny (being high in both masculine and feminine traits). Bear in mind that masculinity and femininity are two separate dimensions, not polar opposites. Sandra Bem, one of the leading researchers in sex roles, has also found a fourth gender role, undifferentiated, which is neither masculine nor feminine. Reflecting on what you have learned in the text about the characteristics of people with each gender role, answer the following questions.

1. On the basis of current research, which status (masculine, feminine, androgynous, undifferentiated) do you think would rank highest on self-esteem? Explain your rationale.

2. Considering your own gender role, what do you think most influenced you to develop in that way? (Consider both nature and nurture—family, individual, culture, and religion.)

3. What would be the benefits of falling into any of the four sex-role categories? Pitfalls?

4. If you chose to change your gender-role status or raise your level of self-esteem, how would you go about doing this? What gender-specific behaviors, attitudes, traits, and interests do you think would help you have a greater level of self-esteem, and why?

Internet Projects

Check out the McGraw-Hill website for this text (www.mhhe.com/santrockessls). You will find numerous activities there, in particular, quizzes. Also, be patient, because there are many very worthy links on each of the sites, but they do take a little time to access. If you do not go to the links many times, you will not get the full value of the site. Please go to all links.

Please note that all website addresses in this Study Guide have been checked and were correct at the time of publication. However, websites may be discontinued or their addresses may change, so when you try to access a given site, it may no longer be viable. If that occurs, please notify the publisher so that it can make appropriate revisions in future editions of this Study Guide.

Internet Project 1:
Talking to Kids about Tough Issues

Kaiser Permanente Health Care has an excellent website titled "Talk with Your Kids," located at www.talkingwithkids.org. It suggests that one start talking with children about tough issues when they are between 8 and 12 years old; if children haven't received guidance by the time they are teenagers, it becomes much harder to establish good communication with them. When you go to the site, consider the following questions.

1. What topics on the site are related to Chapter 8?

2. Are there other topics at this site that you might consider including in a chapter on socioemotional development for elementary school children that weren't already included? (Remember, of course, that no textbook can include everything—students would have to be in the class for a year or two!)

3. What have you learned from this site about ways to talk to children about difficult issues?

Is there someone you know who could benefit from this information? How would you go about approaching such a discussion? Or would you just send them to the website and say, "After you've looked at it, come back and let's talk"?

Internet Project 2:
Testing Your Self-Esteem

Self-esteem refers to your global evaluation of the self. To examine your own self-esteem, go to http://www.queendom.com/tests/access_page/index.htm?idRegTest=720 and complete the Self-Esteem Test. You will have to register on the site (it is free) before taking the test. After taking the test, answer the following questions.

1. How well did you score on this test? How accurate do you think the test is? How are the results of the test useful for you?

2. Do you think someone could fake this test and come out with a high score despite having low self-esteem? What would be the rationale for doing so?

3. What are the benefits of having a positive self-esteem?

4. What can you do to help increase an individual's self-esteem?

Other Relevant Sites on the Internet

Self-Esteem Shop: www.selfesteemshop.com
This is an excellent warehouse carrying hundreds of children's books, games, and toys dealing with emotion skills, social skills, self-esteem, and coping with stress. There is a wide selection of puppets and play therapy tools. You will find products of interest whether you are in the helping professions or have children of your own.

Kohlberg's Stages of Moral Development: www.aggelia.com/htdocs/kohlberg.shtml
This site relates Kohlberg's theory to theology. It references specific biblical passages and ideas in its discussion of morality.

Gender Development: www.psy.pdx.edu/PsiCafe/Areas/Developmental/GenderDev/
This is another page from the Psych Cafe. Here you will find information on lots of theories of gender-role development and research, plus links to all kinds of topics from androgyny to homosexuality.

Divorce Source: http://divorcesource.com
This website offers information on family law, custody, alimony and support, and visitation and includes specific information for all 50 U.S. states. It also includes psychological evaluations for children, various forms to download, chat rooms, and books to buy.

Divorce as Friends: www.divorceasfriends.com
This is the website of Bill Ferguson, a former divorce attorney, who gives solid advice about how to divorce as friends and how to keep a marriage together. He notes that 15% of his clients decided to stay together after working on his "steps for changing your relationship and your life." There is a lot of good advice on here about working with your children, being civil, and related topics.

Stepfamily Association of America: www.saafamilies.org/
The organization is dedicated to helping stepfamilies live well. Its website provides educational information and resources, a catalog of books, information on laws, and much more.
Playing with Self Esteem: The Importance of Social Skills: www.nldline.com/dr.htm
Dr. Stephen Rothenberg presents some case studies of children who have problems with social skills and different therapeutic strategies that could be useful.

Encouraging Social Skills in Young Children: www.humsci.auburn.edu/parent/socialskills.html
Auburn University sponsors this page which features a brief synopsis of some of the best research in the field of children's social skills. It has lots of tips for teachers and parents about how to increase social skills and lists references for some excellent research studies.

Children without Friends: www.canadianparents.com
Read the articles "Children without Friends" and "Improving Social Skills." The articles contain lots of great suggestions for parents and ask some thought-provoking questions. The site also provides parenting advice for just about any other topic you can think of.

The My Hero Project—Jonathan Kozol: www.myhero.com/myhero/hero.asp?hero=jkozol
This page offers a brief biography of Kozol and provides links to excerpts from his writings as well as a link to his Campaign for America's Future website. The fascinating part of this page is its More Featured Teacher Heroes section with profiles of about two dozen teacher heroes throughout the history of American education from Christa McAuliffe (the first teacher in space) to Sequoyah (the inventor of the Cherokee alphabet).

Comer School Development Program: http://info.med.yale.edu/comer
This is the headquarter site for Yale University's Comer School Development Program which aims to bridge child psychiatry with education. It provides some interesting information about the philosophy of psychiatrist James Comer and links to research and evaluation studies on the program and current events at Comer School sites. The FAQs/Fast Facts page is quite valuable.

Chapter 9: Physical and Cognitive Development in Adolescence

Learning Goals

1. Discuss the nature of adolescence.
2. Describe the physical changes involved in puberty as well as changes in the brain and sexuality during adolescence.
3. Identify adolescent problems related to health, substance use, and eating disorders.
4. Explain cognitive changes in adolescence.
5. Summarize the influence of schools on adolescent development.

Chapter Outline

THE NATURE OF ADOLESCENCE

PHYSICAL CHANGES
    Puberty
        Sexual Maturation, Height, and Weight
        Hormonal Changes
        Timing and Variations in Puberty
        Body Image
        Body Art
        Early and Late Maturation
    The Brain
    Adolescent Sexuality
        Developing a Sexual Identity
        The Timing of Adolescent Sexual Behaviors
        Contraceptive Use
        Sexually Transmitted Infections
        Adolescent Pregnancy
            Outcomes
            Reducing Adolescent Pregnancy

ISSUES IN ADOLESCENT HEALTH
    Adolescent Health
        Nutrition and Exercise
        Sleep Patterns
        Leading Causes of Death in Adolescence
    Substance Use and Abuse
        The Roles of Development, Parents, and Peers
    Eating Disorders
        Anorexia Nervosa
        Bulimia Nervosa

ADOLESCENT COGNITION
    Piaget's Theory
        The Formal Operational Stage

Evaluating Piaget's Theory
Adolescent Egocentrism
Information Processing
    Decision Making
    Critical Thinking

SCHOOLS
    The Transition to Middle or Junior High School
    Effective Schools for Young Adolescents
    High School
    Service Learning

Matching Questions

_____ 1. Form of education that promotes social responsibility and service to the community.

A. service learning

_____ 2. Eating disorder in which the individual consistently follows a binge-and-purge pattern.

B. anorexia nervosa

_____ 3. Part of adolescent egocentrism that involves an adolescent's sense of uniqueness and invincibility.

C. bulimia nervosa

_____ 4. Involves adolescents' belief that others are as interested in them as they themselves are.

D. imaginary audience

_____ 5. Eating disorder that involves the relentless pursuit of thinness through starvation.

E. personal fable

Multiple-Choice Questions

1. Since the 19th century, scientists have observed that puberty begins _____ with each passing decade.
a. at a slightly older age
b. at a slightly younger age
c. at about the same age
d. earlier for boys and later for girls

2. Which of the following statements about menarche is NOT true?
a. Menarche is a girl's first menstruation.
b. Menarche marks the beginning of ovulation.
c. Menarche occurs late in the pubertal cycle.
d. Menarche begins a cycle that is quite irregular at first.

3. The _____ is a structure in the brain that monitors eating and sex.
a. hypothalamus
b. pituitary gland
c. thalamus
d. gonads

4. The important endocrine gland(s) that control(s) growth and regulate(s) other glands is/are the
    _____.
a. hypothalamus
b. pituitary gland
c. thalamus
d. gonads

5. The development of genitals, increase in height, and changes in boys' voices is caused by _____, whereas _____ is a hormone associated with breast, uterine, and skeletal development in girls.
a. testosterone/estradiol
b. estradiol/testosterone
c. estrogen/progesterone
d. serotonin/dopamine

6. Henry is a gay teenager. In light of the research in the chapter, which of the following statements about Henry's development is probably FALSE?
a. Henry is also physically attracted to women.
b. Henry does not recall any early childhood same-sex attractions.
c. Henry usually falls in love with his same-sex partners.
d. Henry is unlikely to receive support from his parents, teachers, and peers.

7. Adolescents who engage in homosexual behavior in adolescence _____.
a. will increase their homosexual practices into adulthood
b. do not show a uniformly consistent pattern that shapes their sexual identity
c. may benefit from counseling aimed at helping them become heterosexual
d. should be discouraged from this harmful activity

8. What segment of American adolescents reports being the most sexually active?
a. Asian Americans males
b. African American males
c. Caucasian males
d. Hispanic males

9. Health risks for infants of adolescent mothers include all of the following factors EXCEPT which one?
a. low birthweight
b. neurological problems
c. childhood illness
d. chlamydia

10. Rates of cigarette smoking among U.S. adolescents have _____ since the late 1990s.
a. remained the same
b. dramatically increased
c. gradually declined
d. doubled

11. Anne has an eating disorder that involves the relentless pursuit of thinness through starvation which ultimately may lead to her death. Anne has _____.
a. bulimia nervosa
b. anorexia nervosa
c. body dysphoric disorder
d. failure to thrive syndrome

12. The adolescent who is most likely to suffer from anorexia is _____.
a. Bill, an African American male honor student from a low-income family
b. Kim, an Asian American female honor student from an upper-income family
c. Jarod, a white male from a middle-income family who has dropped out of school
d. Emily, a white female honor student from an upper-income family

13. Victor refuses to use drugs even though many adolescents in his school and neighborhood do so. According to the text, which of the following is NOT likely to be a reason for his refusal?
a. Victor's parents know where he is at all times and so can monitor his behavior.
b. Victor's parents abused drugs when he was in kindergarten, so he has learned about the bad results of drug abuse.
c. Victor's parents monitor the websites he visits and the TV shows he watches.
d. Victor's parents use a lot of verbal reasoning when they talk to him about drugs.

14. Rashmi is exhibiting signs of anorexia nervosa. All the following factors probably contributed to her disorder EXCEPT which one?
a. her Indian heritage and culture
b. her extreme concern for how others perceive her
c. her family's high socioeconomic status
d. her stress over meeting her parents' high standards

15. Although people can have both anorexia and bulimia, which factor typically differentiates the two disorders?
a. People with bulimia are preoccupied with food, but those with anorexia are not.
b. People with anorexia have a strong fear of becoming overweight, but those with bulimia do not.
c. People with bulimia are typically within the normal range of weight, but those with anorexia are not.
d. People with anorexia are typically depressed and anxious, but those with bulimia are not.

16. Adolescents living in _____ get the least amount of exercise.
a. the United States
b. Ireland
c. Germany
d. the Slovak Republic

17. The most typical causes of motor vehicle accidents among adolescents include ALL BUT WHICH ONE of the following factors?
a. speeding
b. tailgating
c. lack of driving experience
d. driving under the influence of drugs or alcohol

18. Julia wants to submit a proposal to her school principal in hopes that he might change the daily school start time. In light of Carskadon's research, which of the following would NOT be a valid justification that Julia might include in her proposal?
a. Later start times are related to fewer discipline problems in teens.
b. Later start times are related to fewer sick days taken by teens.
c. Later start times are related to increased test scores in high school students.
d. Later start times are related to higher levels of college admittances by graduating students.

19. A child in the formal operational thought stage of cognitive development is MOST likely to engage in _____.
a. using building blocks to determine how houses are constructed
b. writing a story about a clown who wants to leave the circus
c. drawing pictures of a family using stick figures
d. writing an essay about patriotism

20. Jean Piaget's ideas on formal operational thought are being challenged in ALL BUT WHICH ONE of the following ways?
a. Not all adolescents are formal operational thinkers.
b. Not all adults in every culture are formal operational thinkers.
c. There is more individual variation in the development of formal operations than Piaget thought.
d. Only those with scientific training use hypothetical-deductive reasoning.

21. Kieran says, "Yesterday I started thinking about who I really am. Then I starting asking myself, 'Why are you thinking about who you are?' " This is an example of the formal operational skill of _____.
a. idealism
b. abstract thought
c. deductive hypothesis testing
d. hypothetical-deductive reasoning

22. Ava, who has been having unprotected sex with her boyfriend, comments to her best friend, "Did you hear about Merri? You know how she fools around so much. I heard she's pregnant. That would never happen to me!" This is an example of the _____.
a. imaginary audience
b. false-belief syndrome
c. personal fable
d. adolescent denial syndrome

23. Syndy calls her best friend, Holli, in a panic. She has a date with Jason, someone she has wanted to date for months, but now she has a blemish on her forehead, which she believes Jason (and everyone else) will notice. This is an example of the _____.
a. imaginary audience
b. false-belief syndrome
c. personal fable
d. personal absorption syndrome

24. Cognitive changes that allow improved critical thinking in adolescents include ALL BUT WHICH ONE of these skills?
a. more breadth of content knowledge in a variety of domains
b. increased ability to construct new combinations of knowledge
c. slower speed of information processing demonstrating focus and concentration
d. a greater range and more spontaneous use of strategies for applying knowledge

25. Research on service learning has shown that because of it, _____.
a. grades decline because students have less time for their studies
b. students' self-esteem improves
c. students reflect less on political issues and more on improving their own neighborhood
d. students are resentful of the extra pressures placed on them

True/False Questions

1. Acting out and boundary testing are time-honored ways in which adolescents move toward accepting, rather than rejecting, parental values.

2. Puberty is occurring earlier and earlier over time. Research indicates that if this trend continues, we will start seeing pubescent toddlers in future decades.

3. The official end of childhood is usually marked by a single, sudden event, such as a boy's wet dream or a girl's starting menarche.

4. Although it is difficult to assess exactly when a boy is beginning puberty, it is easy to assess the first step in a girl's pubertal development, which is marked by the beginning of menarche.

5. Although it is often assumed that girls have more negative body images than boys do, recent research shows that boys actually have much lower opinions of their own bodies.

6. The effects of timing of maturation on children's adjustment depend on when that maturation is assessed. For example, early-maturing girls are happy when assessed in early adolescence but are less satisfied with their bodies by late adolescence.

7. Early-maturing girls are often more easily lured into problem behaviors such as drinking and smoking than are later-maturing girls.

8. Velma, a 15-year-old, recently got a tattoo. Based on the current research on adolescent body art, her parents should be quite concerned as this is a sign of rebellion.

9. By the end of the teenage years (age 19), virtually every adolescent has had sexual intercourse.

10. Low-SES adolescents are more likely to be sexually active and to become pregnant.

11. Although teens in the United States are no more sexually active than their counterparts in other industrialized nations, they have a significantly higher pregnancy rate.

12. Children born to teenage mothers are likely to have lower achievement test scores and more behavioral problems than children of adult mothers.

13. Even though teenagers who have achieved formal operational thought engage in hypothetical-deductive reasoning, they fail to understand the relation between a hypothesis and a well-chosen test of it, stubbornly clinging to ideas that have already been discounted.

14. JaKwon says, "No one can ever imagine how bad this broken heart feels. That girl threw me for a loop that no one could ever understand." He is exhibiting the adolescent cognitive limitation called the imaginary audience.

15. Even though adolescents often progress to being able to think critically and solve problems, the majority of eleventh-graders still do not exhibit critical thinking and often show biased reasoning.

Short-Answer Questions

1. What characterizes adolescent development?

2. What is puberty?

3. What changes characterize the brain during adolescence?

4. Discuss the important aspects of sexuality in adolescence.

5. Discuss Piaget's theory of adolescent cognitive development.

6. Define *adolescent egocentrism*.

7. What changes occur in information processing during adolescence?

8. Explain what the transition to middle school or junior high school is like.

9. Explain service learning, and how it affects adolescent development.

10. Differentiate between anorexia nervosa and bulimia nervosa.

Essay Questions

1. Your former high school counselor has invited you to speak to the students at your old high school. She has asked you to talk to them about high-risk behaviors—what they are, how kids get involved with them, the consequences, and how to avoid getting involved. Which issues are important for you to

address, what would you tell them about each of these, and what suggestions would you have for avoiding them?

2. Your favorite aunt and uncle have come to you because they say they cannot understand their teenage daughter. One minute she's loving and adoring, the next she's a total monster. They try to comfort her when she's upset, but she screams, "You can't possibly understand how I feel"; if she is having a "bad hair day," she refuses to go out in public, even to accompany them to religious services. How would you explain these behaviors to your aunt and uncle, and what would you suggest for helping them work with their daughter? Discuss adolescent cognition, self-regulation, communication, and any other information that will help them understand their teenager better.

Key to Matching Questions

1. A	2. C	3. E	4. D	5. B

Key to Multiple-Choice Questions

1. B	6. C	11. B	16. A	21. B
2. B	7. B	12. D	17. C	22. C
3. A	8. B	13. B	18. D	23. A
4. B	9. D	14. A	19. D	24. C
5. A	10. C	15. C	20. D	25. B

Key to True/False Questions

1. T	4. F	7. T	10. T	13. F
2. F	5. F	8. F	11. T	14. F
3. F	6. T	9. F	12. T	15. T

Key to Short-Answer Questions

1. Most adolescents successfully negotiate the path from childhood to adulthood. Adolescents are a heterogeneous group, with different traits describing different sets of them. One hallmark of adolescence is puberty.

2. Puberty is a period of rapid physical maturation involving hormonal and bodily changes that occur primarily during early adolescence. Sexual maturation is a predominant feature of pubertal change.

3. There are spikes in the electrical activity of the brain around the ages of 9, 12, 15, and 18 to 20 years old. Additionally, the amygdala develops earlier than the prefrontal cortex; this means it is difficult for adolescents to control emotions or refrain from risky, impulsive behavior.

4. Sexual exploration and sexual experimentation are common during adolescence. It is during adolescence that individuals face the challenges of learning to control emerging sexual feelings and developing a sexual identity.

5. According to Piaget, the formal operational stage may develop during adolescence. In this stage, adolescents become capable of increased abstract, idealistic, and logical thought. Additionally, hypothetical-deductive reasoning emerges.

6. Adolescent egocentrism is the heightened self-consciousness of adolescents. Two aspects of adolescent egocentrism are the imaginary audience and the personal fable.

7. Executive functioning—which includes decision making and critical thinking—improves throughout adolescence. Other improvements in information processing include increased speed of processing, automaticity, and capacity; more content knowledge; and a greater range and spontaneous use of strategies.

8. The transition from elementary school to middle or junior high school can be a stressful time. The top-dog phenomenon adds to this stress, as does being in a larger school with an increased focus on achievement. This transition can be particularly difficult if it coincides with the onset of puberty.

9. Service learning involves educational experiences that promote social responsibility and service to the community. Service learning benefits students in several ways, including grade improvement, increased motivation, setting more goals, increased self-esteem, decreased alienation, and reflection on society's political organization and moral order.

10. Anorexia is characterized by starvation for the pursuit of thinness; it is defined as weighing less than 85% of what is considered normal for a person's age and height. Bulimia involves a consistent pattern of binge eating and purging (typically via self-induced vomiting or use of a laxative); many individuals with bulimia fall in the normal weight range.

Key to Essay Questions

1. You need to address the issues of dropping out of school, drugs, adolescent pregnancy, suicide and homicide, accidents, sexually transmitted infections (STIs), and eating disorders. As a backdrop to understanding the issues, briefly present the physiological changes in adolescence, Piaget's notion of formal operations (abstract thought and metacognition—thinking about thinking), and adolescent egocentrism. Then present ways to avoid these problems; such as developing effective ways to cope rather than turning to drugs, learning about contraception, and working on ways to increase self-esteem, improving parent-child communication.

2. To answer this question, you first need to discuss the notion of adolescent egocentrism, with its two components of the imaginary audience and the personal fable. Then go into the suggestions about teaching decision making and critical thinking. Also useful here would be some of the more general discussions of adolescent development, normalizing her behavior, and discussing what role parents can play in positive teenage outcomes. You might also suggest that she become involved in helping others, because service learning has proven beneficial to adolescents as well as the community.

Research Project 1:
Cross-Cultural Comparison of Secondary Schools

PLEASE NOTE: THIS PROJECT OFFERS THE OPTION OF INVOLVING OTHER PEOPLE. PLEASE CHECK WITH YOUR INSTRUCTOR TO SEE IF YOU NEED TO COMPLETE AN INSTITUTIONAL RESEARCH BOARD PROTOCOL BEFORE BEGINNING THIS PROJECT.

The text presents a cross-cultural comparison of secondary schools. Using that information, as well as information you can gather from the Internet, library research, and/or interviews of students or educators from other countries, compare and contrast the following aspects of secondary schools from around the world with the United States, and then answer the questions below.

Country	Mandatory Age	Number of Levels	Entrance/ Exit Exams	Sports	Content and Philosophy	Foreign Languages
United States						

1. What similarities do you see between these countries and the United States? What differences?

2. What effect do you think the differences have on adolescents' intellectual development? What effect do these differences have on social and/or behavioral outcomes?

3. Some educators believe that U.S. students should spend more time in school—that is, the school year and/or school day should be longer so that U.S. students can catch up academically with students in other countries. What do you think about this suggestion? Explain your rationale.

Research Project 2:
Helping Youth Avoid Problem Behaviors

Consider all the problem behaviors presented in this chapter. What do you believe are the antecedents of such behaviors? What are the consequences? What can be done to avoid each of these problem behaviors? What type of interventions would be useful? Use the text as well as information from the Internet to help you.

Behavior	Antecedents	Consequences	Prevention/Intervention
Dropping out of school			
Alcohol and other drug use/abuse			
Sexually transmitted infections			
Adolescent pregnancy			
Accidents and suicides			
Eating disorders			
Other			

On the basis of what you have learned about these problems, design a program that could be implemented in middle schools, junior high schools, or high schools to help confront and eliminate ONE of these problems. Report your findings and your revised (or unrevised) program to your class.

Personal Application Project 1:
Reflecting on and Sharing What You Learned

Consider what you read in Chapter 9, then answer the following questions.

1. What information in this chapter did you already know?

2. What information in this chapter was different from what you previously believed?

3. How was this information different?

4. How do you account for the differences between what you believed and what you learned in the chapter?

5. How can you apply this new knowledge to your own life?

6. Can you use this new information to help teens in your area?

Prepare a resource guide (a brochure, poster, or flyer) that you think would have helped you as a teen, one that can be distributed to teens and preteens, offering them help with problems they face. There are many toll-free numbers for organizations such as; Covenant House (crisis intervention, referral, and information services for troubled teens and their families: 1-800-999-9999), Youth Crisis Hotline (counseling and referrals for teens in crisis: 1-800-448-4663 [1-800-HIT HOME]), and National Runaway Switchboard (24-hour hot line for runaway and homeless youth and their families: 1-800-621-4000). Check out your local phone book and the Internet section for this chapter for some online resources that can be included as well.

Personal Application Project 2:
Consider Your Own Development

Consider your own physical development during adolescence, and then answer the following questions.

Aspects of Physical Development	Early/Late/On Time	Effect on Life Satisfaction	Effect on Self-Image
Menarche (females) Penile growth (males)			
Height spurt			
Weight gain (females)/ Voice change (males)			
Breast growth (females) Testicular development (males)			
Growth of pubic hair			

1. Was your development consistent with that described in the text?

2. Were you early, late, or on time?

3. What effect did that have on your adjustment and satisfaction with yourself and your life?

4. Did you find adolescence to be a time of "storm and stress," or did you have a positive self-image?

5. Did you exhibit (or, if you are now a teen, are you exhibiting) any aspects of David Elkind's notion of adolescent egocentrism (consisting of the imaginary audience and the personal fable)? If so, explain.

6. What other observations can you make when you compare your own development with the information in Chapter 9? Would you change anything in the text? Does the research support your own experience?

Internet Projects

Check out the McGraw-Hill website for this text (www.mhhe.com/santrockessls). You will find numerous activities there, in particular, quizzes. Also, be patient, because there are many very worthy links on each of the sites, but they do take a little time to access. If you do not go to the links many times, you will not get the full value of the site. Please go to all links.

Please note that all website addresses in this Study Guide have been checked and were correct at the time of publication. However, websites may be discontinued or their addresses may change, so when you try to access a given site, it may no longer be viable. If that occurs, please notify the publisher so that it can make appropriate revisions in future editions of this Study Guide.

Internet Project 1:
Teen Pregnancy

Although rates of adolescent pregnancy have decreased somewhat in the past few years, it still remains a major problem, particularly for adolescent girls and their babies. It can also create problems for adolescent fathers, even if they choose not to accept responsibility. Go to the site for Planned Parenthood, at www.plannedparenthood.org, and explore the many options available. In investigating the Planned Parenthood site, what did you learn about the problems inherent in a teenager's having a child (including physical, social, economic, educational, and emotional aspects)? Consider not only the problems encountered by the mother but also those that the child, the child's father, the grandparents, and society will face. What are the risk factors that might predict teen pregnancy? Write up what can be done to offer assistance to adolescent parents, their children, and their families to prevent the negative consequences (for example, dropping out of school) of starting a family so early.

Internet Project 2:
Online Social Networking Sites

Along with the growing popularity of online social networking sites (such as MySpace.com or Facebook.com) is an increasing concern about the impact of this form of communication on adolescents. Read the article "Popular Website MySpace Attracts Teens, But Some Parents Concerned" located at http://seattletimes.nwsource.com/html/living/2002468240_myspace03.html. As indicated by this article, these sites are very popular and equally controversial. After reading the article, briefly explore www.MySpace.com and/or www.Facebook.com. What are the potential advantages and pitfalls for adolescents using online social networks (such as MySpace or Facebook)? In particular, identify the benefits and dangers that are unique to the adolescent population due to the biosocial, cognitive, and psychosocial development relevant to this age group; explain your answers with specific relevance to developmental trends and milestones.

Other Relevant Sites on the Internet

Adolescent Health: www.drkoop.com/search.aspx?pAP=93&searchTxt=adolescent&searchType=0
This page of search results from Dr. C. Everett Koop's excellent medical website dedicated to adolescent health issues from smoking to teenage depression. (Dr. Koop is a former Surgeon General of the United States.) There are innumerable articles here for all aspects of physical and mental health.

Mothers Against Drunk Driving: www.madd.org/home/
This political action group was formed to stop drunk driving, prevent underage drinking, and support those who have been victims of drunk drivers. The site offers information on how to join, the status of new laws and bills, news articles, statistics, victim profiles, chat rooms, and more.

National Clearinghouse for Alcohol & Drug Information: http://ncadi.samhsa.gov/
This site provides information and links regarding all aspects of alcohol and other drug use including fetal alcohol syndrome. Do a search for "adolescent drug use," and see the many excellent links that come up regarding the latest research and statistics on this topic.

David Elkind: www.cio.com/archive/092203/elkind.html
This page, from the website of Chief Information Officers, an organization dedicated to informing the public about the latest in technological and informational influences on humans, describes Elkind's views on the influence of media on children's cognitive development. You can also click on links to his biography and his page on the website of Tufts University's Child Development Department. At the end of the article are some interesting comments parents submitted regarding his arguments.

National Runaway Switchboard: http://www.1800runaway.org/
This program strives to ensure that youth and families have access to resources in their communities. It has links for parents, teachers, students, and teens. It provides runaway prevention kits and gives opportunities to volunteer and donate money to the organization.

National Eating Disorders Association: www.nationaleatingdisorders.org/p.asp?WebPage_ID=337
The NEDA is dedicated to expanding public understanding of eating disorders and promoting access to quality treatment for those affected, along with support for their families through education, advocacy, and research. There is plenty of excellent information on this site.

Chapter 10: Socioemotional Development in Adolescence

Learning Goals

1. Discuss changes in the self and emotional development during adolescence.
2. Describe changes that take place in adolescents' relationships with their parents.
3. Characterize the changes that occur in peer relations during adolescence.
4. Explain how culture influences adolescent development.
5. Identify adolescent problems in socioemotional development, and discuss strategies for helping adolescents deal with these challenges.

Chapter Outline

THE SELF AND EMOTIONAL DEVELOPMENT
    Self-Esteem
    Identity
        What Is Identity?
        Erikson's View
        Developmental Changes
        Beyond Erikson
        Family Influences
        Ethnic Identity

FAMILIES
    Autonomy and Attachment
        The Push for Autonomy
        The Role of Attachment
        Balancing Freedom and Control
    Parent-Adolescent Conflict

PEERS
    Friendships
    Peer Groups
        Peer Pressure
        Cliques and Crowds
    Dating and Romantic Relationships
        Developmental Changes in Dating
        Dating in Gay and Lesbian Youth
        Sociocultural Contexts and Dating
        Dating and Adjustment

CULTURE AND ADOLESCENT DEVELOPMENT
    Cross-Cultural Comparisons
        Traditions and Changes in Adolescence around the Globe
            Health
            Gender
            Family
            Peers

Rites of Passage
Ethnicity
Immigration
Ethnicity and Socioeconomic Status

ADOLESCENT PROBLEMS
Juvenile Delinquency
Causes of Delinquency
Depression and Suicide
Depression
Suicide
The Interrelation of Problems and Successful Prevention/Intervention Programs

Matching Questions

_____ 1. Marcia's term for adolescents who have undergone a crisis and have made a commitment.

A. commitment

_____ 2. Marcia's term for the part of identity development in which adolescents show a personal investment in what they are going to do.

B. identity moratorium

_____ 3. Marcia's term for a period of identity development during which the adolescent is choosing among meaningful alternatives.

C. identity diffusion

_____ 4. Marcia's term for adolescents who are in the midst of a crisis, but their commitments are either absent or vaguely defined.

D. identity achievement

_____ 5. Marcia's term for adolescents who have not yet experienced a crisis or made any commitments.

E. crisis

Multiple-Choice Questions

1. According to Erikson, the adolescent identity crisis refers to a period _____.
a. of confusion during which youth are choosing between attachment and autonomy.
b. when adolescents are actively making decisions about who they want to be.
c. when adolescents actively avoid commitment to ideas or occupations.
d. of intense turmoil and stress that lasts a short time and determines an adolescent's identity status.

2. Which statement regarding identity development is FALSE?
a. Confusion over one's future leads to an inability to synthesize childhood identities.
b. Resolution of identity issues in adolescence does not mean that identity will be stable over time.
c. Identity formation neither begins nor ends with adolescence.
d. Flexibility and openness ensure numerous reorganizations of identity throughout life.

3. Jasper is the life of the party. He is fun to be around but never takes anything seriously. He has not decided to go to college or to get a meaningful job. He has no close friendships and has not had a serious romantic relationship. He seems happy to just live day to day without thinking of such matters. Jasper is probably in which stage?
a. identity achievement
b. identity foreclosure
c. identity diffusion
d. identity moratorium

4. Marcia refers to the part of identity development in which adolescents show a personal investment in what they are going to do as _____.
a. value
b. desire
c. commitment
d. involvement

5. Four students gave the following answers when asked if they had ever experienced doubts about their religion. The student who has arrived at identity achievement is _____.
a. Kristin, who says, "Oh, I don't know. It really doesn't bother me. I figure one's about as good as another."
b. Joe, who says, "No, not really. Our family is pretty much in agreement about these things."
c. Alicia, who says, "Yes, I guess I'm going through that right now. How can there be a god with so much evil in the world?"
d. Phil, who says, "Yeah, I even started wondering if God existed. I've pretty much resolved that by now, though."

6. Tanya is a high school student who has explored all potential employment and educational options and has chosen to attend the state college near home. In terms of vocation, she is experiencing identity _____.
a. achievement
b. moratorium
c. foreclosure
d. diffusion

7. Authoritarian parents are most likely to have adolescents experiencing identity _____.
a. achievement
b. moratorium
c. foreclosure
d. diffusion

8. Research on gender differences in autonomy-granting in adolescence has shown that _____.
a. boys are given more independence than girls
b. girls are given more independence than boys
c. boys and girls are given equal opportunities for independent behavior
d. girls are more likely to demand freedom and independence

9. Research on parenting styles and adolescent identity development has found ALL BUT WHICH ONE of these statements to be true?
a. Permissive parents tend to have adolescents with diffused identities.
b. Authoritarian parents tend to have adolescents in identity foreclosure.
c. Authoritative parents tend to foster identity achievement.
d. Indulgent parents tend to have children with identities that are in moratorium.

10. Erik Erikson's (1968) belief about the relationship between culture and identity development is best described by which of the following statements?
a. Culture plays a critical role in identity development.
b. In some individuals, cultural factors may play a role in identity development.
c. For all individuals, cultural factors play a minor role in identity development.
d. Cultural factors have no influence on identity development.

11. Most ethnic minorities first consciously confront their ethnicity in _____.
a. early childhood
b. middle childhood
c. adolescence
d. young adulthood

12. An enduring, basic aspect of the self that includes a sense of membership in an ethnic group and the attitudes and feelings related to that membership is _____.
a. ethnicity
b. nationality
c. culture
d. ethnic identity

13. Parents who want their adolescents to make a smooth transition into adulthood should _____.
a. relinquish control in all areas and let the adolescent take over
b. maintain control in as many areas as possible for as long as possible
c. relinquish control in areas where the adolescent has shown competence and maintain control in those areas where the adolescent's knowledge is limited
d. maintain control of issues dealing with family and relinquish control for those issues having to do with peer relations

14. Talia, age 16, has a secure attachment with her parents. Therefore, one might expect that she will _____.
a. have trouble breaking away from her parents to form peer relationships
b. tend to be more dependent in her relationship with her best friend
c. have a lower sense of her self-worth
d. have better relations with her peers than will her insecurely attached counterparts

15. The latest research on parent-adolescent relationships confirms that _____.
a. as adolescents mature, they detach from parents and move into a world of autonomy apart from parents
b. parent-adolescent conflict is intense and stressful throughout adolescence
c. everyday negotiations and minor disputes between parents and adolescents are harmful to developmental functions
d. serious, highly stressful parent-adolescent conflict is associated with juvenile delinquency, school dropout, pregnancy, and drug abuse

16. The adolescent who will most likely conform to peer pressure to engage in antisocial acts such as shoplifting or drawing graffiti is _____.
a.   Andrew, who is in seventh grade
b.   Brandon, who is in ninth grade
c.   Charles, who is a high school sophomore
d.   Dale, who is a high school senior

17. Children's groups differ from those formed by adolescents in that children's groups _____.
a.   are more informal
b.   rely more on the leaders of the groups
c.   have more interests in common
d.   include a greater diversity of individuals

18. Bridget is in a crowd at school but does not belong to a clique. Which statement about her group is probably TRUE?
a.   Her group is smaller than a clique.
b.   Her group is probably made up of acquaintances rather than friends.
c.   Members of her group probably do not have anything in common.
d.   Bridget's self-esteem is unlikely to be derived from her crowd membership.

19. Which of the following statements regarding cyberdating is NOT true?
a.   Cyberdating involves dating over the Internet.
b.   Cyberdating is particularly popular among middle school students.
c.   Cyberdating can be hazardous due to the anonymity of those at the other end of the computer.
d.   Cyberdating is more frequent than real-life dating throughout high school.

20. Which of the following statements regarding the rite of passage from adolescence to adulthood in American culture is TRUE?
a.   There are many points of transition to adulthood in American culture.
b.   There is an abrupt entry into adulthood in American culture.
c.   The end of adolescence in American culture is more clearly marked by biological change than by social milestones.
d.   No specific event marks the end of adolescence in American culture.

21. The documented causes of juvenile delinquency include all these EXCEPT which one?
a.   heredity
b.   identity problems
c.   family experiences
d.   boredom

22. A parenting practice that is associated with an adolescent's becoming delinquent is _____.
a.   disciplining an adolescent for antisocial behavior
b.   indulgence of an adolescent's desires
c.   low monitoring of adolescents
d.   restrictively controlling an adolescent's behavior

23. Which of the following statements regarding juvenile delinquency is NOT true?
a. Statistics indicate that 15% of all U.E. youth are involved in juvenile cases.
b. Delinquency rates among minority groups and lower-SES youth are especially high in proportion to the overall population.
c. Adolescent males are arrested more frequently than females for delinquent behavior.
d. Parental monitoring is linked to delinquent behavior in adolescents.

24. All the following factors have been found to be family contributors to adolescent delinquency EXCEPT which one?
a. having a high-achieving sibling who makes a teen feel inferior
b. having delinquent siblings
c. inappropriate parental discipline
d. lack of parental monitoring

25. The method of suicide selected by a male is more likely to be _____.
a. sleeping pills
b. guns
c. knives
d. carbon monoxide poisoning

True/False Questions

1. In general, boys and girls both have high self-esteem in childhood, but as adolescence approaches, girls' self-esteem drops considerably lower than that of boys.

2. Erikson stated that adolescents enter a psychological moratorium, which means that during adolescence, people are unable to really think about issues of psychological importance.

3. Recent research confirms Erikson's idea that adolescents experience an abrupt, dramatic shift called an identity crisis.

4. Erikson may have been incorrect about the sequence of identity development being similar for all people. For example, males and females may follow different stages.

5. The two central issues in determining identity status in adolescence are crisis and commitment.

6. A family atmosphere that limits individuality and emphasizes connectedness is important in the adolescent's identity development.

7. Researchers advise that parents should clamp down and demand conformity from their adolescents in order to prevent teens from performing risky behaviors or becoming out of control.

8. Parent-adolescent conflict is more likely to focus on chores and clothing choices than on major or serious life issues.

9. Parent-adolescent relationships are more positive if the teen lives at home while attending college, because it strengthens the attachment bond.

10. Adolescents are often members of formal and heterogeneous groups.

11. Lara and Christopher are 15 years old and have just started dating each other. Research suggests that they will probably use this relationship to figure out how they should act with dating partners as well as to gauge how attractive they are.

12. Adolescents who date are more likely to be accepted by their peers and judged as physically attractive.

13. Piotr came to the United States from Poland. He identifies with American culture and tries his best to lose his accent. He is embarrassed if his friends see any Polish foods or products in his home, and he tells his mother to always speak English. He has changed his name to Peter. This is an example of pluralism.

14. Because of escalating juvenile crime rates, we must try adolescent offenders as adults in order to deter them.

15. Erikson argued that delinquent behavior is an attempt to establish an identity.

Short-Answer Questions

1. Explain some of the changes in self-esteem that take place in adolescence.

2. How does identity develop?

3. Researchers have found that a family atmosphere that promotes both individuality and connectedness are important in an adolescent's identity development. Describe the dimensions of individuality and connectedness.

4. Explain autonomy and the importance of attachment in adolescence.

5. What may be the purpose of parent-adolescent conflict?

6. Explain the changes that take place in friendship during adolescence.

7. Describe typical adolescent peer groups.

8. Discuss some changes in adolescence around the world.

9. Define juvenile delinquency and outline some of its causes.

10. Give details about the nature of depression and suicide in adolescence.

Essay Questions

1. You are giving a talk to a group of parents about adolescent development. One of the mothers makes the following comment: "My daughter has pink hair one day, wears it in a bun the next day, likes punk rock one week, and hangs out with cheerleaders the next week. I have no idea what's going on with her. She seems so unstable!" How would you respond to her?

2. The principal and the school counselor of your former high school have asked for your advice on dealing with issues of diversity they are facing at school; the formation of cliques, plus growing racial and ethnic conflict. What advice could you give them?

Key to Matching Questions

1. D	2. A	3. E	4. B	5. C

Key to Multiple-Choice Questions

1. B	6. A	11. C	16. B	21. D
2. A	7. C	12. D	17. D	22. C
3. D	8. A	13. C	18. B	23. A
4. C	9. C	14. D	19. D	24. A
5. D	10. A	15. D	20. D	25. B

Key to True/False Questions

1. T	4. T	7. F	10. T	13. F
2. F	5. T	8. T	11. T	14. F
3. T	6. F	9. F	12. T	15. T

Key to Short-Answer Questions

1. In general, self-esteem declines during early adolescence for both girls and boys, but the decline is greater in girls. The degree of this decline is open for debate with some researchers finding the decline significant and others claiming the decline is small and overly exaggerated.

2. Identity development occurs across the lifespan. Marcia has proposed four identity statuses based on two characteristics: crisis (exploration) and commitment. Identity diffusion is a status in which the individual has not yet experienced a crisis or made any commitment. Foreclosure is a status in which the individual has made a commitment but has not experienced a crisis. Moratorium is a status in which the individual is in the midst of a crisis, and commitments are either absent or vaguely defined. Achievement is a status in which the individual has undergone a crisis and has made a commitment. Parents are key figures in an adolescent's identity development.

3. Individuality consists of two dimensions: self-assertion and separatedness. Connectedness also consists of two dimensions: mutuality and permeability.

4. The drive for autonomy increases during adolescence. A secure attachment between an adolescent and his or her parents is predictive of being socially competent.

5. Parent-adolescent conflict increases during this time, but it is typically moderate. This conflict may facilitate the development of autonomy and identity.

6. Friends become increasingly important to meeting adolescents' social needs. Friends provide companionship, intimacy, reassurance of self-worth, and sense of well-being.

7. Two types of peer groups are cliques and crowds. A clique is a small group, averaging around 5 or 6 people, with people who are usually the same sex and age. Members in a clique often share ideas and spend time together. A crowd is larger than a clique and is typically defined by the activities in which adolescents participate.

8. Regarding health, adolescents have different experiences based on culture and location. Overall, death due to infectious disease or malnutrition has decreased for adolescents. However, drug use and unprotected sex is increasing along with HIV cases in some locations. In many areas of the world, females still have less access to educational opportunities, less freedom to pursue various careers or leisure interests, and/or less freedom of sexual expression than do males. Also, the nature of families is changing in various areas of the world. Adolescents are more likely now to grow up in a divorced family or stepfamily environment, in families with fewer children, and in families with a working mother.

9. Juvenile delinquency refers to adolescents breaking the law or engaging in illegal behavior. Some causes of juvenile delinquency include heredity, identity problems, community influences, and family experiences.

10. Depression increases from childhood through adolescence to adulthood. Additionally, adolescent girls have higher rates of depression than adolescent boys. Some risk factors for developing depression include having a depressed parent, emotionally unavailable parents, parents who have high marital conflict, parents with financial problems, and poor peer relationships. Among adolescents, suicide is the third leading cause of death. Many more adolescents contemplate suicide, or attempt it, than succeed in completing it. Females are much more likely to attempt suicide, but males are more successful at it.

Key to Essay Questions

1. Include a discussion of Erikson's and Marcia's ideas about the identity crisis and the different statuses an adolescent may be in with respect to different areas of her or his life; also important are Elkind's notion of adolescent egocentrism discussed in Chapter 9 and the extension of Baumrind's work on parenting styles. For the latter, note that within the culture of the United States, adolescents whose parents use an authoritative parenting style are more socially competent, socially responsible, and cognitively competent than are adolescents whose parents use other parenting styles. (The authoritative parenting style encourages children to make choices and understand the consequences of their choices, an important issue in terms of engaging in potentially harmful activities.) Chapter 10 presents a great deal of information about various activities (for example, peer-tutoring) that have been effective for increasing adolescents' self-esteem and keeping them engaged in prosocial activities. You might note,

however, that although some behaviors that come with identity exploration (such as drinking alcohol) may be both illegal and detrimental, they are not outside the norm in terms of adolescents exploring their identity.

2. Explore the notions of ethnicity and socioeconomic status to understand whether they are dealing with one or both of these issues, so that they know how to proceed. It is important to discuss the stigmas associated with minority status, as well as the cultural differences (for instance, different customs and different values) that may or may not exist, including parenting practices and how they affect the adolescents' behavior. Note the contention that value conflicts are often involved when individuals respond to ethnic issues; thus, it is important to teach students to conceptualize or redefine these conflicts in innovative ways. Also important here is the research concerning the outcome of students' explorations of their ethnic identity, and the finding that students who do explore their ethnic identity tend to have higher self-esteem. Make suggestions, based on the research, for ways to reduce the conflict that is becoming a problem as requested by the principal and high school counselor.

Research Project 1:
Adolescence in Other Cultures

PLEASE NOTE: THIS PROJECT INVOLVES STUDYING OTHER PEOPLE. PLEASE CHECK WITH YOUR INSTRUCTOR TO SEE IF YOU NEED TO COMPLETE AN INSTITUTIONAL RESEARCH BOARD PROTOCOL BEFORE BEGINNING THIS PROJECT.

Interview three people from different countries or from subcultures different from yours. Ask each person to describe his or her experience of being a teenager. Was it an easy or a difficult transition? What was the person's relationship like with parents, siblings, and elders in the community? Did the person feel very different from how he or she felt in late childhood? How did the person's parents handle discussions regarding sexuality, drugs, marriage, careers, and other major issues? Ask each person to explain his or her cultural, ethnic, and/or religious views about the transition to adulthood. Are there formal or informal rites of passage? What is the definition of adulthood where the person grew up? What distinguishing privileges, behaviors, or practices are allowed once a person is no longer a child? Compare each interviewee's responses to your own answers to the same questions. Write a short paper analyzing the cultures you investigated (three others and your own) describing the main similarities and differences. Relate your points to the material in the chapter. What aspects of the reading were confirmed or refuted? What were the most fascinating things you learned, and how do they relate to the research outlined in Chapters 12 and 13?

Research Project 2:
Adolescents in the Media

Examine 3 different newspapers, and look for articles that feature an adolescent. Once you have located several articles, analyze the content. How are adolescents portrayed? Does the media show them in a positive or negative light? Are there gender differences in how males and females are viewed? Provide a critique of the media's coverage of adolescents in your area. How does the media portrayal compare with the information presented in this chapter?

Personal Application Project 1:
Your Adolescent Struggles

Think about your own journey through puberty, the transition to middle and then high school, and your changing relationship with your parents. What was it like for you? Was it a period of "storm and stress," or was it fairly smooth? What parenting style did your parents use when you were a child? Did they modify it when you reached adolescence? What were the most difficult experiences you had as a teenager? Did you engage in risky or dangerous behaviors? What do you think could have prevented you from doing so? What do you think were the most important influences on how you eventually came out of the adolescent period? Integrate your responses with the material in Chapters 9 and 10 (for example, relevant sections on depression, suicidality, violence, eating disorders, the search for identity, relationships with parents and peers, and so on). You should end up with a cohesive and well-organized paper analyzing your own adolescent development in relation to the research in the chapter.

Personal Application Project 2:
Exploring Your Identity

Consider the experiences you have had that stimulated you to think about your identity. Have your classmates, friends, or instructors challenged your view of yourself? Consider your identity in the many domains of your life indicated on the chart, and consider your identity status (achieved, moratorium, foreclosed, or diffused) in each of these different areas. If you are identity diffused or foreclosed, take some time to think about how you might move into a moratorium or achieved status—or consider if that is exactly where you want to be at this time.

Using the chart below, explore your identity status in each of the areas mentioned, explaining how you determined that you are in that status; then state how you might move to moratorium or achieved status if you are not there.

Area	Status	Explanation	Plans for Changing Status
Career			
Political			
Religious			
Relationship			
Achievement			
Sexual			
Gender			
Ethnic/cultural			
Interests			

Personality			
Physical			

1. According to what you wrote in the chart, are you in different statuses for different areas of your life? What does this tell you about yourself? What does it tell you about how Erikson's and Marcia's theories fit adolescent development?

2. Research suggests that people work on moving from diffused or foreclosed to moratorium or identity achieved. Do you believe this is appropriate for you? Is there some reason why it may be more appropriate for you to be in any particular status at this point in your life? Explain your reasons.

Internet Projects

Check out the McGraw-Hill website for this text (www.mhhe.com/santrockessls). You will find numerous activities there, including quizzes. Also, be patient, because there are many very worthy links on each of the sites, but they do take a little time to access. If you do not go to the links many times, you will not get the full value of the site. Please go to all links.

Please note that all website addresses in this Study Guide have been checked and were correct at the time of publication. However, websites may be discontinued or their addresses may change, so when you try to access a given site, it may no longer be viable. If that occurs, please notify the publisher so that it can make appropriate revisions in future editions of this Study Guide.

Internet Project 1:
Being Proactive in Your Own Socioemotional Development

An interesting website that offers a very wide range of socioemotional topics is www.psybersquare.com. Check out this site—the topics covered, the services offered, and so on. Then go to the link for Depression, then check out the articles on suicide, particularly one titled "Suicide: What if Someone You Care About Is Suicidal?" Have you ever had to deal with this situation? If so, what did you do? How might you handle such a situation now? How can you use the information to help the people close to you (including yourself)? Analyze all the information you read on the site. What was new to you? What was most helpful? Did the information on the site lead you to believe something should be added to Santrock's chapters on adolescent development?

Internet Project 2:
Rites of Passage

The text discusses rites of passage, ceremonies or rituals that mark an individual's transition from one status to another, noting that in some cultures they are the avenue through which adolescents gain access to adulthood, but that they seem to be much more nebulous for American adolescents. Using a search engine such as www.google.com or http://www.dogpile.com, do an Internet search for articles on "rites of passage." After exploring several sites, compare the information you found with what Santrock says about rites of passage generally, and more specifically what he says about rites of passage in the United States.

1. Do you agree that rites of passage in the United States are subtler than those in "primitive" cultures? Explain your response.

2. What ceremonies are common in the United States that would fall within the realm of rites of passage?

3. What purpose do these ceremonies serve?

4. What informal events do you think might serve as rites of passage for American youth? Explain.

5. Have you personally experienced a rite of passage (for example, bar or bat mitzvah, quinceañera)? How does this experience compare with what you have learned from the chapter and from the website for the textbook?

6. Before reading this chapter, had you ever thought about any of your experiences as being rites of passage?

7. After reading this chapter and viewing the textbook's website, do you now consider any of your experiences as rites of passage? Explain.

8. Were there any interesting rites of passage described from other cultures around the world?

Other Relevant Sites on the Internet

American Psychological Association: www.apa.org
Do a search on this site for "adolescent depression," and read some of the articles, news items, and resources that come up. You can also order helpful brochures, and the site provides you with people to contact if you need help with depression.

Child, Adolescent & Family: www.mentalhealth.org/cmhs/ChildrensCampaign/
This is the official site for the Children's Campaign run by the U.S. Department of Health and Human Services' Substance Abuse and Mental Health Services Administration. It is a great warehouse for mental health information. It provides resources for children, adolescents, and parents. It also has publications, news articles, and other links. A really helpful article is "Teen Mental Health Problems: What Are the Warning Signs?"

Adults & Children Together Against Violence: www.actagainstviolence.org
This is the site for the early violence prevention program sponsored by the American Psychological Association and the National Association for the Education of Young Children. It has information for parents, professionals, and teachers, along with innumerable resources, from articles to handouts to materials that can be ordered regarding the skills children need to act nonviolently.

Focus Adolescent Services: www.focusas.com/
This excellent website has a lot of great information for parents of teenagers and teens themselves. There are tests to determine whether a child is at risk for mental health problems. The site also provides a state-by-state listing of resources, information on how to find a therapist, hotline phone numbers, leads on books and speakers, and lists of resources for every topic from child abuse to suicide. It also covers new laws and policies that affect teenagers.

Stuart Stotts: www.stuart.stotts.com
This is the personal website of a storyteller named Stuart Stotts who has done extensive research on adolescent development across many cultures.

Chapter 11: Physical and Cognitive Development in Early Adulthood

Learning Goals

1. Describe the transition from adolescence to adulthood.
2. Identify the changes in physical development in young adults.
3. Discuss sexuality in young adults.
4. Characterize cognitive changes in early adulthood.
5. Explain the key dimensions of careers and work in early adulthood.

Chapter Outline

THE TRANSITION FROM ADOLESCENCE TO ADULTHOOD
    Becoming an Adult
        Key Features
        Markers of Becoming an Adult
    The Transition from High School to College

PHYSICAL DEVELOPMENT
    The Peak and Slowdown in Physical Performance
    Eating and Weight
        Obesity
            Heredity
            Leptin
            Set Point
            Environmental Factors
        Dieting
    Regular Exercise
    Substance Abuse
        Alcohol
            Binge Drinking
            Alcoholism
        Cigarette Smoking and Nicotine

SEXUALITY
    Sexual Orientation and Behavior
        Heterosexual Attitudes and Behavior
        Sources of Sexual Orientation
        Attitudes and Behavior of Lesbians and Gay Males
    Sexually Transmitted Infections
    Forcible Sexual Behavior and Sexual Harassment
        Rape
        Sexual Harassment

COGNITIVE DEVELOPMENT
    Cognitive Stages
        Piaget's View

Realistic and Pragmatic Thinking
Reflective and Relativisitic Thinking
Is There a Fifth, Postformal Stage?
Creativity

CAREERS AND WORK
Developmental Changes
Personality Types
Monitoring the Occupational Outlook
The Impact of Work
Work During College
Unemployment
Dual-Career Couples
Diversity in the Workplace

Matching Questions

_____ 1. Coercive sexual activity directed at someone with whom the perpetrator is at least casually acquainted.

A. postformal thought

_____ 2. Diseases that are contracted primarily through sex.

B. date or acquaintance rape

_____ 3. Transition from adolescence to adulthood that involves experimentation and exploration.

C. addiction

_____ 4. Form of thought that involves understanding that the correct answer to a problem can require reflective thinking, that the correct answer can vary from one situation to another, and that the search for truth is often an ongoing, never-ending process.

D. emerging adulthood

_____ 5. Pattern of behavior characterized by an overwhelming involvement with using a drug and securing its supply.

E. sexually transmitted infections

Multiple-Choice Questions

1. Jeffrey Arnett (2000) has termed the age range from 18 to 25 _____.
a. late adolescence
b. early adulthood
c. emerging adulthood
d. adulthood transitioning

2. The most widely recognized marker of entry into adulthood in the United States is _____.
a. getting a full-time job
b. moving out of the parents' home
c. graduating from college
d. getting married

3. Which of the following was NOT one of the key factors Arnett (2000) outlined as a necessary aspect of reaching adulthood?
a. accepting responsibility for one's self
b. finding a life partner
c. becoming capable of making independent decisions
d. gaining financial independence from parents

4. College students today indicate that they feel _____.
a. more excited about their opportunities than their 1980s counterparts.
b. more depressed than their 1980s counterparts.
c. less prepared for college than their 1980s counterparts.
d. more prepared for college than their 1980s counterparts.

5. Peak physical performance is typically reached _____.
a. in early adolescence
b. in late adolescence
c. in early adulthood
d. at different times for men and women

6. How well do college students use their knowledge about health?
a. They are well informed, and a majority uses the information to live healthy lifestyles.
b. Surveys indicate that most of them are aware of what it takes to be healthy, and almost 50% practice what they know.
c. Those who are well-informed also tend to practice what they know.
d. Although most of them know what it takes to be healthy, most do not apply it.

7. Now in her mid-20s, Hayley exercises rarely, skips breakfast to get to work early, and parties hard on weekends to compensate for the long hours of hard work she must put in to support her ambitious career plans. Late in life, when she has achieved success and retired, Hayley will be _____.
a. relatively healthy, because in her youth peak resources protected her against the stress she experienced
b. in satisfactory health, because her stressful living provided her with early success
c. vigorous, because she has trained herself for the demands of a successful career
d. relatively less healthy and dissatisfied with her life, because of her poor lifestyle choices early in life

8. When an individual reaches age 30, he or she for the first time may experience _____.
a. greater muscle tone and strength
b. radical changes in the sensory systems
c. sagging chin and protruding abdomen
d. decrease in the body's fatty tissues

9. Which of the following health habits does NOT worsen from adolescence to emerging adulthood?
a. inactivity
b. substance abuse
c. diet
d. vitamin use

10. Which of the following factors DOES NOT play a role in the development of obesity?
a. heredity
b. metabolism
c. personality
d. environmental factors

11. _____ is a protein that is involved in satiety and is released by fat cells.
a. Leptin
b. Basal
c. Progestin
d. Thalamus

12. While research shows that adults regularly _____ to control weight, experts recommend _____ for more effective weight and health management.
a. exercise; diet
b. diet; exercise
c. meditate; diet
d. exercise; meditation

13. At age 30, you find you are a successful, hardworking executive, but you are also slightly overweight and are having increasing difficulty coping with the tension in your life. To ensure good health, you should _____.
a. diet to lose weight immediately
b. increase stamina by starting a weight-lifting program in which you alternate muscle groups daily
c. get regular aerobic exercise for at least 30 minutes every day
d. increase your sleep to a minimum of 9 hours per night

14. Dante is an alcoholic. Which of the following factors in his life would predict a positive outcome and recovery from alcoholism?
a. Dante enjoys drinking so much, that he will eventually realize how hooked he is.
b. Dante quit drinking and has gained 15 pounds because he eats when he wants to drink.
c. Dante's wife has threatened to leave him, and they fight all the time about his drinking.
d. Dante's lack of affiliation with any kind of religious group allows him to escape feeling guilty and really deal with his alcoholism.

15. A pattern of behavior characterized by an overwhelming involvement with using a drug and securing its supply is _____.
a. drug tolerance
b. addiction
c. drug withdrawal
d. substance abuse

16. Research on alcoholism has found that _____.
a. genetics is the primary contributor to alcoholism
b. the majority of alcoholics recover whether or not they are ever in a treatment program
c. a third of the adults who drink continue on the path to alcoholism
d. both genetics and environmental factors play a role in the development of alcoholism

17. Recent research exploring the biological bases of homosexuality has found that _____.
a. homosexuals and heterosexuals have different physiological responses during sexual arousal
b. if male homosexuals are given male sex hormones, their sexual orientation changes
c. exposure of the fetus to hormone levels characteristic of females might cause an individual to become attracted to males
d. an area of the hypothalamus that governs sexual behavior is twice as large in homosexual males as in heterosexual males

18. The development of homosexuality is a complex process. It probably involves all of these factors EXCEPT which one?
a. parental sexual orientation factors
b. genetic factors
c. cognitive factors
d. environmental factors

19. Andrea and Tom are at a point in their relationship where they will soon become sexually intimate. They would be wise to protect themselves against sexually transmitted infections (STIs) by doing all the following things EXCEPT which one?
a. asking about each other's previous sexual encounters
b. obtaining medical examinations
c. applying petroleum jelly to condoms before using them
d. promising to be monogamous

20. Characteristics of rapists include all the following EXCEPT which one?
a. They use aggression to enhance their sense of power.
b. They have abnormally high levels of sexual desire.
c. They are generally angry at women.
d. They want to hurt and humiliate their victim.

21. Which of the following statements regarding date rape is NOT true?
a. Date rape can occur between strangers or casual acquaintances.
b. The majority of college freshman women report having been involved in a date rape situation.
c. Date rape involves coercive sexual activity.
d. Many college men report that they have forced sexual activity.

22. With respect to adult cognitive processes, psychologist K. Warner Schaie (1977) concluded that _____.
a. adults now enter a postformal operational stage involving more complex strategies
b. many adults revert to a pragmatic concrete stage rather than use formal operational thought
c. adults do not go beyond formal operational thought, but they do progress in how they use their intellect.
d. adults in certain careers (for example, higher education) tend to go into a postformal operational stage, but most others do not.

23. Life-span development students often complain, "Why do we have to learn all these theories? Why don't you just teach us the right one?" According to William Perry, this complaint reflects _____.
a. absolute, dualistic thinking
b. dualistic, reflective thinking
c. reflective, relativistic thinking
d. full relativistic thinking

24. Tamika is very intelligent and often spends a lot of time alone thinking up her next experiment or invention. She has a hard time understanding emotional attachments and would rather read books than go to parties. According to Holland's theory, she is probably a(n) _____ personality.
a. realistic
b. investigative
c. enterprising
d. conventional

25. Recent research on creativity has shown that it _____.
a. is highly correlated with intelligence
b. peaks in adolescence, then declines
c. peaks in adulthood, then declines
d. peaks in late adulthood

True/False Questions

1. Emerging adulthood is a developmental stage that captures the lengthy transition from adolescence to adulthood.

2. The markers of adult status tend to be universal.

3. Most college students experience some level of depression when leaving home and subsequently tend to have pessimistic beliefs about their future health risks.

4. Serena is a 22-year-old obese college student. Recent research suggests that she might benefit from leptin supplements once this treatment is approved for humans.

5. Alex has discovered that he has a very high set point. This means that he uses a lot of energy during resting states.

6. Emerging adults have more than twice the mortality rate of adolescents.

7. Experts recommend that we engage in at least 30 minutes of moderate-intensity exercise on most days of the week.

8. Some researchers believe that once you develop fat cells, they do not go away.

9. Nicotine, the active drug in cigarettes, is addictive because it serves as a tranquilizer, which allows people to relax and better deal with stress.

10. Recent research shows that homosexual people have a very different type of physiological response during sexual arousal than do heterosexual people.

11. Female rape victims often have sexual problems after the rape such as reduced sexual desire and an inability to reach orgasm.

12. Because adolescents have more spare time, their thinking is characterized by reflective and relativistic thinking. Young adults, however, are busier and have to think in absolutes in order to solve problems immediately.

13. Chen is a highly talented artist. He often sits for hours engaged in the creative process, visualizing his next big work of art, and feeling really good about the process to come. This is called being in a state of flow.

14. In projections about the future growth of one's desired career, a good gauge would be whether one needs a college degree to get the job.

15. Working at a full-time job during college is related to being a more mature, responsible student who obtains good grades and graduates on time.

Short-Answer Questions

1. What are the criteria for becoming an adult? What is the nature of emerging adulthood?

2. Explain the transition from high school to college.

3. How does physical development peak and then slow down in early adulthood?

4. Discuss alcohol abuse in early adulthood and the effect that it has.

5. What are some good strategies for protecting yourself against AIDS and other STIs?

6. Describe the effects of forcible sexual behavior and how to facilitate recovery.

7. Explain the changes in young adults' cognitive development.

8. Elaborate on some of the developmental changes in careers and work in early adulthood.

9. Clarify how personality types might be linked to career choices.

10. In which areas are there most likely to be great increases in the number of jobs through 2010?

Essay Questions

1. Jerrilyn is worried about getting a job that is right for her when she graduates from college. What would you suggest that she do to maximize her chances of a good career choice that works well for her and her family of four?

2. You have been asked to talk to a group of college students about sex. Although you know that many have probably been sexually active, you are advised that because you are their peer, they may be more open and honest with you in what they say and the questions they ask. You need to be prepared to discuss the whole range of topics, including sexual orientation, physiological changes, STIs and ways to prevent them, sexual harassment, and rape. How will you address each of these topics?

Key to Matching Questions

1. B	2. E	3. D	4. A	5. C

Key to Multiple-Choice Questions

1. C	6. D	11. A	16. D	21. A
2. A	7. D	12. B	17. C	22. C
3. B	8. C	13. C	18. A	23. A
4. B	9. D	14. B	19. C	24. B
5. C	10. C	15. B	20. B	25. C

Key to True/False Questions

1. T	4. F	7. T	10. F	13. T
2. F	5. F	8. T	11. T	14. T
3. T	6. T	9. F	12. F	15. F

Key to Short-Answer Questions

1. Two of the criteria for adult status are economic independence and independent decision making. The transition period from adolescence to adulthood (18-25 years) is now call emerging adulthood. This period is characterized by experimentation and exploration.

2. There are both positive and negative aspects to the transition from high school to college. There are many parallels between the transition from high school to college and the transition from elementary school to middle school or junior high—for example, the experience of increased stress, the top-dog phenomenon, a more impersonal school environment, a greater diversity of peers, and an increased focus on achievement and assessment. Some positive aspects include feeling more mature, having more freedom to choose classes, having more time with peers, having greater independence, encountering more intellectual stimulation and challenge, experiencing less parental monitoring, and having the opportunity to explore diverse lifestyles and values.

3. Most often, the peak in physical performance and health is achieved between 19 and 26 years. That means that physical performance begins to decline during the latter part of early adulthood. Some markers of this slow down in physical performance include a decrease in muscle tone and strength, a saggy chin, protruding abdomen, a decline in hearing, and an increase in fatty tissue.

4. There is typically a reduction in substance use and abuse between adolescence and the mid-20s. Individuals who go to college after high school tend to drink alcohol more than individuals who do not. Females typically drink less alcohol then do males. Binge drinking among college students is a concern. Binge drinking can result in missed classes, physical injuries, troubles with the police, and unprotected sex. Of all early adults, drinking is heaviest among individuals who are single or divorced. Those that continue to abuse alcohol throughout early adulthood often suffer in their health and social relationships.

5. Strategies for protecting yourself against AIDS and other STIs include knowing your and your partner's risk status; obtaining medical examinations; having protected sex; and not having sex with multiple partners.

6. Rape is forcible sexual intercourse with a person who does not give consent. Rape is traumatic for both the victim and their loved ones. Victims often experience shock, numbness, grief (either externalized or internalized), depression, fear, anxiety, increased substance use, and sometimes sexual dysfunctions. Recovery varies from person to person and depends partially on the victim's coping abilities, social support, and mental health before the attack. Support for recovery can come from mental health professionals, friends, and relatives.

7. Piaget did not theorize a new cognitive stage that began in adulthood. However, if an individual did not develop formal operational thought during adolescence, he or she could still do so during adulthood. Some researchers contend that idealism decreases during early adulthood, whereas realistic, pragmatic thinking increases. Additionally, young adults increasingly think in reflective and relativistic ways.

8. Children often have idealistic fantasies about future careers. During the late teen years and early 20s, individuals begin to consider career options more seriously. On completion of their education or training, many individuals in their early to mid-20s begin their career.

9. Holland developed personality type theory which asserts that the closer the fit between a person's personality and career, the more the individual will enjoy the career and persist in it. He has proposed six career-related personality types: realistic, investigative, artistic, social, enterprising, and conventional. For example, an individual with an artistic personality type would enjoy working with ideas and materials in expressive ways, whereas a person with a realistic personality type would prefer working outdoors or in manual activities.

10. Job growth is forecasted for the service, professional, and business industries; especially in the areas of computers, education, and health. The vast majority of jobs that will experience growth and pay the best will require a college education.

Key to Essay Questions

1. Discuss John Holland's personality type theory and the importance of personal values so that you can help her select a career that matches her personality type and her priorities. You will also need to look at occupational outlook, how to find the right match between student and career, and women's issues in the workforce. Then look at the basic health issues involved with working during college and alcohol and other drug use, as well as how these things might affect Jerrilyn's current school performance and her ability to find and hold a job.

2. Discuss the wide range of sexual orientation (from heterosexuality to homosexuality and all points in between), physiological changes that occur in young adulthood, STIs and AIDS and ways to prevent each of them (for example, abstinence, use of condoms, monogamy), sexual harassment (for instance, what behaviors would constitute harassment, what the consequences of harassment are for victim and perpetrator), and rape (for example, the definition of rape, understanding that rape is an issue of power and control and not of sex).

Research Project 1:
College Drinking Patterns

PLEASE NOTE: THIS PROJECT INVOLVES STUDYING OTHER PEOPLE. PLEASE CHECK WITH YOUR INSTRUCTOR TO SEE IF YOU NEED TO COMPLETE AN INSTITUTIONAL RESEARCH BOARD PROTOCOL BEFORE BEGINNING THIS PROJECT.

This project will assist you in understanding the drinking patterns of college students. Interview six different kinds of students on your campus (different sexes, ages, ethnic groups, majors, etc). Gather basic demographic data, such as students' sex, age, and years of education, and then ask about the students' drinking patterns (for example, how often they consume alcohol, how much they consume at any given time, when they consume it, when they first started drinking) and the problems they encounter from consuming alcohol (refer to the text for common problems). What is the prevalence of alcohol consumption in these six surveys? Who is most likely to abstain from drinking? Who is most likely to engage in moderate or heavy drinking? Is alcohol consumption primarily a social activity, or are many students drinking alone? What specific problems do the students encounter from drinking alcohol? Prepare a chart that indicates who has the problems and specifically what types of problems they have.

1. What did you notice in terms of the specific problems that drinkers have?

2. What patterns of drinking did you notice?

3. Were your observations consistent with what you might expect from the research described? Explain your response.

4. On the basis of your observations, what might you conclude about drinking patterns on your college campus and the problems that may be incurred?

Research Project 2:
Avoiding Sexually Risky Behaviors

Using two professional journal articles and the chapter as your research materials, prepare a 15-minute presentation or a three- to five-page paper on the risk factors that young adults face when engaging in sexual activities. Be specific in stating the potential consequences of various forms of sexual interactions ranging from kissing (minimal risk) to engaging in vaginal or anal intercourse without a condom (high risk). Include in your presentation a discussion of the range of sexual orientations (heterosexual to homosexual), rape (for example, it is a matter of power and control, not sexual gratification; talk about marital rape, date rape, and concerns about whether a person has the mental capacity to consent), and sexual harassment. Relying on the text and two professional journal articles found in the PsycINFO or PsycARTICLES databases at your campus library, provide a good outline of ways to reduce the risks involved in engaging in sexual activities.

Remember to keep your own value judgments out of such a presentation and rely instead on the heavy body of research in this field; however, the members of your audience will be sure to have strong emotional responses to what you say.

Personal Application Project 1:
Reflecting on What You Learned

Consider what you read in Chapter 11; then answer the following questions.

1. What information in this chapter did you already know?

2. What information in this chapter was totally new to you?

3. How can you use that new information in your own life?

4. How do you account for the differences between what you believed and what you learned in the chapter?

5. What is the most important thing you learned from reading this chapter?

6. Write a three-page paper analyzing your own early adulthood development. In what ways did it mirror the material in the book? In what ways did your experience not match up to the research covered? How well do you think you progressed (or are progressing) through this stage of life-span development? What evidence do you have to support your statements?

Personal Application Project 2:
Consider Your Own Development

Chapter 11 provides a lot of information about the transition from adolescence to adulthood and issues inherent in making that shift. Consider some of the topics discussed in terms of your own life; then indicate in the chart below whether they have been (or currently are) important issues for you and, if so, how you have dealt with them (or are currently dealing with them) and whether, from your own experience, you agree with the research the text presented about them.

Aspect of Your Self	Summary of Text	Your Own Experience	Comments
Transition from high school to college			
Peak and slowdown in physical performance			

Substance use/abuse			
Sexuality			
Cognitive development			
Creativity			
Career choices			
Other (describe)			

Internet Projects

Check out the McGraw-Hill website for this text (www.mhhe.com/santrockessls). You will find numerous activities there, in particular, quizzes. Also, be patient, because there are many very worthy links on each of the sites, but they do take a little time to access. If you do not go to the links many times, you will not get the full value of the site. Please go to all links.

Please note that all website addresses in this Study Guide have been checked and were correct at the time of publication. However, websites may be discontinued or their addresses may change, so when you try to access a given site, it may no longer be viable. If that occurs, please notify the publisher so that it can make appropriate revisions in future editions of this Study Guide.

Internet Project 1:
Ensuring Your Health in Later Years

The text cautioned that bad health habits in early adulthood can lead to poor health and lack of satisfaction with life later on. The first section of the chapter makes suggestions for healthier living and presents examples of moderate and vigorous physical activity. Check out the Mayo Clinic website at www.mayoclinic.com. Click on the Healthy Living button at the top of the home page. Look at all the articles available, including those on nutrition and exercise. Also check out the Health Tools button at the top of the home page. This will take you to several valuable health assessments from depression surveys to a heart disease risk calculator. The quizzes and videos are quite interesting.

1. How can you use what you have learned from this website to improve your chances of having a long, healthy, satisfying life?

2. Are you willing to follow their suggestions?

3. Why do you think that so many of us can have this information and, despite wanting to have good health in later years, fail to follow through?

4. How do you think people could be encouraged to take the necessary steps to ensure optimal health throughout their lifetime?

5. What advice would you give someone regarding health who swears that a low-carbohydrate diet is particularly effective?

Internet Project 2:
Lifestyle Factors that Impact Developmental Age

As indicated by the text, there are a variety of factors that can impact your development as you age. The concept "real age" has been proposed to examine the biological age of your body based on how well you have maintained yourself. Go to the Real Age website at http://www.realage.com/ and complete the free Real Age test. After completing the test, answer the following questions:

1. How does your "real age" compare to your chronological age? Do you agree with this analysis?

2. What factors most influenced your real age score?

3. Were you surprised by any of the factors that contribute to your real age? Explain.

4. What 3 factors do you think are most problematic for the "real age" of you and your friends? Explain.

Other Relevant Sites on the Internet

National Clearinghouse for Alcohol & Drug Information:
https://ncadistore.samhsa.gov/catalog/audiences.aspx
The clearinghouse is under the aegis of the U.S. Department of Health and Human Services. This page is a listing of various audiences, so click on the link that best describes you (for example, College Students; African Americans; Lesbian, Gay, Bisexual, Transgender; Parents/Caregivers; Women) and find all kinds of great articles for your group. You can look up information on specific drugs as well.

National Institute on Drug Abuse: www.nida.nih.gov
NIDA is a government-sponsored organization involved in research and prevention of drug abuse. Its website contains information sections for researchers and health professionals, parents and teachers, and students. They have a great listing of "companion websites" relating to things such as "club drugs" and steroids.

Sexually Transmitted Infections: www.plannedparenthood.org/sti/
This is a very informative page of the Planned Parenthood site. It lists all STIs and gives the facts and myths about each one. This site has almost any information you could ever want to find out about sexuality for people of all ages and backgrounds.

The Gay & Lesbian Alliance Against Defamation: www.glaad.org
The website for GLAAD, a national organization, provides information, support, a listing of upcoming events, and current media releases. Click on the Regional Action Map to see what is happening in your area. There are some noteworthy articles on same-sex marriages as well.

Parents, Families and Friends of Lesbians and Gays: www.pflag.org/
This terrific site dedicated to supporting families, friends, and parents of gay and lesbian people.

Rape, Abuse & Incest National Network: www.rainn.org/
Here you will find statistics, counseling resources, and information on what you should do if you are a victim or know a victim of sexual assault.

Facts About Sexual Harassment: www.eeoc.gov/facts/fs-sex.html
This short fact sheet defining sexual harassment is from the U.S. Equal Employment Opportunity Commission and provides information on how to file a sexual harassment claim.

Advancing Women: Dual Career Couples Want Freedom and Control: www.advancingwomen.com/wk_dualcareer.html
This is a great article on dual-career couples, from the Advancing Women Network, which gives women strategies for being successful in business and balancing family life.

NationJob.com: www.nationjob.com/
This is a national job search and employment help website.

Chapter 12: Socioemotional Development in Early Adulthood

Learning Goals

1. Describe stability and change in temperament and attachment from childhood to adulthood.
2. Identify some key aspects of attraction, love, and close relationships.
3. Characterize adult life styles.
4. Discuss key challenges in parenting, marriage, and divorce.
5. Characterize the role of gender in relationships.

Chapter Outline

STABILITY AND CHANGE FROM CHILDHOOD TO ADULTHOOD
    Temperament
    Attachment

ATTRACTION, LOVE, AND CLOSE RELATIONSHIPS
    Attraction
        Familiarity and Similarity
        Physical Attractiveness
    The Faces of Love
        Intimacy
            Erikson's Stage: Intimacy Versus Isolation
            Intimacy and Independence
        Friendship
            Gender Differences in Friendships
            Friendships between Women and Men
        Romantic Love
        Affectionate Love
        Consummate Love
    Falling Out of Love

ADULT LIFE STYLES
    Single Adults
    Cohabiting Adults
    Married Adults
        Marital Trends
        The Benefits of a Good Marriage
    Divorced Adults
    Remarried Adults
    Gay Male and Lesbian Adults

MARRIAGE AND THE FAMILY
    Becoming a Parent
    Making Marriage Work
    Dealing with Divorce

GENDER, RELATIONSHIPS, AND SELF-DEVELOPMENT

Women's Development
Men's Development

Matching Questions

_____ 1. Emotional component of a relationship that involves strong components of sexuality and infatuation.

A. attachment-related avoidance

_____ 2. Explanation of why individuals are attracted to people who are similar to them. Our own attitudes and behaviors are supported and validated when someone else's attitudes and behavior are similar to our own.

B. consensual validation

_____ 3. Involves the extent to which individuals feel secure or insecure about whether a partner will be available, responsive, and attentive.

C. romantic love

_____ 4. States that although we prefer a more attractive person in the abstract, in the real world we end up choosing someone who is close to our own level.

D. attachment-related anxiety

_____ 5. Involves the degree to which individuals feel secure or insecure in relying on others, opening up to them, and being intimate with them.

E. matching hypothesis

Multiple-Choice Questions

1. Personality characteristics _____.
a. are formed during the first five years of life
b. are affected more by later life experiences than by early life experiences
c. appear to change more over long time intervals than over short intervals
d. show little stability over time

2. According to research by Thomas and Chess, well-adjusted young adults likely had a(n) _____.
a. easy temperament as a 3- to 5-year old
b. difficult temperament as a 3- to 5-year old
c. shy temperament as a 3- to 5-year old
d. fearful temperament as a 3- to 5-year old

3. Irene does not like to talk about her relationships with her parents. She feels that those early relationships really did not affect her adult development, but she does mention that she remembers feeling rejected by her father. Irene refuses to rely on anyone else, open up to others or become intimate. Irene is exhibiting signs of _____.
a. attachment-related avoidance
b. insecure-dismissing attachment
c. attachment-related anxiety
d. insecure-preoccupied attachment

4. Which one of the following statements does NOT characterize research findings on the effect of childhood attachment on adult adjustment patterns?
a. Ambivalently attached children often grow up to be jealous and angry.
b. Avoidantly attached children often grow up to engage in one-night stands.
c. Dismissingly attached children often grow up to reject others who show them affection.
d. Securely attached children often grow up to show securely attached romantic relationships.

5. Research findings about close relationships indicate that _____.
a. people who live in glass houses should not throw stones
b. birds of a feather flock together
c. distance makes the heart grow fonder
d. a rose by any other name will smell as sweetly

6. Consensual validation refers to _____.
a. the adolescent's first experiences of sexual intercourse
b. support for one's attitudes and behavior through another person's similar attitudes and behavior
c. parents' acceptance of their offspring as independent adults
d. attraction between similar individuals

7. Erik Erikson believed that the primary crisis of the early adult years is _____.
a. autonomy versus shame and doubt
b. identity versus identity confusion
c. intimacy versus isolation
d. generativity versus stagnation

8. Which of the following factors is NOT typically characteristic of women's friendships?
a. listening at length
b. desire for practical solutions to their problems
c. depth and breadth
d. exchange of mutual support

9. Which of the following factors is NOT typically characteristic of men's friendships?
a. self-disclosure
b. sharing useful information
c. desire for practical solutions to their problems
d. sharing activities

10. Berscheid's (1988) studies show that the most important ingredient of romantic love is _____.
a. sexual desire
b. commitment
c. proximity
d. respect

11. Female friendships in adulthood tend to _____.
a. involve more self-disclosure than male friendships
b. be characterized by depth but not breadth
c. revolve around activities
d. focus on problem-solving

12. Research on falling out of love showed that being in love when the other person does not return love could lead to all the following problems EXCEPT which one?
a. self-condemnation
b. sexual dysfunction
c. violence toward future partners
d. obsessive thoughts

13. Richard and Jamie's only real attraction toward each other is sexual. Sternberg's research would argue that they are _____.
a. experiencing infatuation
b. experiencing companionate love
c. experiencing fatuous love
d. not experiencing love

14. Companionate love can best be described as _____ love.
a. consummate
b. affectionate
c. passionate
d. romantic

15. Most divorces occur in the _____ years of marriage.
a. 1st to 4th
b. 5th to 10th
c. 11th to 15th
d. 16th to 20th

16. Fabiana has just gotten divorced. She is much happier now and feels self-sufficient. She has a successful career, good friends, and interesting hobbies. She has no room in her life for another romantic relationship. Hetherington and Kelly (2002) would call her a(n) _____.
a. enhancer
b. introvert
c. libertine
d. competent loner

17. Which of these is one explanation for the fact that two thirds of stepfamily couples DO NOT stay married?
a. They remarry only for love.
b. They may carry previous negative relationship patterns into the current family.
c. They do not want their new partners to help rear their children.
d. They realize that they keep attracting undesirable partners.

18. Linda and Danielle are a lesbian couple. Which of the following statements about them is likely to be true?
a. One partner is probably masculine and the other feminine.
b. They probably engage in sex daily.
c. They do not want to engage in a long-term relationship.
d. They do not allow each other to have sexual relationships with others.

19. Ron Levant (2002) argues that men should reconstruct masculinity in WHICH ONE of the following ways?
a. attempt to become more emotionally intelligent
b. attempt to use more report talk
c. become more feminine
d. become more passive

20. Which statement is considered a fact and NOT just a myth about parenting?
a. The birth of a child will save a failing marriage.
b. Parenting is an instinct and requires no training.
c. Having a child gives parents a "second chance" to achieve what they should have achieved.
d. Parenting requires a number of interpersonal skills and emotional demands.

21. According to the text, which one of these is NOT a common problem of single adults?
a. intimate relationships with other adults
b. increased risk for sexually transmitted diseases
c. confronting loneliness
d. finding a niche in a marriage-oriented society

22. A benefit of cohabitation is that _____.
a. relationships in cohabitation tend to last longer than marriages, because there are fewer pressures
b. relationships in cohabitation tend to be more equal than they are in marriage
c. cohabitation improves an individual's chances for choosing a compatible marriage partner
d. cohabitation leads to greater marital happiness and success

23. Researchers have found that _____.
a. gay and lesbian relationships are similar to heterosexual relationships in their satisfactions, loves, and conflicts
b. there are more conflicts in homosexual relationships than in heterosexual relationships
c. gay and lesbian partners are generally more open about expressing their love than their heterosexual counterparts are
d. conflict and satisfaction are greater in homosexual relationships than in heterosexual relationships

24. According to Hetherington's research on common pathways in exiting divorce, which type of person is likely to gain in competence and self-fulfillment following a divorce?
a. Enhancers
b. Libertines
c. Competent loners
d. Seekers

25. _____ talk is a more common communication strategy among women; where as men tend to prefer _____ talk.
a. Report; rapport
b. Rapport; report
c. Emotional; factual
d. Factual; emotional

True/False Questions

1. The stability of personality traits appears to be more consistent if we measure people over longer time intervals.

2. The likelihood that childhood temperament is related to adulthood personality often depends on intervening variables such as a child's peer relationships.

3. Shenice constantly worries about whether her partner will be available and attentive; she is demonstrating attachment-related avoidance.

4. Secure attachments in childhood are often related to the security of one's adult romantic relationships, even 20 years later.

5. Because of the strong link between childhood attachment quality and attachment in adult relationships, it is virtually impossible for adults to revise or change their attachment styles later in life.

6. Research has shown that the old saying "Familiarity breeds contempt" is correct.

7. Manuel is politically liberal and enjoys building race cars. When he meets a woman at the car races who also volunteers for the Green Party, he feels he has met his soul mate. Part of why he might be attracted to this woman can be explained by the concept of consensual validation.

8. Erikson describes intimacy as finding yourself and losing yourself in another person at the same time.

9. Adult friendships usually come from the same age group.

10. Sebastian and Marguerite have been together for several years. Their relationship is characterized by psychological intimacy and a strong commitment to each other. However, their passion has diminished. Sternberg would say that they experienced fatuous love.

11. Cohabitation is seen as a universal precursor to marriage.

12. Every marriage has problems. However, the most successful married couples solve their common problems and get them out of the way early in the relationship.

13. Relationships between cohabitating partners tend to be more egalitarian than relationships between married partners.

14. Maria and Juan do not want to become another divorce statistic. They decided not to live together until they got engaged and started planning the wedding. Research shows that this practice is related to lower rates of divorce than living together before engagement.

15. Women and men's communication problems with each other often stem from the fact that women do not like to engage in rapport talk.

Short-Answer Questions

1. How stable is temperament from childhood to adulthood?

2. Describe how much attachment changes from childhood to adulthood.

3. What are some key aspects of what attracts one person to another?

4. What are some different types of love?

5. What characterizes falling out of love?

6. List and explain the six common pathways in exiting divorce.

7. What makes a marriage successful?

8. Explain what the lives of cohabiting adults are like.

9. What are some predictors or risk factors for divorce? How does divorce affect adults?

10. What characterizes the lifestyles of gay and lesbian adults?

Essay Questions

1. You have been asked to address your local community on developing meaningful relationships in young adulthood. Among the topics you have been asked to discuss are developmental norms in young adulthood, ways to recognize healthy and unhealthy relationships, and how to create healthy relationships. What will you tell the participants?

2. You have been caught in the middle of an ongoing argument between the men and the women in your family. Each group says the other is to blame for marital dissatisfaction. They have asked for your wise input to help them deal more effectively with each other. How can you help them?

Key to Matching Questions

1. C	2. B	3. D	4. E	5. A

Key to Multiple-Choice Questions

1. C	6. D	11. A	16. D	21. B
2. A	7. C	12. C	17. B	22. B
3. A	8. B	13. A	18. D	23. A
4. D	9. A	14. B	19. A	24. A
5. B	10. A	15. B	20. D	25. B

Key to True/False Questions

1. F	4. T	7. T	10. F	13. T
2. F	5. F	8. T	11. F	14. T
3. F	6. F	9. T	12. F	15. F

Key to Short-Answer Questions

1. There are some subtle, general changes in temperament in early adulthood. For example, there is a decline in emotional mood swings and risk-taking behavior. Additionally, there is an increase in responsible behavior. Some stability for temperament in early adulthood is also apparent. For example, easy-temperament children are likely to be well adjusted in early adulthood. In comparison to easy-temperament children, difficult-temperament children are less well adjusted in early adulthood, males are less likely to continue with their education, and females are likely to experience marital conflict. Additionally, the temperament characteristics of inhibition and emotional control also demonstrate some stability from childhood to early adulthood.

2. Attachment patterns in infancy tend to be correlated to adult attachment patterns. However, certain experiences, such as death of a parent, can alter attachment patterns.

3. Familiarity, similarity, and physical attraction are all key aspects of attraction.

4. Three types of love are romantic, affectionate, and consummate love. Romantic love is a combination of passion, sexuality, and a diversity of positive and negative emotions. Companionate love includes intimacy, commitment, affection, and a desire to be near the person. Consummate love combines passion, intimacy, and commitment.

5. The experience of falling out of love varies from person to person. Many people find falling out of love to be traumatic, painful, and emotionally intense. If an individual does not have other close relationships to turn to for support, loneliness may result. However, other people find falling out of love to be an opportunity for personal development and can find happiness with this perspective.

6. The six common pathways in exiting divorce are enhancers, good-enoughs, seekers, libertines, competent loners, and defeated. Enhancers grew more competent, well-adjusted, and self-fulfilled following divorce; good-enoughs coped with the ups and downs of divorce and typically remarry individuals very similar to their first spouse; seekers are motivated to find a new mate as soon as possible; libertines pursue sensation-seeking lifestyles; competent loners were well-adjusted but showed little interest in sharing their lives with others; and the defeated struggled significantly to adjust to post-married life.

7. In order for a marriage to work, couples should establish love maps, nurture fondness and admiration, turn toward each other, accept the influence of the partner, solve solvable conflicts, overcome gridlock, and create shared meaning.

8. Cohabitation is defined as living together in a sexual relationship without being married, and it is becoming more common. Cohabitating couples tend to display more equality between the sexes than do married couples. In America, cohabiting arrangements tend to be short; less than 10% last for 5 years.

For the few cohabiting relationships that do last and decide to become married, there is an open question as to whether or not cohabitating before marriage hurts subsequent marital relations. Although some research has found no difference in marital satisfaction between those couples who cohabited and those who did not, other large-scale studies have found that couples who cohabitated before marriage report less happiness in their marriage, less commitment to the marriage, and higher divorce rates than couples who did not cohabitate.

9. The following are predictors/risk factors for divorce: youthful marriage, low educational level, low income, not having a religious affiliation, having parents who are divorced, and having a baby before marriage. Most divorces occur before ten years of marriage. Consequences to the individuals getting divorced include loneliness; decreased self-esteem; anxiety about the uncertainty of the future; and difficulty in developing satisfactory, new, intimate relationships.

10. There is a lack of social and legal barriers to relationship dissolution for same-sex relationships. Same-sex relationships are similar to heterosexual relationships in reports of relationship satisfactions, loves, joys, and conflicts.

Key to Essay Questions

1. Discuss the transition from identity versus identity confusion to intimacy versus isolation, as well as the interaction between independence and intimacy, for both men and women; also include at least the first two stages of the family life cycle. You then need to discuss the different theories of relationships, marriage, and intimacy discussed in the chapter, and relate them to issues of health. While discussing health and relationships, also be sure to look at the single adult as well as adults who are cohabiting and those in homosexual unions. Finally, present what the research has indicated about developing healthy relationships for both men and women as well as the marital and parental myths that were discussed in the chapter.

2. Explore the relationships among gender, parental roles, and intimacy, including suggestions by Gottman for determining whether a marriage will work, strategies suggested for remarried couples living in stepfamilies (having realistic expectations is useful before divorce, too), and how men and women understand the world and communicate differently. Add your own thoughts on how to improve communication and interactions between men and women and how to help partners stop blaming each other for problems. You might also mention that if the relationship does not work out, there are advantages and learning opportunities inherent in the aftermath of a relationship breakup.

Research Project 1:
Checking Out the Myths

PLEASE NOTE: THIS PROJECT INVOLVES STUDYING OTHER PEOPLE. PLEASE CHECK WITH YOUR INSTRUCTOR TO SEE IF YOU NEED TO COMPLETE AN INSTITUTIONAL RESEARCH BOARD PROTOCOL BEFORE BEGINNING THIS PROJECT.

Interview six other college students to assess their beliefs about marriage and parenting. Based on the material in the chapter, develop a 10- to 15-item questionnaire that first asks how they define love; then reword the myths about marriage and parenting so that you can assess how much they know about these two topics. Record your respondents' sex and age and any other demographic information you consider to be relevant (for example, educational level, ethnicity). Classify each participant's definition of love using one of the systems discussed in the text (for instance, Sternberg), which will help you determine whether your respondents have a romantic view of love.

1. What patterns do you notice in your interviews?

2. Were your observations consistent with what you expected based on the research described in the text? Explain your response.

3. What might you conclude about the college students' beliefs and knowledge about marriage and parenting?

4. How do you think college students might gain more realistic perceptions of marriage and parenting before they get married?

Research Project 2:
Improving Male-Female Relationships

Find two empirical studies (professional journal articles) in the PsycINFO or PsycARTICLES databases at your campus library. The articles should focus on adult sex differences in any area that interests you (skills, attitudes, beliefs, practices, and so on). For each article, outline the goals of the study, the sample characteristics of the adults measured (age, ethnicity, socioeconomic status, gender breakdown, and so forth), the methods used to measure their variables (interviews, surveys, observations, and so on), the main results of the study, and the conclusions drawn from these results. Compare the articles and determine what they seem to agree and disagree on. Then compare the articles (especially their introduction and conclusion sections) to the material in the text. Make a table that summarizes the main areas where the three sources agree and disagree. Mark items in the articles that would be good information to add to the textbook chapter. Write a three-page paper based on these articles and on what you have learned in this chapter, outlining the differences that men and women exhibit in terms of relating to each other, dealing with other relationships, dealing with family matters, dealing with work, and other topics of interest to you. Also discuss areas where no sex differences were found at all. Then describe ways that you believe this research might help people improve their relationships and their lives in general.

Personal Application Project 1:
Reflecting on What You Learned

Consider what you read in Chapter 12; then answer the following questions.

1. What information in this chapter did you already know?

2. What information in this chapter was totally new to you?

3. How can you use that new information in your own life?

4. What information in this chapter was different from what you previously believed?

5. How do you account for the differences between what you believed and what you learned?

6. What is the most important thing you learned from reading this chapter?

7. Write a three-page paper about your own early adulthood socioemotional development in terms of the way you conceptualized yourself (for example, mental health, relationship quality) before and then after reading the text. Outline things you wish you would have known sooner.

Personal Application Project 2:
Consider Your Own Development and Relationships

This project will assist you in understanding your own socioemotional development in terms of personality and relationships. First, determine your own temperament characteristics as a child (if possible, get input from the people who knew you when you were growing up), and reflect on your own early attachment. Then look at your current level of adjustment, personality outcomes, and intervening contexts, and your current attachments, including your relationship qualities. Next, observe your relationships (friendships and romantic), and describe them according to Sternberg's classifications.

	Current Level of Adjustment	Personality Outcomes	Intervening Contexts	Current Attachments
Your childhood temperament				

	Sternberg's Classification	Other Relevant Classification(s)	Comments
Your childhood attachment level			
Your romantic relationship(s)			
Your friendship relationships			

1. How consistent were your adult outcomes (current level of adjustment, personality outcomes, and current attachments) with what might be predicted from the research cited in the text?

2. What intervening contexts may have modified the expected links between your childhood temperament or your attachment style and your later adult outcomes?

3. What issues seem particularly relevant to you in terms of the relationship between childhood temperament and attachment with later adult outcomes?

183

4. Were your observations consistent with what you might expect from the research described? Explain your response.

5. What might you conclude about relationships and the development of relationships on the basis of your observations?

6. What other conclusions might you reach on the basis of these observations?

Internet Projects

Check out the McGraw-Hill website for this text (www.mhhe.com/santrockessls). You will find numerous activities there, in particular, quizzes. Also, be patient, because there are many very worthy links on each of the sites, but they do take a little time to access. If you do not go to the links many times, you will not get the full value of the site. Please go to all links.

Please note that all website addresses in this Study Guide have been checked and were correct at the time of publication. However, websites may be discontinued or their addresses may change, so when you try to access a given site, it may no longer be viable. If that occurs, please notify the publisher so that it can make appropriate revisions in future editions of this Study Guide.

Internet Project 1:
Marriage Myths

This chapter discusses Gottman and Silver's (1999) approach to making a marriage work. Marriage myths can be detrimental to a martial relationship. Two different perspectives on marriage myths can be found at the following websites: The article at http://marriage.about.com/cs/myths/a/marmyths from the About.com website outlines several marriage myths. See also the articles linked on the left-hand column to discover more information about marriage that you may not have known. The second viewpoint can be found on a site that supports legally recognized marriages for gay and lesbian couples. See http://www.marriageequality.org/meusa/ for some facts and myths about gay couples and same-sex marriage. Explore both of these websites (check out several of the links at the About.com site and go to the Get the Facts link at the marriage equality site). Reflect on the many myths that are presented at each site and think about your own personal assumptions about marriage.

1. Were any of your own beliefs challenged?

2. How did you come to believe these "myths"?

3. How does gathering more information or a different perspective about an issue change the way you might think about that issue?

4. Were there some items that were suggested as myths that you still believe are, in fact, true?

5. What do you think accounts for the difference in perspective in those instances?

6. How has learning about marriage myths from the text and from these websites affected the way you view marriage?

7. How do you think the websites could be used to help both straight and gay couples live happier lives?

Internet Project 2:
Parenting Myths

As noted in the text, "the needs and expectations of parents have stimulated many myths about parenting." The author then goes on to list different myths, from expecting that "the birth of a child will save a failing marriage" to "parenting is an instinct and requires no training." These two myths involve parental expectations, but myths abound in other areas of parenting as well. The Breakthrough Parenting group (www.breakthroughparenting.com) presents several myths about discipline versus punishment and other topics. Visit this site and then go to a second site, http://www.keepkidshealthy.com/parenting_tips/myths/index.html and read some of the statements made here regarding the myths of parenting. Consider the myths presented in all three places (the text plus both websites)—which of them did you believe to be true and which did you know were myths? Then answer the questions below.

1. Were any of your views challenged?

2. Did gaining new information or new insights change your views?

3. Are there any views you had that were stated to be myths but that you still believe to be true? Which ones? What is keeping you from changing your position?

4. How has learning about parenting myths affected the way you view parenting?

Remember that our parents acted on what they knew and that most of them did the best that they knew how to do, often taking information from the experts of the time. However, today (after many more years of research), these older techniques may not necessarily be considered the most effective forms of parenting. So, if psychologists and developmentalists suggest that young parents today use different methods than their parents used, this does not mean our parents were "bad" people but merely that we know more today than they knew when they were raising a family.

Other Relevant Sites on the Internet

The Gay & Lesbian Alliance Against Defamation: www.glaad.org
The website for GLAAD, a national organization, provides information, support, a listing of upcoming events, and current media releases. Click on the Regional Action Map to see what is happening in your area. There are some noteworthy articles on same-sex marriages as well.

Breaking up Relationships: www.ivillage.com/topics/relation/0,,166872,00.html
This is a great resource for people thinking about breaking up or who have just broken up. The page is sponsored by iVillage and is aimed at women, but men can benefit from the information as well. It has workshops on breakup survival and turning heartache into happiness. It has quizzes to help you find out if you are ready to break up or if you would be better off without the other person. There are also message boards and interesting articles.

Gay and Lesbian Parenting Advocacy and Support Groups:
http://search.looksmart.com/p/browse/us1/us317837/us317919/us10220201/us64144/us540349/

This page from the LookSmart directory focuses on gay parenting and has a lot of information regarding advocacy, support groups, chat rooms, and upcoming events.

Baby Bag Online: www.babybag.com
Baby Bag Online provides a great deal of information on parenting infants and toddlers. It provides helpful articles, books, and listings of baby items recently recalled because of safety dangers or malfunctions.

Substance Abuse and Mental Health Services Administration:
www.mentalhealth.org/cmhs/ChildrensCampaign/
This program is run by the U.S. Department of Health and Human Services. It contains lots of information for parents, teachers, teens, and children on how to help children reach their developmental potential, avoid drug abuse, and maximize mental health.

Parent Soup: www.parentsoup.com/
This section of iVillage has great ideas for parents on such topics as arts and crafts, play activities, day care, health care, and many other parenting-related topics.

Childfree Resource Network: www.freewebs.com/childfreelinks/
This site is for people who are childless, not because of infertility problems, but because they do not choose to have children. What do you think of the humor on this site which claims to have won the "Silver Snip Award for Reproductive Responsibility"? There are cartoons about childfree lifestyles, articles, humor, quotes from famous people, information, links to other sites, and chat rooms.

Childfree By Choice: www.suite101.com/welcome.cfm/childfree_by_choice
This section on the Suite 101website provides a community for childfree adults. It has links to a lot of other articles and organizations. Check the section at the bottom called Recent Articles. There is an interesting argument there for reducing child abuse and neglect by never having children. There is even a World Childfree Day. The point of this section is that not everyone wants children.

Divorce Source: www.divorcesource.com
This website offers information on family law, custody, alimony and support, and visitation and includes specific information for all 50 states. It includes support calculators, step-by-step instructions for divorce, information on how to find an attorney, discussions of issues in family relations, and more. (People contemplating divorce should see an attorney to be sure that they are interpreting the information correctly.)

Divorce as Friends: www.divorceasfriends.com
This is the website of Bill Ferguson, a former divorce attorney, who walks you through the steps to "change both your relationship and your life." Ferguson notes that because he helped his clients "take the conflict out of divorce," 15% of his clients chose not to divorce and the remaining 85% "were able to part as friends." He gives some excellent advice about couple communication and handling divorce in a civil way that harms the children and the couple as little as possible.

Flying Solo: www.flyingsolo.com
This site bills itself as the "Life Management Resource for Divorce and Separation Issues." It provides links to information on divorce and separation (including issues of cohabitation and stepfamilies). It contains good, sound advice, especially for cases in which children are involved.

Chapter 13: Physical and Cognitive Development in Middle Adulthood

Learning Goals

1. Define *middle adulthood*, and explain how it is changing.
2. Discuss physical changes in middle adulthood.
3. Identify cognitive changes in middle adulthood.
4. Characterize career development, work, and leisure in middle adulthood.
5. Explain the roles of religion and meaning in life during middle adulthood.

Chapter Outline

THE NATURE OF MIDDLE ADULTHOOD
    Changing Midlife
    Defining Middle Adulthood

PHYSICAL DEVELOPMENT
    Physical Changes
        Visible Signs
        Height and Weight
        Strength, Joints, and Bones
        Vision and Hearing
        Cardiovascular System
        Lungs
        Sleep
    Health and Disease
    Mortality Rates
    Sexuality
        Menopause
        Hormonal Changes in Middle-Aged Men
        Sexual Attitudes and Behavior

COGNITIVE DEVELOPMENT
    Intelligence
        Fluid and Crystallized Intelligence
        The Seattle Longitudinal Study
    Information Processing
        Speed of Information Processing
        Memory
        Expertise

CAREERS, WORK, AND LEISURE
    Work in Midlife
    Career Challenges and Changes
    Leisure

RELIGION AND MEANING IN LIFE
    Religion and Adult Lives

Matching Questions

_____ 1. Ability to reason abstractly which, according to Horn, steadily declines from middle adulthood on.

A. crystallized intelligence

_____ 2. Developmental period beginning at approximately 40 years of age and extending to about 60 to 65 years of age.

B. menopause

_____ 3. Midlife transition in which fertility declines.

C. fluid intelligence

_____ 4. Accumulated information and verbal skills which, according to Horn, increase with age.

D. climacteric

_____ 5. Complete cessation of a woman's menstruation, which usually occurs in the late 40s or early 50s.

E. middle adulthood

Multiple-Choice Questions

1. According to Santrock, and as reflected in Jim Croce's song "Time in a Bottle," our perception of time depends on _____.
a. how full are our lives
b. where we are in the life span
c. our personal experiences
d. how many deadlines we have to meet

2. Freud and Jung studied midlife transitions around 1900. When comparing their work to that of today's theorists, we see that the boundaries of middle age have _____.
a. moved downward to lower ages
b. moved upward to higher ages
c. become relatively indistinct
d. stayed the same

3. The study of aging has become more prevalent with the aging of the baby-boomer generation. Which of the following statements regarding this cohort is FALSE?
a. It is the largest cohort in U.S. history.
b. It is the most educated cohort in history to pass through middle age.
c. It is the most affluent cohort in history to pass through middle age.
d. It is the cohort with the greatest political power in U.S. history.

4. Which of the following statements does NOT characterize a visible sign of aging?
a. The skin begins to wrinkle and sag.
b. Small, localized areas of pigmentation in the skin develop.
c. Hair becomes thinner and grayer.
d. Fingernails and toenails become thinner.

5. Which of the following is the most accurate perception concerning visible signs of aging in the United States?
a. Most adults gracefully accept the visible signs of aging and take no steps to alter their appearance.
b. Some aspects of aging in middle adulthood are taken as signs of attractiveness in women, but similar signs may be perceived as unattractive in men.
c. Signs of aging in men and women are perceived as unattractive in our culture.
d. Signs of aging in men and women typically elicit increased respect from people in our culture.

6. A typical person between the ages of 40 and 59 years is going to have most difficulty _____.
a. reading a wall chart at the eye-care professional's office
b. reading street signs
c. reading a newspaper
d. watching television at a distance

7. Considering normal aging processes, whose blood pressure would be expected to be highest?
a. Sally, a 60-year-old who is postmenopausal
b. Cindy, a 40-year-old who is premenopausal
c. Carl, a 60-year-old whose prostate was removed
d. Sam, a 40-year-old whose prostate is still intact.

8. An increasing problem in middle and late adulthood is _____.
a. metabolic disorder
b. arthritis
c. eczema
d. ringworm

9. Edgar plans to prevent cardiovascular problems as he nears middle age. His plans should include all the following activities EXCEPT which one?
a. controlling his weight
b. eating a low-carbohydrate diet
c. exercising
d. eating whole grains

10. Exercise can reduce the risks of metabolic disorder which include all the following problems EXCEPT which one?
a. elevated blood pressure
b. low levels of "good" cholesterol
c. abnormal insulin levels
d. excess abdominal fat

11. Ving is concerned about the risks of cardiovascular disease. He wants advice about how to avoid risks and enhance his health. He should do all the following activities EXCEPT which one?
a. exercise
b. control weight
c. eat a diet rich in fruits, vegetables, and whole grains
d. drink moderate amounts of alcohol

12. The main cause of death for individuals in middle adulthood is _____.
a. heart disease
b. diabetes
c. cancer
d. cerebrovascular disease

13. Erroneous beliefs about menopause are based on _____.
a. the fact that a majority of women experience them
b. the fact that such beliefs conform well to gender-typed beliefs about middle-aged women
c. the results of research involving small, select samples of women
d. images promoted by drug companies to sell their products

14. The type of hormonal changes that middle-aged men experience is _____.
a. loss of their capacity to father children
b. modest increase in sexual activity
c. psychological adjustment to declining physical energy
d. a dramatic drop in testosterone levels

15. When compared to that in early adulthood, sexual activity during middle adulthood is _____.
a. more frequent
b. less frequent
c. about the same
d. more dependent on physical activity

16. According to John Horn, in middle age _____.
a. crystallized intelligence increases, whereas fluid intelligence begins to decline
b. fluid intelligence increases, whereas crystallized intelligence begins to decline
c. both crystallized and fluid intelligence increase
d. both crystallized and fluid intelligence begin to decline

17. Data from the Seattle Longitudinal Study have shown that the highest level of functioning for four of the six intellectual abilities tested occurred in _____.
a. late adolescence
b. early adulthood
c. middle adulthood
d. late adulthood

18. Memory decline is more likely to occur when individuals _____.
a. must remember numbers
b. try too hard to organize it in their minds
c. do not use effective memory strategies
d. enter middle adulthood

19. Which of the following is a reason why middle-aged workers may choose to delay retirement?
a. a decline in defined-benefit pensions
b. increased uncertainty about health
c. a lack of satisfaction with their personal life
d. fear over isolation and depression

20. Leisure is particularly important during middle adulthood because it _____.
a. improves the nation's economy
b. helps adults narrow their interests
c. eases the transition from work to retirement
d. gives grandparents something to talk about with their grandchildren

21. The percentage of Americans who believe in God is _____.
a. less than the percentage who attend religious services
b. greater than the percentage who attend religious services
c. equal to the percentage who attend religious services
d. changing in comparison to the percentage who attend religious services

22. Americans generally show a strong interest in religion and believe in God. In addition, they show _____.
a. a declining faith in mainstream religious institutions
b. an increasing faith in mainstream religious institutions
c. less faith in mainstream religious institutions but increased faith in religious leaders
d. no change in terms of their faith in mainstream religious institutions but great disappointment with religious leaders

23. What is the relation between religion and the ability to cope with stress?
a. Religiousness has been shown to be an ineffective strategy for coping with stress.
b. Religiousness can help some individuals cope more effectively with their lives.
c. Religiousness often promotes guilt and anxiety, thus inducing stress.
d. There appears to be little if any relationship between religiousness and the ability to cope with stress.

24. Which of the following statements was NOT proposed as a reason that religion might promote physical health?
a. Religious individuals take fewer drugs.
b. Prayer allows people to fully experience their pain and deal with it.
c. Religion offers comfort and support which helps people deal with stress.
d. Religion promotes social networking.

25. According to Viktor Frankl, which of the following characteristics is NOT a distinct human quality?
a. spirituality
b. freedom
c. responsibility
d. altruism

True/False Questions

1. Hair becomes thinner and grayer with increasing age because of a decline in collagen.

2. "Sarcopenia" refers to age-related loss of muscle mass and strength. This is a normal part of middle adulthood development, and, unfortunately, exercise cannot reduce this loss.

3. In middle age, individuals begin to have trouble viewing objects far in the distance which forces them to wear glasses or contacts.

4. The sleep problems commonly encountered by middle-aged people can be reduced by losing weight.

5. The most common chronic disorders are heart disease for men and arthritis for women.

6. People are typically quite resilient to the effects of chronic stress. In fact, research has shown that the immune system kicks into gear and helps people remain healthy when they are faced with chronic, long-lasting stressors.

7. Health status in middle age is strongly impacted by increases in chronic disease.

8. Although chronic disorders have historically been the primary causes of death for people, today we are much more likely to die from infectious diseases.

9. Most women today become severely depressed after experiencing menopause.

10. Testosterone therapy does not relieve men's lowered sex drive in middle age.

11. One of the side effects of taking Viagra to increase sexual performance is seeing blue.

12. Isabel is 55 years old and feels that she is continuing to learn more and more each day from all the reading she does. However, she notices a slight decrease in her reasoning abilities. This trend supports the pattern Horn and Donaldson (1980) postulated regarding changes in crystallized and fluid intelligence.

13. Unfortunately, even if middle-aged people are trained to use new memory strategies, their ability to remember will continue to decline.

14. Research shows that taking regular vacations can lengthen your life expectancy.

15. Samuel knows that he is a good person and feels that he has been put on Earth to help abused children. However, he feels so overwhelmed by the problem, that he is unable to do anything about it. According to the work of Baumeister, he is lacking self-worth.

Short-Answer Questions

1. How is middle age today different from what it was in past generations?

2. Describe some of the key physical changes in middle adulthood.

3. What are the main causes of death in middle age?

4. Describe the sexual lives of middle-aged adults.

5. Explain how intelligence develops in middle adulthood.

6. What changes take place in information processing during middle age?

7. Name some issues that workers face in midlife.

8. What characterizes leisure in middle age?

9. Explain how religion is linked to physical and mental health.

10. What roles do meaning of life play in middle adulthood?

Essay Questions

1. Your next-door neighbors are a lovely couple whom you like very much. One day they both confide in you that they are fast approaching middle age and are really dreading it. They have heard that once you turn 40, everything begins to fall apart, including your sex life. What would you tell them to help them through this transition period?

2. One of your friends has come to you for advice about his aunt. She was widowed about a year ago, and since then she has become increasingly involved with the church she was brought up in, although neither she nor her husband (nor anyone in your friend's family) ever did much more than celebrate Christmas and Easter. Your friend is worried that this is a sign of her inability to cope with the untimely death of her husband, although she has never before shown any other indications of instability. In fact, he tells you that she worked full time in the fashion industry for many years, has never smoked, drinks only socially, and has had no serious physical illnesses. Your friend asks for your thoughts on how to ensure his aunt's well-being. What do you tell him?

Key to Matching Questions

1. C	2. E	3. D	4. A	5. B

Key to Multiple-Choice Questions

1. B	6. C	11. D	16. A	21. B
2. B	7. A	12. A	17. C	22. A
3. D	8. B	13. C	18. C	23. B
4. D	9. B	14. A	19. A	24. B
5. C	10. B	15. B	20. C	25. D

Key to True/False Questions

1. F	4. F	7. T	10. T	13. F
2. F	5. T	8. F	11. T	14. T
3. F	6. F	9. F	12. T	15. F

Key to Short-Answer Questions

1. What we conceptualize as middle age is occurring later than in previous generations. Additionally, more individuals are now entering middle age than in the past.

2. Some key physical changes that occur during middle age include the appearance of wrinkles and age spots, a decrease in height, and an increase in weight. Additional changes include: a loss of muscle mass and strength; joint stiffness; bone loss; a decline in vision and hearing; and an increase in blood pressure and high cholesterol.

3. The leading cause of death in middle age is heart disease, followed by cancer, and cerebrovascular disease.

4. Women typically experience climacteric and menopause during middle adulthood. Testosterone levels decline for males during this time. Although sexual behavior becomes less frequent during middle adulthood, most middle-aged adults express a moderate to strong interest in sex.

5. There are vast individual differences in intelligence during middle adulthood. Four intellectual abilities reach their highest level during middle adulthood: vocabulary, verbal memory, inductive reasoning, and spatial orientation. Horn's argument that crystallized intelligence continues to increase in middle adulthood while fluid intelligence declines is still debated and further research is needed.

6. Several changes occur in information processing during middle adulthood. Speed of information processing and working memory declines during middle-age. Verbal memory and expertise increase during middle adulthood. Practical problem solving remains stable during middle adulthood. There is some indication that metacognition increases during middle adulthood, but more research is needed.

7. As with many other areas of an individual's life, midlife is a time when an individual reflects, assesses, and evaluates his or her current work. The individual must then decide whether or not to stay in his or her current career or pursue a new goal. Some challenges or changes that middle-aged workers confront include the globalization of work, advances in information technologies, downsizing, early retirement, and pension concerns.

8. Physical changes and preparation for an active retirement make middle adulthood an important time for leisure activities. Additionally, extra income, more free time, and paid vacations increase the opportunities for leisure time.

9. Most research has found either a positive correlation between mainstream religiosity and health, or no correlation at all. However, in cults or religions that refuse medical intervention or even promote dangerous behavior, the relationship between religiosity and health can be negative.

10. With the realization of less time to live and experiencing the death of loved ones, middle-aged adults increasingly seek meaning in life. Baumeister argues that the search for meaning in life involves four primary needs: purpose, values, efficacy, and self-worth.

Key to Essay Questions

1. Describe the specific physical changes (for example, vision, hearing, wrinkles) and the changes in sexuality, noting that most women have a positive attitude toward menopause and providing the recent information about how Viagra (and newer drugs with fewer side effects) is being used by men (as well as some women) to improve their sex life, so long as the desire is still there. Discuss, too, the role that cultural attitudes play in how we feel about aging physically, as well as the differences in people's perceptions of signs of aging in men and in women. Be sure to explain the health issues and the health

practices that will allow aging people to remain vital and active (for instance, do not smoke, stay cognitively active, balance work and leisure, eat a nutritious diet).

2. Assure him that research indicates that religious involvement has been positively correlated with good health, life satisfaction, happiness, and effective coping. Do explore Victor Frankl's research on the meaning of life, and also go over the various health issues that he brought up to let him know that his aunt is on a healthy path.

Research Project 1:
Going to the Source (Reading Real Research)

Search the PsycINFO or PsycARTICLES database at your campus library for scientific articles on middle age. You may choose specific topics (for example, women's midlife transitions, menopause, empty nest, sexuality at midlife) or just look for general information about middle-adulthood development. Find two articles that interest you and read them. Outline the authors' goals and summarize the main sections. If the article is a review of other people's research, outline the main points from each section. If it is a research study, outline the participants' characteristics (age, ethnicity, sex ratio, and so on), the variables measured and the methods used (survey, interview, observation, and so forth), the results found, and the conclusions reached on the basis of those results. Finally, compare the two articles with the material in the text. Make a table comparing the three sources, and note where they agree with one another, where they seem discrepant, and especially where the articles provide new information that could have been included in the text. Write a three-page paper outlining what you now know about middle-adulthood development from these three sources as well as information that seems to be unclear or contradictory.

Research Project 2:
Community Health Brochure

In a community phone book, look through the business pages and the government pages. Also seek out any websites for relevant public health/mental health agencies. Make a detailed list of agencies that seem to be well suited for working with middle-aged clients. Make special note of any agencies that can handle ethnically diverse groups (for example, they speak Spanish; they are tied into Native American health organizations). If the websites do not give enough information, go ahead and call a few of the agencies to ask about the services they provide and whether they serve many middle-aged clients. Considering the information in this chapter, make a brochure for middle-aged adults in the community that would provide them with the information and resources needed to help promote healthy behaviors (for instance, strategies for lowering blood pressure, information on how to stop smoking, culturally sensitive marital counseling). In terms of the diversity that does or does not exist in the community, what types of issues must you consider in addition to the physical and psychological health concerns?

Personal Application Project 1:
Reflecting on What You Learned About Balancing Work, Family, Leisure, and School

While most people desire to effectively balance work, family, and leisure activities, many individuals give priority to one or two of these components. How balanced or unbalanced these factors are in your own life? How do you think your commitment to each of these areas of your life will change? In the chart below, indicate whether each factor has a high, low, or medium priority in your life now, and then indicate the priority you anticipate each will have in the future (state the approximate date). (School has been added as a factor here because that is important in your life at this time.) Then, consider how the priority you place on each of these factors is currently affecting your life.

Factor	Current Priority	Future Priority (Date:)	How It Is Affecting My Life
Work			
Family			
Leisure			
School			

1. What did you notice concerning the balance of these priorities in your life?

2. What did you notice about how these priorities affect your life?

3. How do your current priorities differ from your future priorities? What effect do you think the shift in priorities will have on your life?

4. In terms of the material discussed in this chapter, what patterns did you notice about the four factors?

5. Were your observations consistent with what you expected based on the research described in the text? Explain your response.

6. What do you conclude about your own personal development in light of these observations?

7. What plan might you make for balancing each of these factors in your life to ensure that you stay as mentally and physically healthy as possible?

Personal Application Project 2:
Consider Your Own Development

PLEASE NOTE: THIS PROJECT GIVES YOU THE OPTION OF INTERVIEWING YOUR PARENT. IF YOU WISH TO INTERVIEW YOUR PARENT PLEASE CHECK WITH YOUR INSTRUCTOR TO SEE IF YOU NEED TO COMPLETE AN INSTITUTIONAL RESEARCH BOARD PROTOCOL BEFORE BEGINNING THIS PROJECT.

Depending on your age, consider the issues of physical and cognitive changes in middle age with respect to you, or interview one of your parents to assess the changes that person has experienced. Refer to the text to see what changes typically take place in each of the areas described in the chart below, then indicate your own (or your parent's) experience in that area. Comment on consistencies or inconsistencies between what the text indicates is expected and what has been experienced in real life. Have any measures been taken deliberately or even unconsciously so that middle age is not experienced as a crisis?

Aspect of Yourself/Parent	Expected (as Indicated in Text)	Actual (as Experienced)	Comments
Visible signs of aging			
Height and weight			
Strength, joints, and bones			
Vision and hearing			
Cardiovascular system			
Sleep			
Health			
Sexuality			
Fluid intelligence			
Crystallized intelligence			
Speed of information processing			
Memory			
Expertise			
Problem solving			
Religion/life meaning			

Internet Projects

Check out the McGraw-Hill website for this text (www.mhhe.com/santrockessls). You will find numerous activities there, in particular, quizzes. Also, be patient, because there are many very worthy links on each of the sites, but they do take a little time to access. If you do not go to the links many times, you will not get the full value of the site. Please go to all links.

Please note that all website addresses in this Study Guide have been checked and were correct at the time of publication. However, websites may be discontinued or their addresses may change, so when you try to access a given site, it may no longer be viable. If that occurs, please notify the publisher so that it can make appropriate revisions in future editions of this Study Guide.

Internet Project 1:
Life Coaching

Chapter 13 talks about such issues as retirement, health, and balancing one's life. Often people would like to find balance but do not really know where or how to get started—they are not physically ill and they do not have the types of problems that would send them to a therapist, yet they would like something more out of life. A relatively new service area is life (or personal) coaching. Although not related to sports, it has the same kind of active movement and feedback to help people get the most out of their innate abilities. This type of guidance is undoubtedly not financially feasible for most students, but to get some idea of the kinds of help that are offered (and just for the fun of it), check out some life coaches' websites. The following sites are interesting, although not all are equally attractive. Go to www.reallifecoach.com; click on the Articles to Motivate and Inspire You link and read the article entitled "10 Things between You and a Great Life." Also check out www.benchmarkcoaching.com and www.thepace.org. After checking out these sites, consider how something such as coaching can help people balance their lives, reach goals they had put off to raise a family, or guide them toward achieving a sense of fulfillment in life. How would coaching be consistent with what you read in this chapter? Evaluate the information on these sites in light of what you have learned in the chapter.

Internet Project 2:
Staying Healthy

As stated in Chapter 13,.the major cause of death in middle adulthood is chronic illness. This makes it especially important to remain as healthy as possible. Go to www.nhlbi.nih.gov/, which is the website for the National Heart, Lung, and Blood Institute, a branch of the federally subsidized National Institutes of Health. The site focuses on the many chronic conditions you read about; see the A-to-Z listing of diseases. Check out the health-assessment tools, the educational tutorials, and the opportunity for the public to become involved in real medical research by participating in clinical trials.

1. How does this information supplement what you learned from the text?

2. What do you have to do to ensure that you remain healthy throughout your lifetime?

3. What additional information could you find on these pages about adults' changing hormonal processes and sexual activity? From what you learned, are these changes primarily positive, negative, or neutral?

4. How can you encourage your friends and family members to engage in a healthy lifestyle?

5. What resources are available for individuals who have chronic illnesses or any of the other illnesses mentioned in the chapter?

Other Relevant Sites on the Internet

DrKoop.com: www.drkoop.com
This is the website of former Surgeon General Dr. C. Everett Koop. It is updated daily with the latest medical research findings and health news. Also, search the site for "middle age" and see the plethora of interesting articles that pop up.

U.S. Administration on Aging: http://www.aoa.gov/
This is the site for an agency of the U.S. Department of Health and Human Services. There are great articles, press releases, new legislation updates, and health tips. Look lower on the page for the section with the heading "AoA Supported Web Sites." There are some fascinating links there.

AARP: www.aarp.org
AARP is an especially powerful organization that educates, lobbies, and provides services about and for people age 50 years and older. Especially interesting are the Care and Family, Health and Wellness, and Travel and Leisure sections. These links tie in especially well with the chapter.

MSN Money: http://moneycentral.msn.com/home.asp
MSN's Money has all the information you need for financial advice, retirement planning, wills, insurance, saving for college tuition, budgeting, and so on. It also has some very interesting articles on such topics as getting out of debt and avoiding identity theft.

"Meaning at Mid-Life": www.cedarlane.org/98serms/s980712.html
This is a transcript of a sermon given at a Unitarian-Universalist church in Maryland. Its message is inspiring to people from all faiths and backgrounds. Charlene Belsom Zellmer has many great quotes from sources as diverse as Shakespeare and the Bible, all discussing finding meaning in life at middle age. Her sermon will make you optimistic about becoming middle aged.

Chapter 14: Socioemotional Development in Middle Adulthood

Learning Goals

1. Describe personality theories and development in middle adulthood.
2. Discuss stability and change in development during middle adulthood, including longitudinal studies that address this issue.
3. Identify some important aspects of close relationships in middle adulthood.

Chapter Outline

PERSONALITY THEORIES AND DEVELOPMENT
    Stages of Adulthood
        Erikson's Stage of Generativity Versus Stagnation
        Levinson's Seasons of a Man's Life
        How Pervasive Are Midlife Crises?
        Individual Variations
    The Life-Events Approach
    Stress in Midlife
    Contexts of Midlife Development
        Historical Contexts (Cohort Effects)
        Gender Contexts
        Cultural Contexts

STABILITY AND CHANGE
    Longitudinal Studies
        Costa and McCrae's Baltimore Study
        Berkeley Longitudinal Studies
        George Vaillant's Studies
    Conclusions

CLOSE RELATIONSHIPS
    Love and Marriage at Midlife
    The Empty Nest and Its Refilling
    Sibling Relationships and Friendships
    Grandparenting
        Satisfaction with Grandparenting
        Grandparent Roles and Styles
        The Changing Profile of Grandparents
    Intergenerational Relationships

Matching Questions

_____ 1. Timetable according to which individuals are expected to accomplish life's tasks, such as getting married, having children, and establishing themselves in a career.

A. empty-nest syndrome

_____ 2. Emotional stability, extraversion, openness to experience, agreeableness, and conscientiousness.

B. social clock

_____ 3. Emphasizes that how a life event influences the individual's development depends not only on the life event but also on mediating factors, the individual's adaptation to the life event, the life-stage context, and the sociohistorical context.

C. big five factors of personality

_____ 4. Term that refers to a decrease in marital satisfaction after the children leave home.

D. generativity

_____ 5. Encompasses adults' desire to leave legacies of themselves to the next generation.

E. contemporary life-events approach

Multiple-Choice Questions

1. Hyun-Joo experiences great satisfaction through nurturing, guiding, and teaching skills to her children. Erikson's studies indicate that Hyun-Joo is dealing successfully with the psychological conflict of _____.
   a. industry versus inferiority
   b. identity versus confusion
   c. intimacy versus isolation
   d. generativity versus stagnation

2. An adult who has successfully resolved the conflict of the generativity versus stagnation psychosocial stage is most likely to _____.
   a. donate money to a scholarship fund
   b. buy a piece of a football franchise
   c. start a serious exercise program
   d. hire consultants to increase his or her business's profit margin

3. Daniel Levinson's research found that a major conflict for a middle-aged man is _____.
   a. mortality versus immortality
   b. being young versus being old
   c. empty-nest syndrome
   d. industry versus inferiority

4. Levinson's research found that the success of the midlife transition is dependent on how effectively the individual _____.
   a. accepts polarities of the conflicts as an integral part of his or her being
   b. chooses the most troublesome conflict and resolves it
   c. learns to pay more attention to the needs of others than to his or her own needs
   d. realizes the sense of urgency in his or her life and comes to terms with it

5. Lyle is 25 years old. He is just getting his own apartment and is starting to fulfill his dream of being a schoolteacher by getting his degree. He is dating different women, with no serious commitments, and is volunteering with different youth groups to decide which age group he would like to teach. According to Levinson's theory, he is _____.
   a. becoming his own man
   b. in the novice phase
   c. being constructive versus destructive
   d. incorporating polarities

6. George Vaillant's research shows that _____.
   a. a majority of middle-aged adults go through a midlife crisis
   b. the 40s are a time for reassessing and recording the truth about the adolescent and adulthood years
   c. there is a great deal of empirical research to support Gail Sheehy's observations
   d. individuals between ages 40 and 60 are more nervous and worried than those younger than 40

7. Which of the following statements regarding the midlife crisis is NOT true?
   a. The prevalence of midlife crises has been exaggerated.
   b. It is possible to experience a midlife crisis in one area of life but not in others.
   c. The most common trigger for a midlife crisis is working with attractive younger people.
   d. One-third of midlife crises are caused by stress such as the loss of a job.

8. Stage theories of adult development have been criticized for all of these reasons EXCEPT which one?
   a. Stage theories place too much emphasis on crises in development.
   b. There often is considerable individual variation in the way people experience the stages.
   c. They exaggerate the crises of middle adulthood.
   d. Many of the studies have been flawed by the investigators' questionable research techniques.

9. The contemporary life-events approach emphasizes that how life events influence the individual's development depends not only on the life event but also on all of the following factors EXCEPT which one?
   a. the individual's cohort membership
   b. the sociohistorical context
   c. mediating factors such as physical health and family support
   d. the individual's adaptation to the life event

10. Dr. Stein does not use the life-events approach in his research, because he has several criticisms of it. Which of the following is NOT likely to be one of his criticisms?
    a. It places too much emphasis on change.
    b. It does not emphasize anything about daily uplifts.
    c. It does not consider the effects of one's coping strategies.
    d. It places too much emphasis on major life events.

11. Kanner and colleagues (1981) found in their studies of the daily hassles of middle-aged adults that the adults were most concerned with _____.
    a. weight
    b. rising prices of common goods
    c. misplacing or losing things
    d. crime

12. Neugarten's (1986) "social clock" is a _____.
    a. timetable that people construct for accomplishing life's tasks
    b. way to assess how extraverted or introverted an individual is
    c. way to assess how extraverted or introverted a couple is
    d. biological timetable that guides certain of life's tasks such as bearing children

13. Stage theories of adult development have been criticized for all of the following reasons EXCEPT which one?
a. assuming there is a normative sequence of development
b. not adequately addressing women's concerns
c. not emphasizing career and work achievement as important stage-salient tasks
d. assuming that most people will encounter a given developmental stage

14. When women in nonindustrialized countries reach middle age, their status often improves in all the following ways EXCEPT which one?
a. They are freed from cumbersome restrictions placed on them when they were younger.
b. They have authority over younger relatives.
c. They have opportunities to gain status outside the home that younger women do not have.
d. They do not have to work as midwives or matchmakers any longer.

15. Paul Costa and Robert McCrae have shown that the big five personality factors _____.
a. are characterized by changes during early, middle, and late adulthood
b. became the big three as adults mature
c. are related to whether one dies early in adulthood or not
d. remain constant during the adult years

16. During the middle years, _____.
a. affectionate or companionate love increases
b. romantic or passionate love increases
c. intimate love increases
d. committed love increases

17. After 25 years of a tumultuous and difficult marriage, Andrew and Sarah have found a new lease on life and have decided to stay together. Why do marriages often turn out to be on a more even keel during middle adulthood?
a. Partners have learned to deal with their lack of financial resources.
b. Partners learn to immerse themselves in housework and chores.
c. Partners are able to suppress their negative emotions and enjoy daily life.
d. Partners engage in more mutual activities together.

18. Brad and Tina have just gotten divorced; both are 55 years old. Which reason is Brad more likely than Tina is to cite as the cause of the divorce?
a. cheating
b. falling out of love
c. emotional abuse
d. alcoholism

19. The empty-nest syndrome predicts that parents experience decreased marital satisfaction when the children leave home. Research has found that _____.
a. marital satisfaction does, in fact, decrease
b. marital satisfaction actually increases
c. conflict between parents and their children decreases
d. conflict between parents and their children increases

20. Research on permaparenting has shown that this type of parenting _____.
a. helps ensure that young adult children succeed in college
b. speeds the process by which children become responsible adults
c. has no impact on parents' postparenting lives
d. can impede children's movement toward independence and responsibility

21. Research has consistently found that _____ are more involved grandparents than _____.
a. women; men
b. young adults; older adults
c. older adults; younger adults
d. men; women

22. Which of the following pairs is most likely to have the closest relationship?
a. Margaret, age 65, and her son, Michael
b. Mildred, age 65, and her daughter, Roberta
c. Mort, age 65, and his son, Larry
d. Milton, age 65, and his daughter, Sandy

23. Middle-aged adults have been described as the sandwich generation because _____.
a. they are now responsible for taking care of grandchildren, including preparing their meals, while their adult children are at work
b. as retirees, they now spend more time at home and are able to eat together as a couple
c. they face the demands of caring for both their children and their elderly parents
d. it is now up to them to pass on family traditions to their children and grandchildren

24. If the typical pattern is followed, who is most likely to care for an aging parent?
a. Arthur, a divorced man living alone
b. Beatrice, whose children are now living on their own
c. Candice, whose three teenagers are still living at home
d. Derick, who lives with his wife and their teenage daughter

25. Mario is a proud grandfather. He loves to hear all about his grandchildren's accomplishments and loves to spend time with them. However, he refrains from giving any child-rearing advice. He is a _____ grandparent.
a. fun-seeking
b. distant
c. remote
d. formal

True/False Questions

1. Although the concept of generativity makes intuitive sense, research has not supported its importance for midlife development.

2. Recent research suggests that the struggle for identity does not end after adolescence. Rather, it continues throughout the other stages of Erikson's theory (intimacy and generativity).

3. Levinson's theory emphasizes that success at midlife involves accepting both sides of polar struggles (such as being destructive versus constructive) as being part of one's self.

4. When comparing middle-aged adults to young adults, research shows that middle-agers experience more overload stressors that involve juggling too many activities at once.

5. Older adults experience more stress than both middle-aged and younger adults.

6. Although women do face pressure to remain young, recent research shows that the 50s are considered to be the prime of life for many middle-aged women.

7. Across many cultures, personality research by McRae and others has found that older adults are less agreeable and less conscientious than younger adults are.

8. The cumulative personality model argues that because such diverse experiences have accumulated by middle age, personality tends to change quite a bit during midlife.

9. As people get older, personality is better characterized by stability than by changeability.

10. When children leave home, parents are often at a loss for what to do and feel a deep sense of marital dissatisfaction.

11. If adult children return home, it usually works out best when parents lay the ground rules and children live by them.

12. During middle adulthood, people show a decreased level of interest in friendships.

13. Although most siblings fight a lot during childhood, during adulthood, siblings develop extremely close relationships.

14. Younger grandparents are more likely to show the fun-seeking style of grandparenting than the formal style.

15. The three main reasons that grandparents are now raising their grandchildren include drug use by their own children, a sense of loss for the time they did not spend with their own children, and a desire to be generative after retirement.

Short-Answer Questions

1. Elaborate on some adult stage theories of development.

2. What is the life-events approach?

3. Explain how middle-aged adults experience stress differently from the way younger and older adults do.

4. Expand on how contexts influence midlife development.

5. What conclusions can be reached about personality stability and change during development in middle adulthood?

6. Explain how love and marriage at midlife could be characterized.

7. What is meant by "empty nest" and "refilling"?

8. Describe sibling relationships and friendships in middle adulthood.

9. What is the nature of grandparenting?

10. Describe typical cross-generational relationships.

Essay Questions

1. You have found yourself stuck in the middle of an argument between your two best friends. One says that people never change, that they are the same at age 50 as they were at 15. The other says that people are constantly changing—look at all the famous musicians who have moved on from folk to rock 'n' roll to rhythm and blues to country—even Pat Boone went from bobby socks music to heavy metal. On the basis of what you have learned from this chapter, how would you mediate between these two positions?

2. Your cousin is about to turn 40 and has confided in you his concern that he will go through a midlife crisis. He is also concerned that his wife, who will be 40 next year, will have a similar crisis. He wants to know all that you know about what will and will not predict a crisis for both of them. What will you tell him, and what will you conclude in light of the research that has been conducted?

Key to Matching Questions

1. B	2. C	3. E	4. A	5. D

Key to Multiple-Choice Questions

1. D	6. B	11. A	16. A	21. A
2. A	7. C	12. A	17. D	22. B
3. B	8. D	13. C	18. B	23. C
4. A	9. A	14. D	19. B	24. B
5. B	10. C	15. D	20. D	25. D

Key to True/False Questions

1. F	4. T	7. F	10. F	13. T
2. T	5. F	8. F	11. F	14. T
3. T	6. T	9. T	12. F	15. F

Key to Short-Answer Questions

1. Two main adult stage theories of development are Erikson's theory and Levinson's theory. Erikson argues that the seventh stage of generativity versus stagnation occurs during middle age. There are four areas for generativity: biology, parenthood, work, and culture. Levinson's theory argues that there are four conflicts that are central to middle adulthood: being young versus being old, being destructive versus being constructive, being masculine versus being feminine, and being attached to others versus being separated from them.

2. The contemporary life-events approach stresses that how life events influence the individual's development depends not only on the life event but also on mediating factors, adaptation to the event, the life-stage context, and the sociohistorical context.

3. In general, young adults and middle-aged adults experience more stress than do older adults including more stressful days, more multiple stressors, and more overload stressors.

4. Neugarten asserts that the social clock of a particular cohort can be altered by the social environment. The concept of middle age varies across cultures, and a woman's status improves with age for many nonindustrialized societies.

5. The idea of personality stability or change in middle adulthood is hotly debated. Some theorists believe that personality stabilizes around 30, whereas others see it stabilized in the 50s or 60s, and still others for even a later age. One indisputable fact is that some people show more change than do others.

6. Married middle-aged adults often state that their marriage is good or excellent. There is an increase in affectionate love at midlife, particularly for long-term marriages.

7. *Empty nest* is the term used to describe a home in which all the children have grown up and moved out. An empty nest typically is correlated with an increase in marital satisfaction. However, an increasing number of young adults are returning home to live with their parents; hence, refilling it.

8. Sibling relationships continue throughout life and vary in closeness. Friendships continue to be important throughout middle adulthood.

9. Most individuals are satisfied in their role as a grandparent. Grandparents can be fun-seeking, traditional, or distant in their style. Grandmothers typically spend more time than grandfathers do with their grandchildren. The number of United States grandchildren living with their grandparents is increasing.

10. Family members typically maintain contact across the generations. Mothers and daughters have the closest relationships. The middle-aged generation plays an important role in linking generations.

Key to Essay Questions

1. Examine all the personality studies (for example, Costa and McCrae's Baltimore study, the Berkeley longitudinal studies, and Vaillant's studies). Indicate what each study says about what does and does not change. Then come to a conclusion, based on the evidence presented, about change over the life span. What elements are most likely to change, and what aspects are probably more stable?

2. Address all the theories presented about adult development (for instance, Erikson's, Levinson's, the life-events approach) to discuss their different positions on whether a crisis is experienced by all, some, or no adults. Be sure to address gender differences and cultural differences in answering this question. Explain the difference between midlife crisis and the search for generativity, and discuss the concept of midlife consciousness.

Research Project 1:
Restructuring Perceptions of Parents

PLEASE NOTE: THIS PROJECT ASKS YOU TO STUDY OTHER PEOPLE. PLEASE CHECK WITH YOUR INSTRUCTOR TO SEE IF YOU NEED TO COMPLETE AN INSTITUTIONAL RESEARCH BOARD PROTOCOL BEFORE BEGINNING THIS PROJECT.

This project will assist you in understanding the relationship between parents and their children across the life span. Recall from the chapter that parents and their children (at all ages) do not typically have the same perception of the parent-child relationship. Develop a short questionnaire, based on the research findings described in this chapter, to assess respondents' perceptions of their parents and their relationship with their parents (and you can participate as well). Gather demographic data, such as age, sex, cultural background, and other information you think is important to understand your findings. Interview six people—two adolescents, two young adults, and two middle-aged adults. Create a chart to assist you in assessing the similarities and differences in the ways that adolescents, young adults, and middle-aged adults view their parents and their relationships with their parents. On the basis of your findings, answer the following questions:

1. What similarities did you notice among adolescents, young adults, and middle-aged adults in terms of how they perceive their parents and their relationships with their parents?

2. What differences did you notice among adolescents, young adults, and middle-aged adults in terms of how they perceive their parents and their relationships with their parents?

3. What patterns of development did you notice when comparing the three groups in terms of the material discussed in this chapter?

4. Were your observations consistent with the research described in the textbook? Explain.

5. What might you conclude about the development of relationships between children and their parents in light of your observations? Write up your results in a three-page paper discussing these issues, and support your points with material from the text and the interviews.

Research Project 2:
Assessing the Social Clock

PLEASE NOTE: THIS PROJECT ASKS YOU TO STUDY OTHER PEOPLE. PLEASE CHECK WITH YOUR INSTRUCTOR TO SEE IF YOU NEED TO COMPLETE AN INSTITUTIONAL RESEARCH BOARD PROTOCOL BEFORE BEGINNING THIS PROJECT.

The text presents a figure that shows a comparison of individuals' conceptions in the late 1950s and the late 1970s of the right age for major life events and achievements. Using the questions in that figure and those from the chart following, survey two college students, two members of your family, and two people in your community, being sure to record their age, ethnicity, education level, and gender. Look at the ages of your respondents to determine if there is any major difference from one age category to another—if there is, use age as an additional variable in your chart. Compare the responses you receive with those given in the late 1950s and late 1970s. (Because the original research was begun in the 1950s, some of the career-related Activities/Events are tied to men only. It was assumed in the 1950s that few women would pursue careers.) Record the number of your respondents who agree with the findings of each survey shown in the figure. Then answer the questions below.

Activity/ Event	Appropriate Age Range	Number Agreeing (Late 1950s Study)		Number Agreeing (Late 1970s Study)		Number Agreeing (Current Study)	
		Men	Women	Men	Women	Men	Women
Best age for man to marry							
Best age for woman to marry							
When most people should become grandparents							
Best age to finish school and go to work							
When men should settle on a career							
When most men hold their top job							
When most people should be ready to retire							
When a man has the most responsibilities							
When a man accomplishes the most							
The prime of life for a man							
When a woman has the most responsibilities							
When a woman accomplishes the most							

1. What similarities did you notice across the different studies?

2. What differences did you notice across the different studies?

3. What gender similarities and differences did you notice in all three time periods? What might you conclude about how men and women view activities/events within the context of social clocks?

4. What patterns did you notice when comparing the three time periods in terms of the material discussed in this chapter?

5. Were your observations consistent with what you expected based on the research described in the textbook? Explain.

6. What might you conclude, on the basis of your observations, about changes in attitudes about social clocks and the time frame within which society believes certain activities or events must take place?

Personal Application Project 1:
Reflecting on What You Learned

Consider what you read in the chapter; then answer the following questions.

1. What information in this chapter did you already know?

2. How can/do you use that information in your own life?

3. What information in this chapter was different from what you previously believed?

4. How was this information different?

5. How do you account for the differences between what you believed and what you learned in the chapter?

6. What is the most important thing you learned from reading this chapter?

7. Write a three-page paper analyzing your personal views about middle-aged people both before and after you read the chapter. What would you tell a loved one who was afraid of getting older and especially of having a midlife crisis? Refer to specific information from the text.

Personal Application Project 2:
Looking at Your Own Personality

The first section of this chapter presents a debate about whether personality traits over time remain relatively stable or change. Consider the various elements involved in each of the theories (for example, Erikson's crisis of generativity versus stagnation, Levinson's seasons of life [see if you can apply this to females as well], Costa & McCrae's big five), and illustrate how they do or do not describe your own experience. You can use the following chart to organize your data. Then answer the questions below.

Theory	Concepts	Do or Do Not Apply	Discussion
Erik Erikson			
Daniel Levinson			

George Vaillant			
Paul Costa and Robert McCrae			

1. What parts of your personality have remained most stable since childhood?

2. What parts of your personality have changed quite a bit over time? How do you account for these changes?

3. Which longitudinal study found results that most closely match your experiences relating to personality change and stability over time?

4. Do you think you can actively change your personality to match some of the results of these findings about people in middle age? If you are already middle-aged, did you play an active role in the changes you have experienced in your personality?

5. Write a three-page paper discussing your personality stability and change over time. Relate your experience to the longitudinal findings in the chapter, and explain why your experience either confirms or disconfirms the results of the various studies.

Internet Projects

Check out the McGraw-Hill website for this text (www.mhhe.com/santrockessls). You will find numerous activities there, in particular, quizzes. Also, be patient, because there are many very worthy links on each of the sites, but they do take a little time to access. If you do not go to the links many times, you will not get the full value of the site. Please go to all links.

Please note that all website addresses in this Study Guide have been checked and were correct at the time of publication. However, websites may be discontinued or their addresses may change, so when you try to access a given site, it may no longer be viable. If that occurs, please notify the publisher so that it can make appropriate revisions in future editions of this Study Guide.

Internet Project 1:
The Sandwich Generation

The chapter briefly discusses the sandwich generation—middle-aged adults who are sandwiched between caring for their adolescent or younger children and their aging parents. Check out the Sandwich Generation website at http://www.sandwichgeneration.info/.

1. What are the expectations of middle age? What information did you gather from the website that added to what you learned in our text?

2. Do you think the term "sandwich generation" is an appropriate one? Explain.

3. How can the information on this website help you deal more effectively with midlife (and, possibly, with the midlife crisis)

Internet Project 2:
To Change or Not to Change, That Is the Question

A major debate discussed in the first sections of the chapter deals with the stability versus the continuity of personality as we go through adulthood. Go to MIDMAC at http://midmac.med.harvard.edu/. There you will find midlife research. This site summarizes work done by the Research Network on Successful Midlife Development and offers links to research, publications, bulletins, and other useful information. After exploring this site, state your conclusions about the stability–change/continuity–discontinuity debate on personality in adulthood, and discuss your reasons for those conclusions. Support your points with specific information gleaned from the website and the chapter. What did you learn on the website that helped clarify your thinking about middle age? Should some of the information from the site be added to the text's discussion of middle age?

Other Relevant Sites on the Internet

Midlife Crisis Support for Men and Women Club: www.midlifeclub.com/
This organization provides an online support group and chat room dealing with the struggles of midlife. There are some interesting articles and books. Do you think that the people who sponsor this site know about the research on the rarity of midlife crises that was cited in the chapter?

ThirdAge: www.thirdage.com
This is a forum for adults over age 40 that presents a wide range of topics from dating to dieting to family issues.

AARP: www.aarp.org
AARP is a powerful organization that educates, lobbies, and provides services about and for people age 50 years and older. Check out the sections on Health and Wellness, Travel and Leisure, and Money and Work.

Chapter 15: Physical and Cognitive Development in Late Adulthood

Learning Goals

1. Characterize longevity and the biological theories of aging.
2. Identify health problems in older adults and how they can be treated.
3. Describe the cognitive functioning of older adults.
4. Discuss aging and adaptation to work and retirement.
5. Describe mental health problems in older adults.

Chapter Outline

LONGEVITY, BIOLOGICAL AGING, AND PHYSICAL DEVELOPMENT
    Longevity
        Life Span and Life Expectancy
            Differences in Life Expectancy
        Centenarians
    Biological Theories of Aging
        Cellular Clock Theory
        Free-Radical Theory
        Hormonal Stress Theory
    The Aging Brain
        The Shrinking, Slowing Brain
        The Adapting Brain
        The Nun Study
    Physical Development
        Physical Appearance and Movement
        Sensory Development
            Vision
            Hearing
            Smell and Taste
            Touch and Pain
        The Circulatory System and Lungs
    Sexuality

HEALTH
    Health Problems
        Causes of Death in Older Adults
        Arthritis
        Osteoporosis
        Accidents
    Exercise, Nutrition, and Weight
        Exercise
        Nutrition and Weight
    Health Treatment

COGNITIVE FUNCTIONING
    Multidimensionality and Multidirectionality

Matching Questions

_____ 1. Concentrating on more than one activity at the same time.   A. life span

_____ 2. Upper boundary of life, the maximum number of years an individual can live.   B. divided attention

_____ 3. Focusing on a specific aspect of experience that is relevant while ignoring others that are irrelevant.   C. sustained attention

_____ 4.Refers to the number of years that will probably be lived by the average person born in a particular year.   D. life expectancy

_____ 5. State of readiness to detect and respond to small changes occurring at random times in the environment.   E. selective attention

Multiple-Choice Questions

1. With improvements in medicine, nutrition, exercise, and lifestyle, our _____.
   a. life span has increased
   b. life expectancy has increased
   c. life expectancy has stayed the same, but our lives are healthier
   d. life expectancy has dropped, but the quality of life has improved

2. Gender differences in longevity can be attributed to _____.
   a. social factors
   b. lifestyle choices
   c. biological factors
   d. social, lifestyle and biological factors

3. Hiromi lives on the island of Okinawa in Japan. She is 97 years old and very healthy. According to research on the citizens of Okinawa, which factor might NOT explain Hiromi's longevity?
   a. She has never been tempted to commit suicide.
   b. She continues to work at her fruit-stand job.
   c. She prays daily.
   d. She eats a healthy diet of eggs and dairy products.

4. Hayflick's research indicates that as we age, our cells become increasingly less capable of dividing, and that our cells will divide a maximum of about _____ times.
   a. 25 to 50
   b. 50 to 65
   c. 75 to 80
   d. 80 to 90

5. Research expanding Hayflick's cellular clock theory found that cells die because _____.
   a. they disintegrate over time
   b. they become too large and are no longer able to sustain themselves
   c. the telomeres, or DNA sequences that cap the chromosomes, become shorter over time
   d. the RNA in our bodies is programmed to stop sending nutrients to the cells over time

6. People age because inside their cells normal metabolism produces unstable oxygen molecules that ricochet around the cells, thus damaging DNA and other cellular structures. This is the _____.
   a. free radical theory of aging
   b. cellular clock theory of aging
   c. hormonal stress theory of aging
   d. mitochondrial theory of aging

7. All the following are normal declines in vision due to aging EXCEPT which one?
   a. diminished tolerance for glare that reduces night vision
   b. slower dark adaptation, taking longer to recover vision when going from light to dark areas
   c. decreased ability to detect events in the center of the visual field
   d. reduction in the quality or intensity of light reaching the retina

8. Rosa's eyes have cloudy, opaque areas in the lens that prevent light from passing through, causing her to have blurred vision. Rosa's visual problem is _____.
a. macular degeneration
b. cataracts
c. glaucoma
d. presbyopia

9. The leading cause of death among the elderly is _____.
a. heart disease
b. cancer
c. influenza
d. diabetes

10. A disorder of old age associated with calcium and vitamin D deficiencies, estrogen depletion, and lack of exercise is _____.
a. arthritis
b. osteoporosis
c. pernicious anemia
d. depression

11. To prevent osteoporosis and broken bones, middle-aged women should do all the following things EXCEPT which one?
a. talk to their doctor about possibly taking estrogen replacement therapy
b. eat foods rich in calcium
c. avoid smoking
d. stop lifting weights, because it increases the chance of breaking bones

12. Who is most likely to get osteoporosis?
a. Veronique, who is a voluptuous Frenchwoman
b. Virginia, who is a large-framed Mexican woman
c. Velma, who is a petite Englishwoman.
d. Victor, who is an average-sized Italian man

13. Which statement regarding the decline in processing speed in older adults is FALSE?
a. It is probably due to a decline in functioning in the central nervous system.
b. Exercise may affect the extent to which processing speed declines.
c. Aerobic exercise can improve reaction time.
d. It is associated with declines in social support.

14. Pablo is 80 years old and finds that when he has Sunday dinner with his extended family of 15 people, he cannot focus on one person's voice in all the noise. This is a fairly typical decline in _____.
a. auditory processing speed
b. divided attention
c. selective attention
d. sustained attention

15. Evelyn, who is 105 years old, is active in her community and continues to play the piano at social gatherings. She loves to tell stories about when she was a little girl. On the basis of the research on memory and aging, we could expect that _____.
   a. she believes her memory to be accurate, but in reality it has become increasingly inaccurate as she has aged
   b. her memory of the events is accurate, and she is telling the stories as they happened
   c. her memory of the events is accurate, but she is probably adding a lot to her stories that did not happen
   d. she can no longer remember these events very well, but she wants to entertain her audience, so she pretends her memory is good

16. As we proceed into late adulthood, we can normally expect the least amount of decline in _____.
   a. episodic memory
   b. working memory
   c. semantic memory
   d. perceptual speed

17. Older adults are most likely to forget _____.
   a. the bottom items on a written list of items they need from the hardware store
   b. how to drive a car
   c. what items they wanted to buy at a grocery store
   d. how to play golf

18. Which of the following statements about memory and aging is FALSE?
   a. Positive or negative beliefs about one's memory skills are related to actual memory performance.
   b. Health, education, and socioeconomic status can influence an older adult's performance on memory tasks.
   c. Research has found that maintaining good health can eliminate memory decline.
   d. Using familiar tasks in research reduces age decrements in memory.

19. Wisdom is required in which of the following?
   a. remembering a grocery list
   b. braking when a pedestrian steps out in front of your car
   c. helping a son keep his marriage from falling apart
   d. helping a granddaughter with her algebra homework

20. The research on wisdom suggests that _____.
   a. wisdom involves the ability to use abstract ideas
   b. although not all old people are wise, generally speaking, wisdom comes with age
   c. older adults who demonstrate wisdom are faster at processing ideas than those who are less wise
   d. there are no age differences in wisdom

21. Which of the following statements concerning cognitive skills in the elderly is the most appropriate?
   a. Training has little effect on slowing declines.
   b. An increasing number of developmentalists have found that the elderly can be retrained.
   c. Memory is the only cognitive skill that can be improved by training.
   d. A shift from factual knowledge to wisdom occurs in most elderly adults.

22. Regarding older workers and younger workers, all of the following statements are true EXCEPT which one?
a. Older workers have better attendance records.
b. Older workers have fewer accidents.
c. Older workers have more disabling injuries.
d. Older workers are more productive.

23. What percentage of the average worker's life can he or she expect to spend in retirement?
a. 1% to 5%
b. 6% to 9%
c. 10% to 15%
d. 16% to 20%

24. The retiree who would be expected to have the POOREST adjustment to retirement is _____.
a. Zachary, who has a Ph.D. in sociology and has been saving for retirement for the past 30 years
b. Yoel, a widower who has worked in a minimum-wage construction job since high school graduation
c. Xanath, an interior decorator who has decided to move to France to attend art school at the Sorbonne
d. Wilma, a widow who volunteers as a guide at the art museum

25. Although depression is not found in higher levels in the elderly than in the middle-aged, after about age 85, we do find higher levels. Which of the following factors has NOT been suggested to explain this trend?
a. changes in neurotransmitter levels
b. cognitive impairments
c. women making up the majority of those in this group
d. socioeconomic status

True/False Questions

1. The United States boasts the highest life expectancy at birth today.

2. The gender disparity according to longevity is particularly evident in people older than 85 of whom 70% are female.

3. Recent research suggests that overeating helps destroy free radicals by flooding the cells with carbohydrates.

4. Free-radical decay is thought to be one of the causes of aging which happens when oxidative damage occurs in the cell.

5. Physical activity can increase brain volume in older adults.

6. Because loss of muscle mass is a normal part of the aging process, exercise cannot slow down this process.

7. When elderly adults in nursing homes were given more control over their daily lives, they felt happier and died sooner, because they were finally at peace.

8. Older people's sustained attention abilities do not decline with age.

9. Eighty-five-year-old Faisal tells his neighbor that he remembers what happened before World War II better than what happened last week. However, research finds that older people do not have very accurate memories of things that happened a long time ago.

10. Because implicit memories are hidden so much deeper below the cognitive surface, they are more likely to be forgotten than are explicit memories.

11. Recent research suggests that older people take longer to retrieve semantic memories, but their accuracy is just as good as younger individuals.

12. Although intelligence centers on practical knowledge systems and solving everyday problems, research suggests that wisdom comes only when one has found a spiritual center and can help others.

13. Because cognitive decline is a normal part of aging, cognitive training has been shown to be ineffective in improving the mental functioning of older adults.

14. If an older person is very flexible and comfortable without a structured environment, he or she will probably adjust well to retirement.

15. Early-onset Alzheimer's disease is rare and affects people 30 to 60 years of age.

Short-Answer Questions

1. Distinguish between life span and life expectancy.

2. List some common health problems and the leading causes of death in older adults.

3. Explain how exercise, nutrition, and weight influence development in late adulthood.

4. Elaborate on some options and issues in the health treatment of older adults.

5. Explain the changes in cognitive processes that take place in aging adults.

6. How do education, work, and health affect cognition in aging adults?

7. Discuss the concept of "use it or lose it."

8. To what extent can older adults' cognitive skills be trained?

9. What characterizes the work of older adults?

10. Explain how individuals can adjust effectively to retirement.

Essay Questions

1. Your next-door-neighbor is an 87-year-old woman who knows you have been taking this class in life-span development. She confides in you that she feels she is slowing down and cannot quite do the things she used to do. Also, she feels that her doctors do not listen to her; they just say, "Rose, you're in

great shape for a woman your age." What would you tell Rose about the aging process, how to keep healthy, and how to get the best possible medical assistance?

2. Your mother is CEO of a large corporation that offers an excellent retirement package. However, after evaluating a survey conducted of the employees, she is now concerned that relatively few employees have made any plans for their retirement. Because you are taking this life-span development class, she has asked you to address her employees about retirement, their need to plan for the future (including both continuing work and retirement), and what they can expect once they do decide to retire. What will you tell them?

Key to Matching Questions

1. B	2. A	3. E	4. D	5. C

Key to Multiple-Choice Questions

1. B	6. A	11. D	16. C	21. B
2. D	7. C	12. C	17. C	22. C
3. D	8. B	13. D	18. A	23. C
4. C	9. A	14. C	19. C	24. B
5. C	10. B	15. A	20. D	25. A

Key to True/False Questions

1. F	4. T	7. F	10. F	13. F
2. T	5. T	8. T	11. T	14. T
3. F	6. F	9. T	12. F	15. T

Key to Short-Answer Questions

1. Life expectancy refers to the number of years that will probably be lived by an average person born in a particular year. Life span is the maximum number of years any member of a species has been known to live.

2. The most common chronic disorder in late adulthood is arthritis. Osteoporosis is another health problem of concern in late adulthood. Another concern is accidents, since they are usually more debilitating in old age then earlier in life. The majority of adults die of heart disease, cancer, or stroke.

3. Exercise can help mitigate the physical decline experienced during late adulthood. Being overweight is correlated with an increased morality rate. Some research indicates that calorie restriction can increase the life span in animals, but most nutritional experts do not recommend calorie restriction at this time. Proper nutrition is important for slowing the aging process, improving health, and maintaining cognitive performance.

4. Although the majority of older adults prefer to maintain independent living or live with loved ones, this is not always possible. About 3% of adults over 65 and 23% of adults over 85 reside in a nursing home. The quality of nursing homes varies tremendously. For optimal health, nursing homes should provide residents options for control, teaching of coping skills, and personnel with positive attitudes toward older adults.

5. Cognitive mechanics are more prone to decline with aging, whereas cognitive pragmatics may remain stable or even improve. For example, the brain decreases in volume with age, but attention span remains stable.

6. Education, a cognitively oriented job, good health, and exercise are associated with higher cognitive functioning in older adults.

7. Older adults who engage in cognitive activities have higher cognitive functioning than those who do not.

8. Training can increase the cognitive abilities of many older adults; however, there is some loss of plasticity.

9. Fewer men over 65 continue to work full-time than at the beginning of the 20th century. However, more men now work part time.

10. Individuals who are healthy, have adequate income, are active, are well educated, have an extended social network of friends and family, and are satisfied with their lives before they retire adjust best to retirement.

Key to Essay Questions

1. Summarize everything in this chapter, including age changes in the brain and in the sensory, circulatory, and respiratory systems; also let her know there is no need to expect a reduction in her sexual activity. Then let her know about the various health issues, including the diseases that are common, and what she can do to reduce her risk factors (for example, positive emotions, taking calcium, exercising), also explaining what has and has not yet been determined about the use of supplements ("yes" on calcium and antioxidants, but either too little is known about some of the others or they pose potential risks). Finally, help her develop techniques to talk effectively with her physicians, pharmacist, and family members about her health needs and how to find the types of information and health care that are appropriate for her. Do be sure to let her know about the research by Langer, Rodin, and Schultz about the importance of maintaining control (or at least the perception of control) for living a longer, healthier life.

2. First address changes in work patterns from the early 20th century through today, and look at how many older adults are not continuing to work either full time or part time, noting that as the Age Discrimination Act now stands, unless there is an issue of safety (for example, fire or police departments), employers are prohibited from firing older workers. Address the issue of who adjusts best to retirement, pointing out ways to retain a sense of control and self-determination, which are so important for continued health and well-being—something people are sure to want when they finally have time to enjoy life. You might also talk about mental health issues such as depression and spirituality as they relate to the aging population.

Research Project 1:
The Nuns' Study and Other Research

Do a search for two articles on the aging brain using the PsycINFO or PsycARTICLES database at your campus library. Search for terms such as "brain and old age" or "aging brain." Find two articles in professional research journals and read them. You might even come across one from the Nun Study by Dr. Snowden discussed in the chapter. Outline the goals of each article, the characteristics of the samples used (age, ethnicity, gender, education level), the methods used (survey, interview, observation, intelligence tests, and so on), a brief summary of the results, and the conclusions the authors come to regarding the aging brain. Compare these two articles with the research described in the text, especially that from the Nun Study. One thing you might find as you delve further into this topic is that remaining active does not necessarily prevent Alzheimer's, but it does appear to delay the onset of symptoms. What advantage do you see to that? Another thing you'll find is that early life experiences and abilities seem to be connected to later life lucidity on the one hand, but, on the other hand, keeping your mind and body challenged acts as a buffer. As you read more about this topic, consider what you have read in Chapter 15, and answer the following questions:

1. What did you notice in your reading of the research articles that was consistent with what you read in the chapter?

2. What differences did you notice between the articles and what you read in the chapter? How would you explain those differences (if there were any)?

3. What might you conclude, on the basis of your reading, about cognitive changes with age?

4. Was there anything intriguing or important that you would add to the textbook's coverage of this topic?

Research Project 2:
Retirement Planning

PLEASE NOTE: THIS PROJECT ASKS YOU TO INTERVIEW PEOPLE. PLEASE CHECK WITH YOUR INSTRUCTOR TO SEE IF YOU NEED TO COMPLETE AN INSTITUTIONAL RESEARCH BOARD PROTOCOL BEFORE BEGINNING THIS PROJECT.

First, consider your own present situation with regard to career planning and retirement planning in light of the material presented in the text. Then, interview three people of different ages (for instance, middle-aged, young-old, and already retired), asking them about the type of job they currently hold or if they are currently retired, the type of career path that they see for themselves or that they followed while employed, the plans they have made for their retirement (whether still working or retired), and what they expect they will be doing or expected they would be doing at retirement. Ask those who have already retired what they are currently doing with their time and if they are doing what they anticipated. Look, too, at the factors that predict good adjustment to retirement (for example good health, adequate income, better education, support system, flexibility). Chart what you learn from these interviews in a way that makes it easy to understand the relevant factors and progressive steps you noticed for adjusting well to retirement. Were your findings consistent with what you expected based on the text (for instance, people who are further away from retirement having not yet begun to plan)? What have you learned in terms of your own retirement plans?

1. What similarities did you notice among your respondents in terms of how they have planned for retirement? Was age a predictive variable?

2. What differences did you notice among your respondents in terms of how they have planned for retirement? Was age a predictive variable?

3. How did personal factors (for example, personality traits, support system, health) affect people's retirement plans in terms of the material discussed in this chapter?

4. Were your observations consistent with what you might expect from the research described? Explain your response.

5. What might you conclude about retirement planning on the basis of your observations, combined with the information in the chapter? What would you advise people so that they can have a positive retirement experience??

Research Project 3:
Maintaining a Challenging Life in Old Age

PLEASE NOTE: THIS PROJECT ASKS YOU TO OBSERVE AND INTERVIEW PEOPLE. PLEASE CHECK WITH YOUR INSTRUCTOR TO SEE IF YOU NEED TO COMPLETE AN INSTITUTIONAL RESEARCH BOARD PROTOCOL BEFORE BEGINNING THIS PROJECT.

Visit two local senior centers. Your choices might include a nursing home, an assisted living center, a senior day care, or a center for active older adults. Note which people are active and involved and which seem isolated and withdrawn. Get permission to interview an elderly person of each type. Determine from them what it is that they believe keeps them active or withdrawn, involved or isolated, happy or unhappy, and so on. Note what the text says about keeping mentally active, staying physically healthy, reducing cognitive decline, adapting to work and retirement, maintaining good mental health, and having an interest in religion or the meaning of life. Combining your observations and interview findings with the information in the text, and design your ideal programs to help older adults maximize and enjoy their lives by remaining as active and involved as their health allows. Also include responses to the following questions.

1. Did you notice that some of the people who have a sense of well-being may have more physical handicaps and chronic health problems than do some who seem unhappy? What would account for this?

2. What part does religion play in your respondents' sense of well-being and satisfaction with life?

3. Is what you learned from these interviews consistent with what you read in the text? Explain your response.

4. What might you conclude, on the basis of your observations, about maintaining a challenging life in old age?

Personal Application Project 1:
Can You Live to Be 100?

PLEASE NOTE: THIS PROJECT ASKS YOU TO STUDY OTHER PEOPLE. PLEASE CHECK WITH YOUR INSTRUCTOR TO SEE IF YOU NEED TO COMPLETE AN INSTITUTIONAL RESEARCH BOARD PROTOCOL BEFORE BEGINNING THIS PROJECT.

Take the Longevity Test at http://www.hbhealthonline.com/longevity-test.html to predict your longevity. Where do you rank? Ask family members and friends to take the test to see where they rank. How does your score compare with theirs and with the scores of your classmates? What steps could you take to extend your life expectancy? Have you already taken any steps to increase your chances of aging well? Write a three-page paper that deals with these issues. Also, discuss the lifestyle choices you have made in the past, what your current lifestyle is like, and what steps you are going to start to take right now after having read this chapter, to increase your chances of a long life. Or do you feel that you do not really want to live a long life? If not, explain your reasons. Moreover, comment on some of the items in the test and how you feel about the fact that some are controllable and some are not. How would you summarize your overall perspective on your own aging?

Personal Application Project 2:
Your Aging Relative

PLEASE NOTE: THIS PROJECT ASKS YOU TO INTERVIEW ANOTHER PERSON. PLEASE CHECK WITH YOUR INSTRUCTOR TO SEE IF YOU NEED TO COMPLETE AN INSTITUTIONAL RESEARCH BOARD PROTOCOL BEFORE BEGINNING THIS PROJECT.

Interview an elderly person in your own family. This person should be over 70 and be able to answer questions. Devise a 10-item questionnaire based on 10 issues of interest in the text. Think of questions that would help you determine whether your family member's experience mirrors or disagrees with research findings in the text. You want to ask your family member what keeps him or her going at his or her age, how important a positive attitude is (or is it all the luck of our genes?), whether religion is an important part of his or her life, and how he or she adjusted to retirement. Write a three-page paper describing the experiences of your family member and analyzing how positive or negative his or her aging process has been. Compare the person's experiences to those described in the text, and explain why you think they are consistent or why they seem divergent.

Personal Application Project 3:
Consider Your Own Development

Chapter 15 presents many factors relevant to healthy cognitive development in later years. Evaluate these factors in your own life to assess whether you are currently engaging in activities that are likely to promote a satisfying later life for you (and what you are doing), what aspect of your life would be affected, and if there are any changes you might consider making to offer the greatest opportunities for enjoying your later years. Complete the chart; then answer the following questions.

Aspect of Your Self	Current Status and Current Activities	Aspect of Life Affected	Changes to Enhance Later Years
Education/learning/training			
Work			
Health (exercise, nutrition, etc.)			
Use/disuse			
Retirement plans (financial, social, etc.)			
Mental health			
Safety needs			
Spiritual self			
Other (describe)			

1. What aspects of your current life do you see as leading toward satisfying later years? Explain why.

2. What aspects of your current life do you see as needing change in order to provide you with optimum satisfaction in later years? What specific changes do you plan to make?

3. You may see that making some changes in your life right now could help lay the foundation for a more satisfying life as you get older, but you choose not to make those changes. If that's the case, what is holding you back from making the changes? What might motivate you to make changes?

4. What have you learned about yourself by doing this project?

Internet Projects

Check out the McGraw-Hill website for this text (www.mhhe.com/santrockessls). You will find numerous activities there, in particular, quizzes. Also, be patient, because there are many very worthy links on each of the sites, but they do take a little time to access. If you do not go to the links many times, you will not get the full value of the site. Please go to all links.

Please note that all website addresses in this Study Guide have been checked and were correct at the time of publication. However, websites may be discontinued or their addresses may change, so when you try to access a given site, it may no longer be viable. If that occurs, please notify the publisher so that it can make appropriate revisions in future editions of this Study Guide.

Internet Project 1:
Check Out the Biological Theories of Aging

There are a host of websites that deal with aging. One that offers particularly useful and up-to-date information is sponsored by the Health and Aging Organization: www.healthandage.com/. Here you will find some fascinating articles on topics related to health and aging. In addition to featured articles, there is a "Health Centers" menu where you can investigate topics that interest you. Investigate what this site has to offer, and answer the following questions.

1. What did you learn that supplemented the information in Chapter 15?

2. Was there anything you learned that was different from the information contained in the text? How would you explain the differences (if any)?

3. What were your feelings about aging before you read the chapter? What were your feelings about aging before you checked out this website?

4. Did your exploration of these links make you more or less concerned about your own aging or the aging of your loved ones? Or did this information not change your feelings?

5. Having read Chapter 15 and explored the links on this site, how might you change your own lifestyle to reduce risk factors for poor health and shortened longevity? What is the first step you might take?

6. Do you think it would be worth changing your lifestyle to live a longer, healthier life? Explain your response.

Internet Project 2:
Research on Aging

Perhaps one of the best sites on the Internet for information about aging is that of the National Institute on Aging, which is one of the NIH (National Institutes of Health) programs sponsored by the U.S. government. Go to http://www.nia.nih.gov/ and do a search for "anti-aging." Search under the Health Information link for topics you find of particular interest, and compare what you read with the briefer versions in the text. Write a three-page paper in the form of an explanation to your parents or grandparents. What suggestions would you have for them? What comments would you make to them about their past, present, and current lifestyle choices? Support your points with information from the chapter and the website.

Internet Project 3:
Dealing with Alzheimer's Disease

There are many sites on the Internet that deal with the subject of Alzheimer's disease. One that presents a spectrum of diverse offerings is the Mayo Clinic site (http://www.mayoclinic.com/health/alzheimers/AZ99999); take the Alzheimer's Quiz at http://www.mayoclinic.com/health/alzheimers/QZ00017.

1. In view of what you have read in these articles, how would you describe the current state of research on the origins, management, treatment, and possible cure of Alzheimer's disease?

2. Why do you think researchers take so long to put a drug on the market? What are some of the obstacles they face?

3. What information did you find on the site that should be added to the text's discussion of the disorder? Write a three-page paper analyzing the current state of information regarding this disorder as represented by what you learned on the website and in the text.

4. Are there any steps a person could take to reduce the risk of getting Alzheimer's disease, or at least to delay the onset of symptoms?

5. By the time Alzheimer's might pose a problem for you, will there be effective ways to treat this disease? To cure it? To prevent it? Explain your response.

Other Relevant Sites on the Internet

Health and Aging Organization: www.healthandage.com
You can find some fascinating articles here on topics related to health and aging. In addition to featured articles, there is a "Health Centers" menu where you can investigate topics that interest you.

Alzheimer's Disease Education & Referral Center: www.alzheimers.org/
This site covers the symptoms, causes, and treatments of Alzheimer's disease and provides lots of helpful information for families.

American Parkinson Disease Association: www.apdaparkinson.org/user/index.asp
This group's aim is to "ease the burden and find the cure." It provides free information kits, and the website has good links to news and research articles, local chapters for people to join, and lots of publications and videos.

American Academy of Anti-Aging Medicine: www.worldhealth.net/p/96.html
This is the website for the physicians and the scientists of the Alzheimer's Disease Education and Referral Center (A4M), who "are committed to the belief that aging is not inevitable." A nonprofit organization with a membership of 11,500 physicians and scientists from 65 countries, the A4M is the sole medical society dedicated to the advancement of therapeutics related to the science of longevity medicine. See their 101

Tips of Antiaging Wisdom to Living to a Fit, Vital and Robust Age 101, at www.worldhealth.net/p/4227,5678.html, and interesting articles on stem cell research and other topics.

"MIT Helps Unlock Life-extending Secrets of Calorie Restriction":
www.sciencedaily.com/releases/2004/01/040101090959.htm
This article is from Science Daily, a comprehensive site covering all areas of science. It is updated daily with the latest science news. This article discusses work on calorie restriction and longevity.

American Psychological Association: www.apa.org
Do searches on this site for any topic related to aging and psychology. A search on "memory and aging" brings up articles on successful aging, cognitive decline, and guidelines for assessing dementia. A search on "dementia" and "depression and the elderly" brings up a plethora of informative articles.

Administration on Aging: http://www.aoa.gov/
This agency is part of the U.S. Department of Health and Human Services. It covers the latest legislation, news on aging, and issues for families and professionals.

AARP: www.aarp.org
The AARP is a powerful organization that educates, lobbies, and provides services about and for people age 50 and over. There are interesting links for travel and leisure, health and wellness, and financial advice.

Chapter 16: Socioemotional Development in Late Adulthood

Learning Goals

1. Discuss key theories of socioemotional development and aging.
2. Describe links between personality and society in late adulthood.
3. Characterize the families and social relationships of aging adults.
4. Summarize how ethnicity, gender, and culture are linked with aging.
5. Explain strategies to promote successful aging.

Chapter Outline

THEORIES OF SOCIOEMOTIONAL DEVELOPMENT
    Erikson's Theory
    Activity Theory
    Socioemotional Selectivity Theory
    Selective Optimization with Compensation Theory

PERSONALITY, THE SELF, AND SOCIETY
    Personality
    Older Adults in Society
        Stereotyping Older Adults
        Policy Issues in an Aging Society
        Income
        Technology

FAMILIES AND SOCIAL RELATIONSHIPS
    Lifestyle Diversity
        Married Older Adults
        Divorced and Remarried Older Adults
        Cohabiting Older Adults
        Romance and Sex in Older Adults' Relationships
    Older Adult Parents and Their Adult Children
    Friendship
    Social Support and Social Integration
    Altruism and Volunteerism

ETHNICITY, GENDER, AND CULTURE
    Ethnicity
    Gender
    Culture

Matching Questions

_____ 1. View that our aging society is being unfair to its younger members because older adults pile up advantages by receiving inequitably large allocations of resources.

A. socioemotional selectivity theory

_____ 2. Prejudice against others because of their age.

B. selective optimization with compensation theory

_____ 3. Theory that successful aging is related to three main factors: selection, optimization, and compensation.

C. generational inequity

_____ 4. Theory that older adults become more selective about their social networks.

D. activity theory

_____ 5. Theory that the more active and involved older adults are, the more likely they are to be satisfied with their lives.

E. ageism

Multiple-Choice Questions

1. Erik Erikson believed that the final life-cycle stage that characterizes late adulthood is _____.
   a. integrity versus despair
   b. trust versus mistrust
   c. generativity versus stagnation
   d. intimacy versus isolation

2. When Rosaria sold her business and retired, she gradually became less active and began to withdraw from society. This supports the _____ theory of aging.
   a. activity
   b. life review
   c. socioselectivity
   d. disengagement

3. Omar is an older retired adult. The fact that he maintains his interest in friendships, politics, and the stock market illustrates the _____ theory of aging.
   a. engagement
   b. disengagement
   c. activity
   d. social construction

4. Activity theory holds that when one of an older person's roles is taken away, that person should _____.
   a. withdraw from society
   b. become self-preoccupied
   c. lessen emotional ties with others
   d. find a replacement role

5. Socioemotional selectivity theory argues that older adults deliberately withdraw from social contact with _____.
   a. individuals peripheral to their lives
   b. close friends
   c. family members
   d. all but a few close family members and health-care professionals

6. In socioemotional selectivity theory, an older adult narrows his or her social circles _____.
   a. because he or she is preparing for death
   b. to have social partners who satisfy his or her emotional needs
   c. because it is more difficult for him or her to maintain large social networks
   d. as he or she becomes increasingly depressed

7. Agatha is an aging actress. She can no longer do eight shows a week, but she continues to take parts in shows that play four or five times a week. Because her memory is not what it once was, she takes smaller parts with fewer lines to remember. She also takes more comedy and "character" parts so that she does not have to worry so much about seeming like a realistic person, as she knows that ageism often prevents people from taking elderly actresses seriously. This would be a good example of the _____ theory of aging.
   a. disengagement
   b. integrity
   c. socioemotional selectivity
   d. selective optimization with compensation

8. Research on changes in emotion across adulthood found which statement to be true?
   a. Older adults report experiencing more positive emotions and fewer negative emotions than younger adults.
   b. Older adults report experiencing fewer positive emotions and fewer negative emotions than younger adults.
   c. Older adults report experiencing fewer positive emotions and more negative emotions than younger adults.
   d. Older adults report experiencing more positive emotions and more negative emotions than younger adults.

9. All the following are examples of ageism EXCEPT which one?
   a. not being hired for a new job because of one's age
   b. older adults having less tasks assigned at work due to their declining cognitive ability
   c. older adults being asked to serve as "grandparents" for teenage parents
   d. being eased out of one's job because one is perceived as feebleminded due to their age

10. One special concern over the current medical system is that it is _____-oriented, whereas most health problems of the elderly are _____.
    a. care; chronic
    b. care; acute
    c. cure; chronic
    d. cure; acute

11. Because of the increase in chronic illnesses as people age, many older people are cared for in their homes. This necessitates _____.
    a. more Medicare assistance
    b. cooperation among health-care professionals, patients, and family members
    c. that doctors return to the practice of making house calls
    d. improved facilities for placing elders so that their adult children can live their lives

12. A policy issue that focuses on the greater amount of resources received by the elderly compared with those received by younger adults is referred to as _____.
a. generational inequity
b. elder care
c. ageism
d. role preoccupation

13. Anna is a typical elderly widowed African American woman living in the United States. Most likely, Anna is _____.
a. emotionally depressed
b. among the physically disabled
c. poor
d. more in control of her life

14. Generational inequality has been blamed for _____.
a. producing intergenerational conflict
b. promoting increased attention to the unique demands of the working older adults
c. reducing the allocation of resources available to older adults
d. avoiding issues about who is responsible for eldercare

15. In the United States, the older people who tend to be the poorest are _____.
a. African American females
b. Latina females
c. Asian American females
d. ethnic American males who must depend on religious organizations for assistance

16. The marriages of older adults tend to be _____ compared to younger couples.
a. more satisfying
b. based more on friendship
c. less satisfying
d. based less on shared activities

17. In most cases, when older adults choose to cohabitate, it is for _____.
a. love
b. convenience
c. independence
d. companionship

18. The number of older adults choosing to divorce has _____ since the early 1990s.
a. remained about the same
b. decreased significantly
c. decreased slightly
d. increased considerably

19. Researchers have found that adult children are more likely to have ambivalent feelings about their relationship with aging parents when ALL BUT WHICH ONE of the following characteristics were present?
a. There earlier had been a poor parental relationship.
b. There was elder abuse.
c. The relationship involved in-laws.
d. The parents were in poor health.

20. Which of the following is NOT a component of the triple jeopardy facing older female ethnic minorities?
a. ageism
b. sexism
c. racism
d. purism

21. According to the trends discussed in the chapter, all the following support systems help elderly ethnic minority individuals survive in the dominant White world EXCEPT which one?
a. families
b. income from Social Security
c. churches
d. neighbors

22. Eula is typical of elderly African American women in cities. Consequently, we would expect her to put a high value on all of the following things EXCEPT which one?
a. solitude
b. her family
c. the American work ethic
d. her church

23. Which of the following terms describes perceived control over the environment and the ability to produce positive outcomes?
a. self-esteem
b. self-control
c. self-efficacy
d. self-satisfaction

24. Researchers have found that many older adults _____.
a. are ineffective in maintaining a sense of control
b. have a negative view of themselves
c. no longer desire self-efficacy
d. are effective in maintaining a sense of control and have a positive view of themselves.

25. Which of the following is NOT a factor that is likely to predict high status for older adults in a culture?
a. Older persons have valuable knowledge.
b. Older persons control key family and community resources.
c. Older persons are permitted to engage in useful and valued functions.
d. Older persons provide flexible care for the young generation.

True/False Questions

1. Erikson would argue that for a life review to end positively, an older adult must have completed early stages of adult development positively as well.

2. Research suggests that because older adults' lives are somewhat empty, it is beneficial for them to spend most of their time thinking about the joys of their past.

3. When older adults engage in more "solitary" activities, they are happier and function better than do those older adults who engage in "productive" activities.

4. As people get older and their children move on, they have fewer needs to reach emotional goals and strive more to reach knowledge goals before the end of life.

5. Seniors tend to have more positive and balanced emotional lives than do younger adults.

6. The process of selective optimization with compensation is more likely to be effective when a person has experienced some form of loss in his or her life.

7. A recent study found that the personality traits of low conscientiousness and high neuroticism predict earlier death.

8. Being pessimistic has no effect on longevity.

9. Self-esteem remains steady throughout adulthood.

10. "Generational inequity" refers to the idea that the baby boom generation is so large that we will eventually have unequal numbers in society, with too many older people and too few children to grow up and work the jobs necessary for the economy to thrive.

11. Women are more likely to negatively stereotype older adults than are men.

12. Older adults are more satisfied with their marriages than are young and middle-aged adults.

13. Older adults tend to report closer relationships with adult daughters compared to sons.

14. Volunteering in older adulthood is associated with a number of positive health and social outcomes.

15. People who provide social support to others live longer than those who do not help others.

Short-Answer Questions

1. Discuss the selective optimization with compensation model.
2. Explain the final stage of Erikson's theory of psychosocial development.

3. What is activity theory?

4. Define the socioemotional selectivity theory, and explain how research supports it.

5. Describe some of the key challenges with eldercare.

6. What are some negative stereotypes of older adults?

7. What characterizes the relationships of older adult parents and their adult children?

8. Define and expand on the roles which social support and social integration play in late adulthood.

9. List four factors likely to predict high status for the elderly in a culture.

10. List and explain the factors that are linked with aging successfully.

Essay Questions

1. Your friend is pregnant, and her mom has confided in you that she is afraid of becoming a grandparent. She is concerned about how family relationships change as people get older. She does not want to be one of those old, isolated widows without any reason to live. Using the research in this chapter, what can you tell her about family relationships, friendships, and social support in the aging population?

2. Your classmate is confused about the different theories of aging described in the text. Which one is "correct" in terms of describing the real lives of seniors in the United States? What would you tell her to keep in mind regarding these theories and the research in the text?

Key to Matching Questions

1. C	2. E	3. B	4. A	5. D

Key to Multiple-Choice Questions

1. A	6. B	11. B	16. A	21. B
2. A	7. D	12. A	17. D	22. A
3. C	8. B	13. C	18. D	23. C
4. D	9. C	14. A	19. B	24. D
5. A	10. C	15. A	20. D	25. D

Key to True/False Questions

1. T	4. F	7. T	10. F	13. T
2. F	5. T	8. F	11. F	14. T
3. F	6. F	9. F	12. T	15. T

Key to Short-Answer Questions

1. This model proposes that aging is related to three main factors: 1. selection—reduced capacity and loss of functioning require selection of activities to continue; 2. optimization—performance in some areas

can be maintained by practice and use of new technologies; 3. compensation—occurs when life tasks require capacity beyond level of older adult's performance potential.

2. The eighth and final stage of Erikson's theory is the conflict between integrity and despair. Integrity is achieved when one looks back on their life with a positive review; despair occurs when one believes that their life was not well-spent.

3. Activity theory states that the more active and involved that older adults are, the more likely they are to be satisfied with their lives.

4. Socioemotional selectivity theory asserts that the older adults become, the more selective they are about their social networks. Individuals place a higher value on emotional satisfaction and spend more time with familiar individuals with whom they have had rewarding relationships. Research has found that older adults have smaller social networks than younger adults but about the same number of close emotional relationships. Researchers have also found that older adults, when compared to younger adults, prefer seeking emotional satisfaction in many cultures.

5. Eldercare is the physical and emotional caretaking of older members of the family (either via day-to-day physical assistance or responsibility for arranging and overseeing such care). There is ongoing concern over how eldercare can best be provided.

6. Some negative stereotypes of older adults include the perception that they are incapable of thinking clearly, learning new things, enjoying sex, contributing to the community, and holding responsible jobs.

7. The majority of older adults have living children, which play an important role in the parent's social network. Adult daughters are more likely than adult sons to be involved in the lives of an aging parent. Adult children can assist with daily living activities (such as eating, transportation, housework), as well as provide companionship. Emotional ambivalence is sometimes found in the adult child caring for in-laws, people in poor health, or if there had been an early poor parental relationship.

8. Social support is correlated with improved coping, lessening of symptoms of disease, reduced likelihood of being institutionalized, and lower rates of depression. Social integration may increase longevity, and engagement in social activities may slow cognitive decline.

9. Factors that improve an older adult's status:
a. Older persons have valuable knowledge.
b. Older persons control key family or community resources.
c. Older persons are permitted to engage in useful and valued functions as long as possible.
d. There is role continuity throughout the life span.
e. Age-related role changes involve greater responsibility, authority, and advisory capacity.
f. The extended family is a common family arrangement.
g. The culture is more collectivistic than individualistic

10. Older adults may age better by:
a. being socially active and involved.
b. maintaining or developing positive close relationships.
c. staying connected in positive ways with children and grandchildren.
d. engaging in life review.
e. knowing factors involved in successful aging and including them in life's activities.

Key to Essay Questions

1. Address the five theories of aging discussed in this chapter (Erikson's, activity, socioemotional selectivity, and selective optimization with compensation), noting that older adults' active participation in society is beneficial. Discuss the effects that health, income, gender, culture, and relationships have on an elderly person's well-being; then address the personality factors noted by Erikson and Peck. Discuss the importance of a life review and the strategies presented for successful aging (for example, Baltes's selective optimization with compensation model). Be sure to underscore the importance of relationships and support systems in maintaining optimum life satisfaction and well-being. Tell her especially about the research on siblings and friends in later life. Point out that women are particularly likely to maintain close family relationships as they age.

2. Because human lives are complicated, it is doubtful that one psychological theory will ever be considered the "right" one. However, we do know that the disengagement theory is wrong. It is not beneficial for older adults to disengage from life. All the other theories have something in common. They suggest remaining active, choosing relationships that are meaningful and investing your time into those, and optimizing the health and skills you currently have so that your life is fulfilling. Go over each theory with your classmate and point out the research findings that support each one. Also talk about the diversity that exists in different aging populations. For example, poor, ethnic minority, and female seniors may have fewer resources, lack of medical care, and poor health, which can affect the aging process. So even if we believe activity theory is a good one, it still might have drawbacks, such as not applying to certain populations who have a hard time being active because of social or health constraints. However, the active mind is always possible. Even in groups that have been marginalized, social support from family and religious organizations provide wonderful buffers against the stressors they face in life, so even they are selecting things they can do, optimizing their current skills, and compensating for areas they lack (hence, this theory seems pretty applicable).

Research Project 1:
Dealing with Diversity

PLEASE NOTE: THIS PROJECT ASKS YOU TO INTERVIEW AN INDIVIDUAL. PLEASE CHECK WITH YOUR INSTRUCTOR TO SEE IF YOU NEED TO COMPLETE AN INSTITUTIONAL RESEARCH BOARD PROTOCOL BEFORE BEGINNING THIS PROJECT.

Interview an older person who has experienced marginalization in some form (for example, is poor, is female, is an immigrant, is an ethnic minority). Ask this person how he or she feels his or her aging experience has been the same as and/or different from that of the "typical" older person. What stressors has the person faced that others might not have faced? How did the person overcome these stressors? Consider the person's risk factors and strengths. and note them in the chart below. Consider what the consequences of those risk factors could have been and then actually were for the person you interviewed. Compare what you wrote about your interviewee in the chart to information presented in Chapter 16.

As pointed out throughout this chapter, and elsewhere throughout the text, being female, ethnic, and old places women at high risk for all the problems associated with poverty and aging. Consider the various factors that may put these women at risk (for example, low educational level, prejudice) and the potential consequences that each may have (for instance, inability to access services). Write these risk factors in the left-hand column of the table. Then consider the strengths that have been noted that these women often have (such as family support) and the consequences that these may have (such as caregiving support). Chart these risk and strength factors and consequences for your interviewee and those in the text, and then answer the questions that follow.

Risk Factors	Potential/Actual Consequences
Women's role is unimportant	
Low income	

Strengths	Potential/Actual Consequences
Family support	
Religious/spiritual	

1. What did you notice about the risk factors your interviewee faced as well as their potential and actual consequences?

2. What did you notice about the strengths and their potential and actual consequences?

3. What patterns did you notice when comparing these risk factors and strengths and the information discussed in this chapter regarding ethnic minority older females?

4. Were these patterns consistent with what you might expect from the research described? Explain your response.

5. What might you conclude, on the basis of your observations, about the issues that older women (particularly minority women) and other marginalized seniors face?

6. What type of interventions (individual, community, federal, etc.) would you suggest for alleviating the problem of double and/or triple jeopardy that these women and/or men experience?

Research Project 2:
Issues in the Media

Monitor the media (newspapers, talk/news radio, and television) for a week, and keep track of when and in what context senior citizens' issues are raised. Note how often each specific issue was discussed and which issue was raised most often. How it was presented? Did you notice biased reporting? Was it presented in terms of the life-span perspective? Was it fully covered?

Throughout the life span, people are affected by different age-related stereotypes. To assess the extent of the stereotypes and myths that are perpetrated by the media, for one week keep a record of the television shows you watch and the print media (newspapers, magazines, books, and so on) that you read. Note instances of ageism and stereotypic depictions of the elderly.

1. How many elderly people appeared in the TV shows? Did they play a major role or merely have supporting or minor roles? What traits characterized each person? Were these traits positive or negative? Were they stereotypical? Describe how their portrayal could be either beneficial or detrimental to the well-being of elderly people as a group.

2. In all the media that you kept track of, what ethnic, socioeconomic, and gender differences did you notice, and how did they affect the portrayal of the elderly?

3. What social policy issues were raised, and how were they handled?

4. How much of the information meshed well with the research in the text? Or was it mostly erroneous or not based on research?

5. Discuss your findings in a three-page paper.

Personal Application Project 1:
Reflecting on What You Learned

Consider what you read in Chapter 16, and then answer the following questions.

1. What information in this chapter did you already know?

2. How can/do you use that information in your own life?

3. What information in this chapter was different from what you previously believed?

4. How was this information different?

5. How do you account for the differences between what you believed and what you learned in the chapter?

6. What is the most important thing you learned from reading this chapter?

7. Write a three-page paper on how your views of the socioemotional lives of seniors changed after reading this chapter. What messages do you think are important to tell other people regarding socioemotional development of the aging population? Did the chapter make you feel more hopeful about your own development, or are you afraid of aging? Explain your answer.

Personal Application Project 2: Engaging in a Life Review

Refer to the discussion in Chapter 16 of life reviews, and use the chart below to conduct your own life review (even if you have not reached middle age). Consider every aspect of your life, using—for example, what was most important about your childhood; what major events changed your family; what aspects of your family life are you most and least satisfied with right now; how would you like your family life to be in the future, and what can you do to bring it there; how did you get into the work you are currently in; how far along have you progressed with respect to your personal goals; what can you do to make the progress you want; do you need to adjust your goals for the future? Add other questions concerning education plans, travel, financial security, and religion/spirituality, and remember to include questions about plans for fun.

Aspects of Life	Past	Present	Future	What I Need to Change
Family				
Friends				
Education				
Career				
Travel				
Financial security				
Religious/spiritual				
Fun and leisure				
Other				

1. What have you learned about yourself, your goals, and how you have been achieving your goals from reviewing your life so far?

2. How can looking at your life help you understand how things are, why they are that way, and how you can get where you want to go?

3. What other ways could help you examine your life and who you are? Explain what they are.

4. What has been the most useful outcome of doing a life review?

Internet Projects

Check out the McGraw-Hill website for this text (www.mhhe.com/santrockessls). You will find numerous activities there, in particular, quizzes. Also, be patient, because there are many very worthy links on each of the sites, but they do take a little time to access. If you do not go to the links many times, you will not get the full value of the site. Please go to all links.

Please note that all website addresses in this Study Guide have been checked and were correct at the time of publication. However, websites may be discontinued or their addresses may change, so when you try to access a given site, it may no longer be viable. If that occurs, please notify the publisher so that it can make appropriate revisions in future editions of this Study Guide.

Internet Project 1:
The Latest on Aging News

Go to the American Psychological Association website, at www.apa.org, and do a search on "aging." What types of publications are included (for example, journal articles dealing with research, books, reports at symposia, policy papers)? What are the different topics that are covered? As you browse through the different titles, read three articles that interest you. How do these articles compare with the information in the chapter? Were there any areas that were discrepant or did not seem to agree? Take notes on the most important points from each of the articles you read. Did you come away with a more positive or more negative view of what it is like to grow old? How did this search add to what you had already learned from reading the chapter? Should anything important be added to the chapter?

Internet Project 2:
Grandparenting in the Twenty-First Century

The AARP (formerly known as the American Association for Retired Persons) is probably the strongest political voice for older adults in the United States. The Grandparenting page on the group's website, www.aarp.org/life/grandparents/, offers a wide range of information for and about grandparents. As you browse through the document titles, what types of articles do you notice, and how do you think they relate to the material in our text? What questions come to mind as you consider these articles in the context of successful aging? As you browse through the different titles, read three articles that interest you. How do these articles compare to the information in the chapter? Were there any areas that were discrepant or that did not seem to agree? Take notes on the most important points from each of the articles you read. Did you come away with a more positive or more negative view of what it is to be a grandparent? How did this search add to what you had already learned from reading this chapter and the ones before it? On the basis of what you read, what do you conclude about grandparenting today? How do the issues discussed in the grandparenting articles illuminate new trends, new roles for grandparents, and new ideas about being a grandparent? Outline the most important points and your own plan for ensuring the best possible relationships between you and your grandparents and between you and your own grandchildren, if you have any.

Other Relevant Sites on the Internet

Gray Panthers: www.graypanthers.org/
The Gray Panthers (Age and Youth in Action) is a social activism and lobbying group. The site covers the organization's history, its achievements, and its current campaigns. The group's philosophy is the motto of its founder, Maggie Kuhn, "The best age is the age you are!"

Help the Aged: www.helptheaged.org.uk/default.htm
This British organization deals with policy and social movements benefitting the elderly. It is enlightening to see what steps are being taken in the United Kingdom. The information on this site is helpful for people in the United States, because it covers topics relevant to all of us such as the effects of poverty on the elderly.

Ageism Resources: http://falcon.jmu.edu/~ramseyil/ageism.htm
This page from the website of the International School Library Media Center is a great resource for teachers and families. It provides curriculum guides and lesson plans for teachers to discuss aging issues. There are also links to literature and research on ageism.

Health and Aging Organization: www.healthandage.com
You can find some fascinating articles here on topics related to health and aging. In addition to featured articles, there is a "Health Centers" menu where you can investigate topics that interest you.

American Academy of Anti-Aging Medicine: www.worldhealth.net/p/96.html
This is the website for the physicians and scientists of the Alzheimer's Disease Education and Referral Center (A4M), who "are committed to the belief that aging is not inevitable." A nonprofit organization with a membership of 11,500 physicians and scientists from 65 countries, the A4M is the sole medical society dedicated to the advancement of therapeutics related to the science of longevity medicine. See their 101 Tips of Antiaging Wisdom to Living to a Fit, Vital and Robust Age 101, at www.worldhealth.net/p/4227,5678.html, and interesting articles on stem cell research and other topics.

Administration on Aging: http://www.aoa.gov/
This agency is part of the U.S. Department of Health and Human Services. It covers the latest legislation, news on aging, and issues for families and professionals.

Chapter 17: Death, Dying, and Grieving

Learning Goals

1. Evaluate issues in determining death and decisions regarding death.
2. Describe the roles of sociohistorical and cultural contexts in understanding death.
3. Explain the psychological aspects involved in facing one's own death.
4. Identify ways to cope with the death of another person.

Chapter Outline

DEFINING DEATH AND LIFE/DEATH ISSUES
    Issues in Determining Death
    Decisions Regarding Life, Death, and Health Care
        Natural Death Act and Advanced Directive
        Euthanasia
        Needed: Better Care for Dying Individuals

DEATH AND SOCIOHISTORICAL CULTURAL CONTEXTS
    Changing Historical Circumstances
    Death in Different Cultures

FACING ONE'S OWN DEATH
    Kübler-Ross' Stages of Dying
    Perceived Control and Denial

COPING WITH THE DEATH OF SOMEONE ELSE
    Communicating with a Dying Person
    Grieving
        Dimensions of Grieving
        Dual-Process Model of Coping with Bereavement
        Coping and Type of Death
    Making Sense of the World
    Losing a Life Partner
    Forms of Mourning

Matching Questions

_____ 1. Kübler-Ross' third stage of dying, in which the dying person develops the hope that death can somehow be postponed.

A. denial and isolation

_____ 2. Kübler-Ross' first stage of dying, in which the dying person refuses to believe that he or she is really going to die.

B. acceptance

_____ 3. Kübler-Ross' fourth stage of dying, in which the dying person comes to accept the certainty of his or her death; a period of preparatory grief may appear.

C. bargaining

_____ 4. Kübler-Ross' second stage of dying, in which the dying person may   D. anger
experience resentment, rage, and envy.

_____ 5. Kübler-Ross' fifth stage of dying, in which the dying person   E. depression
develops a sense of peace with his or her fate.

Multiple-Choice Questions

1. Elvira was brought into the hospital after a car accident. She has had a flat electroencephalogram for more than 20 minutes, and the doctors have informed her parents that there is no longer any electrical activity in her brain, but that she is still breathing. She would be considered dead from both a _____ and a _____ perspective.
   a. neurological/cortical death
   b. coma/neurological
   c. vegetative/cortical death
   d. surgeon's/neurologist's

2. Dylan watched his father suffer for a year before he died of cancer. Now Dylan wants to be sure that he retains control over any decisions made concerning how, when, and under what circumstances life-sustaining treatments will be used or withheld in the case of his own final illness. To ensure this, Dylan should prepare a _____.
   a. living trust
   b. living will
   c. last will and testament
   d. power of attorney

3. Advance directives reflecting an individual's wishes concerning life-sustaining procedures when death is imminent requires _____ physicians to diagnosis the individual as terminally ill.
   a. no
   b. one
   c. two
   d. three

4. "Active euthanasia" means _____.
   a. the self-administration of a lethal dose of a drug
   b. letting patients die naturally
   c. the intentional administration of a lethal drug dose by medical personnel to dying patients
   d. allowing dying patients to decide when painkilling drugs should be administered

5. Most people tend to find fewer ethical problems with _____ if the individual is old and terminally ill.
   a. involuntary euthanasia
   b. active euthanasia
   c. passive euthanasia
   d. assisted euthanasia

6. The only state in the United States that allows active euthanasia is _____.
a. Florida
b. California
c. Kansas
d. Oregon

7. The debate over whether or not to remove the feeding tube of Terri Schaivo, who was in a long-term coma, highlighted the controversy surrounding _____.
a. active euthanasia
b. passive euthanasia
c. palliative care
d. hospice

8. Hospice care typically does all of these EXCEPT which one?
a. make every effort to prolong life
b. bring pain under control
c. help dying patients face death in a psychologically healthy way
d. include the dying individual's family

9. The view of most societies is that death is _____.
a. the end of existence
b. a biological end to the body but not an end to the spirit
c. a time to celebrate the person's life
d. a terrifying experience

10. The members of what culture react angrily to death, because it is believed to be caused by magic and demons?
a. United States
b. Gond culture of India
c. Tanala culture of Madagascar
d. Mexican culture

11. Denial of death in the United States takes ALL BUT WHICH ONE of the following forms?
a. use of phrases like "passing on"
b. the never-ending search for a fountain of youth
c. the emphasis on human suffering rather than on prolonging life
d. rejection of the elderly

12. According to Kübler-Ross's theory, the stage of death when a person is most likely to request to be alone is _____.
a. denial
b. bargaining
c. anger
d. acceptance

13. When a terminally ill patient becomes depressed, others should _____.
a. attempt to cheer up the patient
b. talk about anything other than death
c. tell the medical staff about it
d. accept the depression as normal

14. All the following are criticisms of Kübler-Ross's stages of dying EXCEPT which one?
a. Research shows that people rarely experience the feelings she laid out.
b. Kübler-Ross neglected to take into account the patients' support systems.
c. The existence of the five-stage sequence has not been demonstrated in research.
d. Reactions to death take many forms, all of which can be considered to be "normal."

15. A major concern with long-term grief is the potential for _____.
a. suicide and violent behavior
b. isolation and keeping one's feelings locked away
c. sadness turning to uncontrollable rage
d. negative consequences on physical and mental health

16. Cross-cultural research indicates that healthy grieving involves _____.
a. breaking bonds with the deceased
b. survivors returning to their autonomous lifestyles
c. forgetting the deceased as quickly as possible
d. a wide range of patterns with no one ideal way to grieve

17. When mourners repeatedly go over all the events that led up to the death, they are _____.
a. trying to make sense of their world
b. creating a potentially harmful situation for their recovery
c. setting themselves up for continuing depression
d. trying to escape blame for the loved one's death

18. The typical experience of grieving in the United States is best explained as _____.
a. a series of predictable stages
b. an emotional roller coaster
c. the depths of despair and suicidality
d. the emotions described in Kübler-Ross' theory

19. Which of the following is NOT associated with the Amish mourning ritual?
a. holding the funeral ceremony in a barn in warmer months
b. a horse-and-buggy "hearse"
c. the deceased's body dressed in white
d. support for bereaved family members

20. The _____ model of coping with bereavement consists of two main dimensions: 1) loss-oriented stressors, and 2) restoration-oriented stressors.
a. complicated
b. dual-process
c. active-directive
d. palliative care

21. _____ involves reducing pain and suffering, while helping individuals die with dignity.
a. Palliative care
b. Advance directive
c. Active euthanasia
d. Terminal care

22. _____ euthanasia occurs when a person is allowed to die by withholding available treatment, while _____ euthanasia occurs when death is deliberately induced.
a. Mercy; passive
b. Passive; active
c. Active; passive
d. Active; mercy

23. Which of Kubler-Ross' stages of dying is represented by a patient that states, "I will accept death gracefully, if I can just see all of my children one last time"?
a. denial and isolation
b. anger
c. bargaining
d. acceptance

24. Which of Kubler-Ross' stages of dying is seen as the final resting stage before death?
a. anger
b. bargaining
c. depression
d. acceptance

25. Which of the following is NOT a reason that widows outnumber widowers by a ratio of 5 to 1?
a. Women live longer than men.
b. Women tend to marry men older than themselves.
c. A widowed man is more likely to remarry.
d. Widowed women have increased money and resources to ensure a long life.

True/False Questions

1. Brain death from a neurological perspective includes having no heartbeat or respiration.

2. The definition of brain death currently followed by most physicians includes the death of both higher cortical functions and the lower brain stem functions.

3. The difference between being in a coma and being brain dead is that a comatose person may recover and still shows electrical activity in the brain.

4. Supporters of the cortical death policy argue that once the person is in a coma, he or she is not using the brain cortex and so should be allowed to die.

5. When a person has been told by a physician that he or she is terminally ill, the person can sign an advance directive telling the physician how to dispose of the body when he or she dies.

6. Janet is terminally ill and does not want to be resuscitated if she goes into cardiac arrest. Therefore, she is advocating a form of active euthanasia.

7. Passive euthanasia is illegal in most countries around the world.

8. As with hospitals, the goal of hospices is to prolong life. The difference is that hospice care occurs at home.

9. Kübler-Ross's stage called "depression" is so severe that when dying people experience it, we should try at all costs to cheer them up and help them see the positive side of what remains of their lives.

10. Although individual reactions to a diagnosis of terminal illness may vary widely, research suggests that denial is never a positive response style.

11. Experts suggest that when conversing with a dying person, we focus not on preparation for death but on the strength of the individual and preparing mentally for the remainder of life.

12. Grieving is best conceived of as a flexibly defined response to death based on whatever is considered appropriate within a cultural context.

13. Studies on widows show that they decline financially when their spouse dies.

14. Cremation is more popular in Canada and Japan than in the United States where only 20% of bodies are cremated.

15. Complicated grief typically involves enduring despair that is still unresolved after an extended period of time.

Short-Answer Questions

1. Why do some medical experts argue that the criteria for death should include only higher cortical functioning?

2. Discuss the two types of euthanasia, and give an example of each.

3. List three recommendations for preparing for one's own death.

4. What is a hospice program?

5. List four ways that Americans try to avoid and deny death.

6. Explain the role of perceived control as an adaptive strategy for dealing with death.

7. List, in order, Kübler-Ross's five stages of dying.

8. List five effective strategies for communicating with a dying person.

9. Define grief and its course.

10. Briefly describe traditional Amish mourning of the death of a group member.

Essay Questions

1. A good friend has approached you with a difficult decision—his father is in the last stages of a terminal illness, and the medication he is on is not controlling the excruciating pain he experiences. Your friend tells you that his father has asked for help in dying, and your friend is torn between the anguish of watching his father suffer and his own moral reluctance to help his father die. He asks for your help in deciding what he should do. Take a totally objective perspective on this, on the basis of what you have read in the chapter on euthanasia, and discuss under what circumstances a person in the medical profession might consider terminating a patient's life, and when it would not be appropriate to do so. Include in your answer a discussion of when a person is considered dead from a clinical perspective, and how you might advise your friend under those circumstances. Finally, take a stand on the issue of euthanasia and support your position with research findings from the chapter.

2. You have just learned from your mother that your favorite aunt is dying. Having no children of her own, she has always been extremely close to you. Your mother says the doctor, a young oncologist, has not yet told your aunt of her diagnosis, wanting to discuss it with the family first. To achieve the best possible outcome for your aunt and for the family who loves her, what should be done? Should she be told? If so, why; if not, why not? How should the rest of the family be told? How should family members deal with her and with one another? How would you expect your aunt and other members of the family to react during her death, and the family members to react after her death? Would you recommend hospice care? In light of the information in the text, what would you suggest the family do to enable a grieving experience to end positively? Explain the reasons for your answers.

Key to Matching Questions

1. C	2. A	3. E	4. D	5. B

Key to Multiple-Choice Questions

1. A	6. D	11. A	16. D	21. A
2. B	7. B	12. A	17. A	22. B
3. C	8. A	13. D	18. B	23. C
4. C	9. B	14. A	19. C	24. D
5. C	10. B	15. D	20. B	25. D

Key to True/False Questions

1. F	4. F	7. F	10. F	13. T
2. T	5. F	8. F	11. F	14. T
3. T	6. F	9. F	12. T	15. T

Key to Short-Answer Questions

1. Supporters of cortical death policy argue that the functions associated with being human (such as thinking and personality) are located in the higher cortical part of the brain. They believe that when these functions are lost, the "human being" is no longer alive.

2. Active euthanasia occurs when death is induced deliberately; for example, an injection of a lethal dose of a drug. Passive euthanasia occurs when a person is allowed to die by withholding an available treatment; for example, by turning off a respirator.

3. Some ways to prepare for your death include:
   • Make a living will and sharing it with family and doctors.
   • Give someone power of attorney, and make sure this person knows your medical care wishes.
   • Give your doctors specific instructions for specific circumstances.
   • If you want to die at home, talk it over with your doctor.
   • Check to see if your insurance plan covers home and/or hospice care.

4. A hospice program is a humanized program committed to making the end of life as free from pain, anxiety, and depression as possible. It is a program for terminally ill patients that deemphasizes the use of medical intervention.

5. a. The glossing over of death and fashioning lifelike qualities in the dead by the funeral industry; b. use of euphemistic terms for death—passing on, exiting, passing away; c. persistent search for a fountain of youth; d. rejection and isolation of the aged; e. the concept of a pleasant and rewarding afterlife; f. medical community emphasis on prolonging biological life instead of diminishing suffering.

6. When individuals are led to believe they can influence and control events, they become more alert and cheerful.

7. 1. Denial and isolation, 2. anger, 3. bargaining, 4. depression, 5. acceptance

8. Effective strategies for communicating with a dying person:
   • Establish your presence.
   • Eliminate distraction.
   • Don't overstay your visit.
   • Don't insist that the dying person feel acceptance.
   • Encourage the expression of feelings.
   • Appropriately discuss the expected outcome of their illness and any unfinished business.
   • Ask if there is anyone that the dying person would like to see.
   • Encourage the dying person to reminisce.
   • Be available and reliable.
   • Express your regard for the dying individual.

9. Grief is the emotional numbness, disbelief, separation, anxiety, despair, sadness, and loneliness that accompanies the loss of someone we love. The course of grief is often like a roller coaster—up and down.

10. The funeral service is held in a barn or a home. Calm acceptance through deep religious faith is characteristic. A high level of support is given to the bereaved family for at least a year including frequent visits, service projects, and giving of sentimental and household items.

Key to Essay Questions

1. Whatever your personal biases for or against euthanasia, you will need to put them aside to answer this question. Explain the terms *euthanasia*, *passive euthanasia*, and *active euthanasia*, and explain when they are used. Address the issues of assisted suicide and Dr. Kevorkian including the patient's suffering, moral/ethical concerns (both sides of that issue), and legal concerns. Also consider here the financial, physical, and emotional drain on the family as well as their feelings about the dying patient. Then explain exactly what constitutes death. Is it the cessation of breathing? Of brain function? Discuss the issues involved in brain death. Be sure to discuss all the research findings (for example, the survey of physicians' thoughts about the issue). After addressing all these issues, explore your own feelings about them. Are your feelings supported by the research in the text?

2. Discuss the reasons psychologists suggest that it is best to tell a terminal patient of his or her impending death (for example, putting affairs in order, making decisions such as creating advance directives regarding his or her own life and death). Discuss the importance of being honest with family members, taking their age into account in terms of how they are told. Family members should be encouraged to talk to one another and to the dying person, using the suggestions throughout the chapter on how to communicate with someone who is dying. Then, to predict how your aunt and other family members will react, discuss Kübler-Ross's stages of dying, noting the limitations of that theory and that there is no one right way to die or to grieve. Explore the notion of hospice care—what it does and does not offer—taking into consideration your aunt's wishes. Also discuss the issues of a living will and preparing a durable power of attorney to ensure that your aunt's wishes will be carried out. Assure your family that any feelings they have are normal and should be validated and talked about. There is no right way to grieve, and as long as there is social support (and professional help if necessary), grieving can lead to personal growth and a closer family in the long run.

Research Project 1:
Observing Developmental Periods in Grieving

PLEASE NOTE: THIS PROJECT ASKS YOU TO INTERVIEW TWO INDIVIDUALS. PLEASE CHECK WITH YOUR INSTRUCTOR TO SEE IF YOU NEED TO COMPLETE AN INSTITUTIONAL RESEARCH BOARD PROTOCOL BEFORE BEGINNING THIS PROJECT.

Interview two people, one who lost a close family member during childhood and one who lost a close family member in adulthood. If they are willing to discuss this event and it is not too painful for them, ask them about the circumstances of the person's death: Was it slow, sudden, or expected? Was it an older person or a young person? How was it discussed with the victim and the family? What type of funeral proceedings took place? How was your interviewee included or excluded from the rituals that took place? How did the grieving process feel to your interviewee? How did the interviewee "get over" this death and grieving experience? Did the experience make the interviewee stronger? Compare the answers and see if they are consistent with the developmental trends discussed in the text regarding how children versus adults view and deal with death. Did their experiences vary widely, or were there similar patterns? Compare both people' answers to the information in the text. Do you think some of the differences were based on gender, age, ethnic or cultural background, marital status, support system, or religious orientation? Explain these differences, and what you can conclude about how each of these variables affected the individuals' ability to cope with loss. What might you conclude, on the basis of your observations, about coping with one's own death or the death of a loved one? Did this project make you more comfortable thinking about death and grieving, or did it make you fearful? Explain.

Research Project 2:
Integrating What You've Learned

Do a literature search in the PsycINFO or PsycARTICLES database of your campus library on any topic from this chapter that appeals to you (for example, children and death, dealing with miscarriage, funeral rites in Jewish families, grieving, hospice care). Find two scientific journal articles on your chosen topic, and read them. Outline the goals of each study, the participants' characteristics (age, gender, ethnicity, socioeconomic status), the methods used (survey, observation, and so on), a brief summary of the results, and the conclusions the authors drew. Compare these two articles with the material discussed in the text. Outline the similarities and the disagreements. What were some of the most important things you learned from each source? What new material was covered in the articles that you think would be important to add to the text? What final conclusions can you make about your chosen topic? What do you believe everyone should know about this topic?

Personal Application Project 1:
Your Experience with Death

Think about how much experience you have with death. Have you ever seen a dead person? Have you ever visited a terminally ill person in the hospital or at home or hospice care? What were the characteristics of the conversations you had with that person? Think about every person you have known who has died. How did each experience differ for you? Why were you more upset about some deaths than others? Why did it take you longer to "get over" some deaths versus others? What did you learn from each exposure to death? Have your experiences made you more or less fearful of your own death? Do you think your religious or spiritual beliefs (or lack thereof) have influenced these processes in your life? For each question answered, include your personal ideas, but also support those ideas with research and theory from the chapter. Compare your personal experiences with those described in the text. How did your grieving process(es) compare to those outlined in the chapter? Are some things in the chapter that could have helped you deal with a person's death? Outline those things you think are most helpful and least helpful in the text.

Personal Application Project 2:
Pictorial Life Review

In the previous chapter of the Study Guide, you created a life review. After considering all the issues that are relevant to your life review, present them pictorially. You may draw or paint your life or a self-portrait containing the answers to your questions, put together a collage, or do any other type of visual project that will assist you in reviewing your life. After completing the visual project, answer these questions.

1. Is there another method that would be more helpful in doing a life review? Explain; then use that approach.

2. What has been the most useful outcome for you in doing a life review?

3. What has been the most harmful outcome for you in doing a life review?

4. Butler (1996) noted that, "as the past marches in review, the older adult surveys it, observes it, and reflects on it." Did you find this to be so in evaluating your life review? Explain.

5. Butler (1996) also noted that, "this reorganization of the past may provide a more valid picture for the individual, providing new and significant meaning to . . . life. It may also help prepare the individual for death, in the process reducing fear." In doing your life review, did you find this to be true?

6. What might you conclude, on the basis of your life review, about development in late adulthood?

Internet Projects

Check out the McGraw-Hill website for this text (www.mhhe.com). You will find numerous activities there, in particular, quizzes. Also, be patient, because there are many very worthy links on each of the sites, but they do take a little time to access. If you do not go to the links many times, you will not get the full value of the site. Please go to all links.

Please note that all website addresses in this Study Guide have been checked and were correct at the time of publication. However, websites may be discontinued or their addresses may change, so when you try to access a given site, it may no longer be viable. If that occurs, please notify the publisher so that it can make appropriate revisions in future editions of this Study Guide.

Internet Project 1:
Funeral Rites around the World

Check out this website: www.thefuneraldirectory.com/ancientrites.html. It has funeral rites and rituals from all over the world and throughout history, from Aztec to Celtic to American historical rites. Choose three cultures, and explore their rites and rituals in depth. Write down the ideas, beliefs, philosophies, and practices that interest you and that either confirm or refute information about death, grieving, and dying in this chapter. Write a three-page paper describing the similarities and differences between what you found in these three cultures and the material covered in the text. You may also use the rest of the website to help you put your comments into perspective regarding the material in the chapter. For example, if you go to the site's home page, you will see articles on such topics as how to deal with the death of children, on grief in families, on how to arrange your own funeral.

Internet Project 2: Grieving

Go to Compassionate Friends at www.compassionatefriends.org, Grief Net at www.griefnet.org, or Counseling and Education at www.hospicegso.org/html/education.html. These sites were developed to give grieving people throughout the Internet community a place to access information, exchange ideas, and share their own personal experiences in regard to the grieving process. Your participation in this website may help others, as well as yourself, to better cope with the painful but necessary grieving process. For this project, read as many of the articles as you can found through links on this page. Pay particular attention to the personal stories, grief resources, and information to help children with grief. Write down things that come to mind as you read that relate well to the material in the chapter. What things seem to disagree with material in the chapter? Which articles were most informative and interesting to you and why? Was there some information that should be covered in the text that is not? In light of the information on these websites and the chapter in the textbook, what are the three most important things you think the public needs to know about the grieving process?

Other Relevant Sites on the Internet

Hospice Foundation of America: www.hospicefoundation.org/
The foundation's website provides information on locating hospice care near you, stories of families who have used hospice, home study courses for professionals, and newsletters and other publications.

Compassion & Choices: www.compassionandchoices.org/
Compassion & Choices (formerly the Hemlock Society and then End-of-Life Choices) emphasizes dying with dignity and compassion by being in control. The site has information on the latest legislative and social policy actions from the right-to-die movement. There is a lot of information here that most people never think about, so it is worthwhile spending some time on this site.

TreeGivers: www.treegivers.com/index-m.html
This memorial organization that will plant trees in memory of your loved one on public lands in the United States and Canada. Planting trees is a terrific alternative to sending flowers that will soon wilt.

Bereavement: http://medlineplus.nlm.nih.gov/medlineplus/bereavement.html
This MedlinePlus page from the website of the U.S. National Library of Medicine, a part of the National Institutes of Health, has a collection of links to articles on dealing with the death of a child, dealing with the death of a parent, how to healthfully grieve, and much more. It also offers many links to articles and organizations that deal with grief and bereavement for all age groups.